D1625358

Secret Love Affairs

Secret Love Affairs

Morris Mandel

JD | JONATHAN DAVID PUBLISHERS, INC.
MIDDLE VILLAGE, N.Y. 11374

SECRET LOVE AFFAIRS

by
Morris Mandel

Copyright © 1975
by
JONATHAN DAVID PUBLISHERS

No part of this book may be reproduced in any manner without written permission from the publisher. Address all inquiries to:

Jonathan David Publishers
68-22 Eliot Avenue
Middle Village, New York 11379

Library of Congress Cataloging in Publication Data
Mandel, Morris, 1911-
    Secret love affairs.

    1. Love.   2. Biography.   I. Title.
HQ801.A2M25   301.41'092'2   75-14242
ISBN 0-8246-0201-3

Printed in the United States of America

Table of Contents

FOR SHIRLEY

Introduction

SECRET LOVE AFFAIRS is about the surge and drive for love. Though it is an emotion that properly belongs to the private domain of each individual, in the case of famous men and women, it belongs to the world-at-large. The public hungers to find out all it can about its famous men and women, be they artists, musicians, dancers, writers, scientists, government leaders, kings, queens or presidents. Yet, despite this wide interest, no book has been published that deals exclusively with this enticing subject.

Secret Love Affairs is selective rather than encyclopedic, and concentrates on presenting a portrait of some of the one-time secret, amorous love affairs and patterns of behavior of the great and the near great. From a reading of these pages the reader will develop an insight into the type of infidelity, and the degree of infidelity that obtained in social circles over the years.

Much has been said about what is called, "the affair." Frank Caprio, M.D., author of *Marital Infidelity* said: "Infidelity, like alcoholism or drug addiction, is an expression of a deep basic disorder of character." Dr. Leon Saul, author of *Fidelity and Infidelity*, wrote: "Infidelity is often a neurotic and sometimes psychotic pursuit of exactly the man or woman one imagines one needs . . . It is primarily a return to behavior characteristic of adolescence or earlier."

After reading this volume, I am confident the reader will be able to pen his own definitions. He will understand, fully, the heartaches, disappointments and difficulties experienced by those who involved themselves in extra-marital relationships and secret amorous involvements.

Much work went into the preparation of this book, and my gratitude is hereby expressed to my colleagues with whom I have had the opportunity to discuss the subjects portrayed in this volume. My profound thanks are also extended to Shirley Horowitz for her help and suggestions, and to Debbie Koenig, for her thorough researching.

MORRIS MANDEL

1

Lillie Langtry --
Mistress of Royalty

The name Lillie Langtry means very little, if anything, to most of us. But there was a day when the name Lillie Langtry made hearts beat faster. She was truly the desire of every man—and the envy of every woman. Artists, royalty, musicians, poets and essayists, men of business and commerce—all looked to Lillie for love.

"Lillie Langtry," said John Everett Millais, the distinguished painter, "happens to be, quite simply, the most beautiful woman on earth."

"To look at Lillie," said James McNiell Whistler, "is to imagine one is dreaming. She is so extraordinary that not even I can do her justice in a painting."

Theodore Roosevelt, America's rough riding President, said of Lillie: "That woman is a real marvel. And she's so pretty she takes away a man's breath."

Walt Whitman, the famous poet wrote: "There shines in Lillie Langtry a purity of spirit. Therein lies the essence of human poetry."

Frederick Gebhard, the most celebrated of her American millionaire lovers said, "I don't give a damn if Lil did sleep with the Prince of Wales. I love her, and I issue a public appeal to her. Marry me, Lillie!"

Even W. S. Gilbert wrote a lyric about her which his partner, Sir Arthur Sullivan, put to music:

> Oh, never, never, never since we joined the
> human race
> Saw we so exquisitely fair a face.

George Bernard Shaw, who often reduced women to mere sex, said of Lillie, "I resent Mrs. Langtry. She has no right to be intelligent, daring, and independent as well as lovely. It is a frightening combination of attributes."

Lillie was a born winner, being endowed with almost everything a lady could pray for. She became a renowned actress. She was a clever capitalist, possessing a rare business instinct and ability. She was hailed as the world's best-dressed woman. And she was the mistress of many men—men of art, men of wealth, men of royal blood, men of commerce—men who had already made their own mark in life.

1

She was a truly remarkable woman. Whatever she did made news! Whatever she wore became the style! There were Lillie dolls, Lillie sketches, Lillie paintings, Lillie statues. She made men sit up and take notice—men like Churchill, William Gladstone, Whistler, Oscar Wilde, Albert Edward, Prince of Wales, son of Queen Victoria and Prince Consort Albert, and the future King Edward VII of England.

Who was Lillie? How can the most beautiful woman in the world be described? She was a composite of Elizabeth Taylor, Jacqueline Kennedy, Zsa Zsa Gabor, Marilyn Monroe and perhaps a few more Hollywood beauties; and she was remarkable in that she utilized her beauty, brains, independence, desire and hope to make herself into the most desirable woman in the world. Even hard-hitting Roy Bean of Texas, the self-styled hanging judge, named a town in Texas after her, saying, "I dare any man alive to tell me a better name for a town than Langtry."

And she was an excellent actress.

Sarah Bernhardt praised her as "superb."

Ellen Terry, one of the first ladies of the English theatre, said "Lillie breathes life into a theatre." In truth Lillie was living art, living poetry, living music, a veritable symphony of all that is beautiful.

Lillie was born on October 13, 1853 to Dean Le Breton, a pious and conservative Anglican clergyman, and to his modest wife, Emile Martin Le Breton. Lillie was one of seven children. She was the sixth child to be born to her parents, and the first and only girl.

Her early years were spent on the Isle of Jersey, located several miles off the coast of Saint-Malo, France. Today, the residents consider themselves Englishmen. In Lillie's time, the population numbered approximately 30,000.

With five older brothers, Lillie was not a typical girl. A full-fledged tomboy, she climbed cliffs, rode bareback, and held her own with the roughest of boys. She joined the boys in whatever mischief they planned, once helping them tar and feather a statue of Queen Victoria.

At 15, she already possessed an almost flawless beauty. She was 5' 8", weighed 130 pounds, and was endowed with shapely, full breasts. Her chestnut hair was worn in a bun at the nape of her neck. Her deep blue eyes attracted immediate attention. Even at 15, she knew that she could get men and boys to do her bidding merely by smiling at them. And smile she did!

Lillie's mother was determined that her daughter's cultural experiences be broadened and decided to take her to London for an extended visit. It was there that Lillie became aware of her social handicaps. She found herself unable to cope with the people she met. They were aristocratic in manner, speech and appearance. They could dance; she tripped over her own feet. They knew how to eat elegantly. They knew which piece of silverware to use for each course; she had never known that so many forks and spoons could be used at one meal. Lillie's visit to London was a disastrous experience, and it was abbreviated.

As they grew older, her brothers fled the Island of Jersey. They felt that there was no room for advancement in its limited and stifling environment. Lillie was determined to do the same. But how?

Her only possible means of escape was through marriage! She knew that the aristocratic men of the island would not admit a girl lacking formal education to a prestigious school. Her future husband would have to be an outsider! Lillie watched the yachts steaming into the harbor, and dreamed of the man who would come into her life and claim her.

One day, the *Red Gauntlet* sailed into Saint Heilier. The owner was Edward Langtry, a good-looking young man dressed in tailored clothes. His dark hair and black eyes were attractive. Edward was a widower, a friend of one of Lillie's brothers. Best of all, the yacht on which he came, measuring 80 feet long, with a crew of six including the captain, was his own. And this was but one of several yachts belonging to him. It was obvious that Edward Langtry was wealthy.

Langtry was invited to the Le Breton household and soon a new Lillie emerged. No longer the tomboy, she put on her prettiest dresses. She acted ladylike and demure. She was out to get her man, the man who represented freedom and escape. It didn't take long before Langtry asked Lillie to marry him. Her parents urged patience, but Lillie's mind was not to be changed. Without the consent of her parents, she had already accepted a large diamond ring as a betrothal gift.

On March 9, 1874, Edward and Lillie were married. It was a small morning wedding. Dean Le Breton performed the ceremony and only one of Lillie's brothers attended. The wedding breakfast was held at the yacht club, and the newly-married couple went off for a month long honeymoon on the *Red Gauntlet*. After the honeymoon, the couple moved into their house in Southampton, and Lillie became mistress of Cliffe Lodge. She knew absolutely nothing about housekeeping and was quite inept at it. But it mattered little because the preoccupation of the young couple was with the yachting set.

Very early in their marital years, Lillie told friends that her husband was not arousing her sexually. This was an astounding statement to make in those days, when women were not expected to enjoy marital intimacy.

Lillie was not happy at Cliffe Lodge. Southampton offered her little in the way of a social life. To her, women's talk was dull, as were the hours playing cards. She wanted to live in London.

Lillie was determined and, with the help of her doctor, convinced Edward that Southampton was not the place for Lillie; it was adversely affecting her health. On their first wedding anniversary, they moved to London, then the hub of the civilized world. And it is in London that the story of Lillie's rise to world fame and fortune begins.

It was during a visit to the Royal Aquarium in Westminister that their first break came. While wandering through the building they came face to face with Lord and Lady Ranelagh, one of the wealthy couples who at times visited the Island of Jersey. Lady Ranelagh recognized Lillie immediately and that very day an invitation was extended to them to attend a tea party to be held the following Sunday afternoon.

A stiff, awkward Edward Langtry and a frightened Lillie came for tea and there mixed with England's most elegant people. Little did Lillie realize that, dressed in her black gown, she was creating a sensation. And little did the other guests realize that this was the only gown Lillie owned. After all, her husband was not at all wealthy by their standards, and was living on a not too generous allowance from Langtry's father.

The following week she received an invitation from Lady Sebright of the elegant set to attend a party at her home. Edward preferred not to go through a second ordeal, but Lillie insisted and had her way. She usually did.

She altered her one and only gown by lowering the neckline. She changed her hair style by twisting it into a single braid and arranging it in a figure 8 at the back of her neck. She looked positively beautiful and breathtakingly ravishing.

The men surrounded her. Everyone gravitated toward her. John Everett Millais asked that she sit for him at a future date, and Lord Frederick Leighton, the noted sculptor, made an appointment to do a bust of her in marble. Whistler, the artist; Henry Irving, the actor; William Yardley, the poet—all crowded around her. She was immediately voted into the Professional Beauties group, a group of well-dressed aristocratic ladies who had enthusiastic followings. They were not professional, however, in any sense.

Edward Langtry went unnoticed. Only Whistler took the trouble to nod to him. Edward was both hurt and bored, while Lillie walked on a cloud. She felt she had finally arrived.

The next day, the Langtrys were deluged with invitations, the most important one coming from Lord Randolph Churchill. Lillie was delighted as coach after coach drove up, and invitations were delivered. Despite Edward's protestations, she insisted on accepting every one of them.

They went everywhere, and everywhere they went she was the center of attraction, and Edward was neglected. Lillie was the focus of attention at as many as four parties in a single day. She was gay, interesting, beautiful; she bubbled with enthusiasm.

In addition to this excitement, she was busy posing for Millais, for Frank Miles, for George Frederic Wates, and for Edward Burne-Jones. In her first year of discovery not less than 11 oils were painted of her, and many hundreds of pen and ink sketches were made and sold. Soon, photographs of Lillie appeared in shop windows throughout England.

At 24, Lillie was the most sought after young woman in all of England. Dante Gabriel Rossetti painted her portrait; Algernon Charles Swinburne, the brilliant poet, attached himself to Lillie; Oscar Wilde wrote and published poems about her, and for her.

The more popular Lillie became, the more did her marriage deteriorate. Soon, it was rumored, husband and wife had moved into separate bedrooms. Edward Langtry had lost his wife, and for solace he turned to the whiskey bottle.

All England now wondered how long it would take before Albert Edward, Prince of Wales, the eldest son of Queen Victoria and Prince Consort Albert, would attach himself to Lillie. Edward had an eye for beauty and it was speculated that he would set out to meet her. Lillie did spy him once riding through the park. "He is a very large man, but appeared to ride well for one of his bulk," she wrote.

The question in everyone's mind was, "What would happen when Prince Albert Edward met Lillie?" There was no doubt that he would meet her; he always sought out beauty. Some felt that the prince would be absolutely smitten, and she would be easy game for him. Others said that Lillie was moral, and her sense of propriety would be respected by the prince. Oscar Wilde said "I will predict, accurately, all human behavior, except that which governs the human heart. Man is constant in his infidelity, and woman puts him to shame because she is, by nature, fickle."

Oscar Wilde was not wrong.

But Prince Albert Edward and Lillie did not meet for a long time. One novelist, Marie Louise de la Ramée, who used the pseudonym of Ouida, remarked that the prince was avoiding Lillie because he was afraid to meet her.

When Lillie did meet Albert it was at the home of Sir Allen Young, and the meeting was unplanned. Lillie had gone there for a supper of 10 people. Suddenly, in the midst of the meal, the

Prince of Wales appeared, demanding a dish of the famous Young lobster curry. At the time, he was 36 and Lillie was 24. He had been married for 14 years to Princess Alexandra of Denmark.

Little is known about the first meeting except that the prince, upon leaving Lillie, told her that she was far more beautiful than her photographs and portraits. The next meeting was not long in coming, and it was followed by many others.

Evidently, both Lillie and the prince knew what they wanted. Soon, they were meeting often at the home of Mr. C. J. Freake, a multimillionaire who was a friend of the Prince of Wales. Up to this point, Lillie had remained faithful to her husband, even though the marriage had deteriorated to the point that marital togetherness was completely absent. But now she became restless; a new spirit had come over her. She began to abhor her loveless marriage.

With the prince she became involved in her first real affair. Whether she loved him or not, no one could really tell. She did not even mention it in her autobiography. Undoubtedly, she was flattered by the attention of a man soon to become a king. And she surely admired his gifts. The rings, bracelets, pendants and earrings that he gave Lillie became part of the world's largest private jewelry collections. After all, he was one of the richest men in Europe.

By 1879, her name was on the tongue of every Englishman.

The couple was seen everywhere together. They went riding, attended the theatre, shopped, dined. Where Lillie was, the prince was sure to be found. Once, at a dinner which they attended, honoring Victor Hugo, the 78-year-old author toasted Lillie by saying, "Madam, I can celebrate your beauty in only one way: by wishing I were three years younger."

In the meantime, Edward Langtry seemed to be having a stroke of good luck. The prince's wealthy friend, Freake, advised him on some choice investments that paid off. The whispers that were heard in London was that this was the prince's way of bribing Edward to hear nothing and see nothing, so that he and Lillie could enjoy their close association in peace.

Now, when the prince and Lillie met at functions, there was no need to hide the fact that they were good friends. And even though she was still married to Langtry, and until this time had put off all her suitors and admirers with a warm smile, the thought of extramarital romance was no longer a remote possibility.

Why the sudden change in Lillie's attitude? For one thing, her popularity began to swell her head. Being young and romantic, the thought of a "knight on a white horse" coming along and sweeping her off into a dream world was more than she could withstand. She was vulnerable and quite ready for an extramarital affair.

Lillie began to dress in extremely stylish clothes. She was determined to utilize her femininity to the utmost for she realized that her relationship with Edward VII could bring her world renown.

Though the proprieties were always observed, and Lillie was usually seen with her husband, the prince was ever present. It was evident that the Prince of Wales had arranged his own affairs so as to give him the latitude to spend as much time as he wished with the woman he now loved. Though he and the princess attended official functions together, it was an open secret that they led separate and private lives.

Lillie now crashed the headlines more and more often. She dazzled Benjamin Disraeli at a government reception. She enchanted King Leopold of Belgium who came daily, for a full week, to have coffee with her. She favorably impressed Queen Victoria to whom she was presented at a formal court reception. Her activity was always newsworthy.

At what moment Lillie actually became the mistress of the prince is anybody's guess. They handled the situation with discretion. Of course, there were always rumors—and they were especially juicy because they involved a future king and his mistress.

Lillie, realizing that her good fortune might be only temporary, made the most of the situation. The prince was reputed to tire of his ladies. He had never maintained a prolonged interest in any of them.

Lillie now mixed with royalty. She met the King and Queen of Denmark, various members of Austrian royalty, and assorted German princes. She was now the favorite of the Prince of Wales. What surprised many was that she now often appeared at official functions. They were amazed at how quickly she had acquired an international reputation. Her husband, now a confirmed drinker, faded into the background. By this time, the marriage was meaningless, and no effort was even made to maintain the facade that they had originally erected.

London society was shocked by Lillie's behavior. Though no fault could be found with their prince and his extramarital affairs, they did find fault with her. Her visitations with the Crown Prince Rudolph of Austria-Hungary, the heir to the throne of the Hapsburg Empire, added fuel to the fire.

The Crown Prince of Austria-Hungary, son of Emperor Franz Joseph, was one of Lillie's admirers. A playboy with an international reputation, he met Lillie at a ball given in his honor by Baron Ferdinand de Rothschild. The Crown Prince went wild.

Though he knew of her relationship with the Prince of Wales, and though the prince was present, Prince Rudolph danced with her repeatedly, refusing to give her up.

Each day, after their meeting, Prince Rudolph called on Lillie at her Norfolk Street apartment. His advances were bold and insistent. Lillie maintained an air of innocence, though she was truly furious. She had done nothing to incite the young prince.

"Lovely Lillie Langtry," the *New York Tribune* reported, "has added another royal scalp to her fast-growing collection." But the affair ended when Emperor Franz Josef summoned his son back to Vienna.

At this point in her life, Lillie Langtry was forced into retirement. She discovered that she was pregnant and could no longer carry on socially; but she was not neglected. Alexandra, Princess of Wales, called on Lillie at her Norfolk Street apartment, and Albert, the Prince of Wales himself, maintained contact as well.

The next few months of Lillie's life are shrouded in mystery. She was reported to have been in Lille, Paris, in Rouen, in Wales. In either March or April of 1881, Lillie Langtry gave birth to her child. No record of the infant's birth or baptism appeared in London, Wales, or in Jersey. There was no record in Paris or in any of the smaller French cities. But the baby was a girl and was named Jeanne Langtry.

Very few knew of the child's existence. One person, above all, had no idea of the birth of a daughter, and that was Edward Langtry, now a lost soul. Had he known of the child, he could have caused Lillie tremendous difficulties.

Lillie now decided to become an actress, and once again left London. No sooner was her decision made public that offers began to arrive from the United States. She rejected them all claiming that she wasn't ready for so demanding a move.

She began taking drama lessons with Henrietta Hodson Labouchère, a retired actress. Lillie played a minor role in *A Fair Encounter*. Whenever she was announced to be appearing in a play, the house was oversold.

The newspaper critics gave her good reviews. "She will become a star," wrote the *Daily Telegraph*. Oscar Wilde, enthusiastic as ever, announced that he would write a part especially for her. In all, she received acclaim beyond all expectations. Soon, she was earning 250 pounds a week.

Financially, the cloud was beginning to lift. Her personal life, however, had become more complicated than ever. She was now fair game for every man in London. The ladies often shunned her, but not their husbands. The best advice she received came from Prime Minister Gladstone, who, visiting her backstage after a performance, said, "Mrs. Langtry, you have become a truly public person, so you will be attacked, maligned, and slandered, in your professional life, and in your personal life as well. Never reply to your critics! Never explain, no matter what you've said or done! If you attempt to defend yourself, you'll keep alive a controversy. As the French say, 'speech is silver, but silence is golden'."

By the summer of 1882, Lillie was a strong box office attraction. It was then that her husband visited her, demanding money, and threatening her life if she did not pay. She agreed to pay him a monthly sum provided that he would promise never to see her again.

Lillie now acted in many English cities. Manchester had never had so successful an opening night as when Lillie appeared. Every performance in Edinburgh was sold out. The Prince of Wales sent flowers for each of her opening nights.

Lillie was even asked to endorse a commercial product, something no woman had ever been asked to do. She now was ready for a tour of the United States. She set sail for Liverpool on October 14, 1882 and was due to reach New York nine days later.

Wilde was on hand to greet Lillie. The day prior to her arrival he told the *New York World*, "I would rather have discovered Mrs. Langtry than to have discovered America. You have asked whether she is indeed a beauty, and I can reply to such nonsense only by saying that you will see for yourself. No, I will go further. She is the most beautiful woman in the world, and will be a beauty still at eighty-five. It was for such as she that Troy was destroyed, and well it might have been!"

There was such a demand for tickets for her opening night that box seats sold for $325 each. When the publisher of the *New York Herald* assigned a reporter to accompany her and write reports, he promptly fell madly in love with her. Opening night found Chester A. Arthur, Jr., the son of the President of the United States, in the audience. He was representing his father.

Lillie's opening night in *As You Like It* was not the success she had hoped for. The reviews were the worst she had ever received. Despite her poor reception, the box office announced an advance sale of $65,000 for the next few weeks.

It was a short time after her New York opening that Lillie met the man she later described as "the great love of my life." He was Frederick Gebhard, Jr., a young man of 22. He had inherited a fortune of at least $5,000,000 and his annual income was in the vicinity of $100,000 a year. He was tall, a real athlete. He played tennis, boxed, fenced, and engaged in almost every activity. With all his wealth and good looks, Frederick had somehow eluded marriage.

Fred fell in love with Lillie almost immediately. She was

seven years his senior, but that made no difference to him. He invited her everywhere. Soon he was sending her huge bouquets of flowers. Hidden in the bouquets were necklaces and bracelets of matching diamonds.

Soon, Lillie was the talk of America. The public disapproved of a married woman spending so much time with a young bachelor, and accepting such expensive gifts. The gossip only served to increase the interest of the public in Lillie. In an act of independence, she announced that Fred Gebhard would accompany her on her tour. To make it more acceptable, she announced that he would act as her bodyguard.

It was shocking in the 1880's for a young married woman to be seen in the company of a wealthy, handsome young bachelor who was proclaiming his love for her. Lillie didn't care about the gossip, and, in any event, scandal was good for business.

It was at this time in Lillie's career that Diamond Jim Brady entered her life. Diamond Jim Brady was a character known throughout the country as a generous spender. He always wore a huge diamond stickpin and cuff links. Eating was his hobby. No sooner did he meet Lillie that he gave her a large diamond ring and a diamond brooch. All he wanted in return was to be seen with her.

During her Boston tour, Lillie was discreet. She did not want to upset the morals of the city, and so she dined with Fred Gebhard alone in her hotel suite. In this way the newspapers did not mention him at all.

Philadelphia was a repeat of Boston. The critics panned the show, but the theater was sold out nevertheless. Lillie herself was the attraction; the critics didn't matter at all. In Chicago, the audiences went wild.

It was in St. Louis that Lillie once again made international headlines. One morning Fred Gebhard was having breakfast in her room. He was fully dressed. Lillie wore a peignoir. Colonel A. B. Cunningham, one of the editors of the *St. Louis Globe-Democrat* chose that hour of that day to call on Lillie. Though he was refused entrance by the maid, he pushed his way through and came upon Lillie and Fred. The next day he wrote a blistering article condemning Lillie as immoral, naming Fred as her lover, and urging the citizens of St. Louis to boycott her performances. When that same evening Fred Gebhard confronted A. B. Cunningham, it made news around the world. Tension mounted when Cunningham challenged Fred Gebhard to a duel with pistols.

This was no laughing matter; Cunningham was a crack shot. Lillie did not want Fred to enter the duel, fearing he might be killed. The crisis passed when Diamond Jim Brady interceded. In the meantime, despite the threatened boycott, the theater company grossed a record $31,539.80 during a two-week stay in St. Louis.

By the time Lillie reached Buffalo, her affair with Fred was an open book. Fred arrived in the evening, went directly to her hotel room and was soon in pajamas. Agnes Langtry, Lillie's sister-in-law, who was in the same hotel, found Lillie dressed in her peignoir, drinking champagne with her lover.

Agnes departed the next morning, but not before writing her sister-in-law a scathing note.

The tour ended late in March. Lillie had earned somewhere between $100,000 and $150,000. She was the strongest box office draw in the United States. In June 1883, Lillie Langtry ended the busiest season of her life. She celebrated it by having dinner with Fred Gebhard. A few days later she sailed for England.

There, she assembled a group of players for a second visit to the United States. The play to be presented was *The Highest Bidder.* This time, she rented an apartment, which made it easy for Fred Gebhard to come and go without being seen by reporters.

By June 1884, Lillie was $100,000 to $125,000 richer.

In August 1884, she returned to England to act in several plays. The Prince and Princess of Wales attended each performance. There was no doubt that Lillie and the prince had quietly resumed their former relationship.

Lillie was now wealthy and successful. She decided to bring her daughter to live with her. Her daughter, in public, addressed her as "aunt." Fred wanted to visit Lillie in London, but Lillie procrastinated.

Lillie was fast becoming an accomplished actress. She scored in *Macbeth,* was a great hit in *As You Like It,* and brought the house down in *Cleopatra.*

By this time her romance with Fred Gebhard was over, and a new lover had appeared on the scene. He was George Alexander Baird, Baron Auchmeddon, one of the wealthiest men in England with an annual income of more than a quarter of a million pounds. He was a gambler, and Lillie met him when she played *Cleopatra.* She was 38 at the time, but appeared to be in her mid-twenties. He was younger.

Lillie and Baird plunged into an affair immediately. She never bothered to conceal the fact that she was sleeping with Baird. She was not in love with him, nor would she think of marrying him. Yet, she allowed him to kiss her and caress her in public.

Lillie and her new lover had several things in common. They both loved horses and fine jewelry. Each time Baird won at the horse races, Lillie sprouted new jewelry.

Baird was a jealous lover, and this led to the most shattering experience of Lillie's life. When Baird left for a hunting trip, Lillie went to Paris to purchase a new wardrobe. There, she met Robert Peel. They dined together one evening and, a few days later, he came to Lillie's suite for a chat.

In the meantime, George Baird had discovered that Lillie was in Paris. He found the hotel, burst into her room, and found the pair together. He beat Robert Peel and physically threw him out of the room. In his anger, he assaulted Lillie, blackening both her eyes and inflicted a bruise on her cheeks. When she screamed for help, he choked her until she lost consciousness.

His anger still unabated, he made a shambles out of her apartment. He ripped the tapestries, slashed the paintings, over-turned the furniture, ripped her new gowns into shreds. Four policemen had to subdue him before he could be arrested. Lillie spent 10 days in a hospital and the newspapers made much of this scandal, speculating that if the vicious beating Lillie had received would cause her death, Baird was certain to face the guillotine.

The charges were dropped when Baird showed remorse and completely refurbished Lillie's apartment. She remained in Paris for two weeks. Each day new gifts arrived. One afternoon, 50 gowns from Worth were delivered. The next day a ruby pendant arrived. She received as a gift three magnificent race horses.

One day she was told that her lover awaited her. She was led to a magnificent boat, 220 feet long. It was named *The White Lady*. On deck stood a docile George Baird. Title to the yacht and a check for fifty thousand pounds were given to her. All in all, he was making her a gift of one-half million dollars.

After placing some restrictions on his drinking and on her freedom, she once again accepted him. They spent several days at sea before *The White Lady* put into harbor. The press called the boat *The Black Eye*. Lillie's friends were disappointed in her. They were distressed to see that she could be bought.

It was in March 1893 that Lillie learned that Baird had died in New Orleans.

In 1896, Lillie received news about her husband, Edward Langtry. They had been quietly divorced. The information came from a young reporter for the *New York Journal*, who had located Edward Langtry. The reporter who interviewed Langtry reported that he had said, "However cruel it may be, I affirm that I never heard that my wife gave birth to a child of which I am reputed to be the father, until I learned of our divorce."

In 1897, Langtry was found wandering on the railroad tracks near Chester. He was in desperate condition. Drunk, he was taken to the jail where he became sober, but his talk was still incoherent. The court had him committed to a county asylum for the feebleminded, where he died, insane and penniless.

After the death of Edward Langtry, Lillie announced her retirement from the stage. She was now 45 years old and she was worth over $2,000,000. Her horses were earning more money for her than she could earn on the stage. In 1898, she and her daughter, Jeanne Marie, were seen in public more and more often. There was a strong resemblance between them, as well as a new bond that was being forged.

At this time her favorite was Prince Paul Esterhazy, an enormously wealthy widower. He made no secret of his infatuation with her. In fact he asked her to marry him. Lillie put him off, and at the same time saw other men; one of them was Hugo de Bathe. He was tall, slender, and only 27 years old. What she saw in him was a mystery to her friends. Yet, in the summer of 1899, they were quietly married.

The marriage astounded her friends. Hugo had little to offer her. He had no estate of his own, did not earn a living, had achieved no status whatsoever. Oscar Wilde, a long time friend of Lillie, was said to have remarked: ". . . a famous actress, who, after tragic domestic life, has married a fool. She thought that because he was stupid, he would be kindly, when, of course, kindliness requires both intellect and imagination."

Despite this remark, when Wilde was convicted on a morals charge, and sentenced to imprisonment at hard labor, Lillie came openly to his defense. The same cannot be said about other of his friends who deserted him.

Lillie, meanwhile had her own troubles. Hugo's family disinherited their son. His sisters made it clear that they would not receive Hugo and his wife. The *New York Journal* described Hugo as "an empty-headed young noodle." The *Chicago Inter-Ocean* called him "a typical English saphead."

For a while the marriage seemed to be working out. Lillie resumed her acting career, and Hugo would accompany his actress-wife. Lillie's daughter, Jeanne, now 18, accompanied them. Jeanne was beautiful, and onlookers who saw the three of them, believed that Hugo and Jeanne were married. When Hugo went off, late in 1899, to offer his services to the British in the Boer War, Lillie decided to reconquer the United States.

She arranged for a tour with her play, *The Degenerates*. The critics remarked that both the play and the actress were degenerate. This led to increased attendance, and her attraction at the box office remained intact. She played for 18 weeks in New York; then played in Philadelphia, as well as other major cities.

In the meantime, Jeanne Marie was being invited everywhere. It was evident that the Prince of Wales and Princess Alexandra were interested in her. Late in 1900, Jeanne Marie was presented to Queen Victoria at a formal Buckingham Palace audience. This was clearly an expression of approval of her respectability.

Back in England, Hugo had returned from the army. He had been discharged for medical reasons. Within a week after his return to London, in December 1900, Hugo was already escorting other women. In the forefront was a London chorus girl who was a noted sex symbol.

Lillie showed little concern. One time, she was seated in one part of a fashionable restaurant with some friends, and Hugo and his chorus girl in another. Lillie and Hugo waved to one another as though nothing was amiss.

Late in 1901, Jeanne was betrothed to Sir Ian Malcolm, a prominent, wealthy heir of a Scottish family. Jeanne was accepted by his family, but not so Lillie. Loyal Jeanne, however, refused to attend any function to which her mother was not invited.

The Prince of Wales was now King Edward VII. At a ball given by the Duchess of Devonshire, Alexandra, the queen, showed royal approval by personally seeking out Jeanne, chatting with her for a few minutes, and then leading her to King Edward to make her curtsy. Jeanne was now an "insider."

Jeanne was married at St. Margaret's of Westminster on June 30, 1902. Hundreds of people attended, including the most distinguished English families. But no recognition of the occasion was given by King Edward VII. Several newspapers did report that he had given Jeanne "a splendid jewel," and had sent her a handwritten letter. The press hinted that she was a girl "in whom he had been strongly interested since her birth."

Lillie, always practical, asked Hugo not to attend the wedding. After all, he was younger than the groom and his presence could prove to be embarrassing. He complied.

Lillie continued with her career. She originated a tour and once again was immensely successful. She charmed Theodore Roosevelt, had an entire Texas town named after her, and captivated Rudyard Kipling. Reporters insisted that Lillie looked like a woman in her twenties. Asked by a reporter for the *New York Sun* if she was happy, she replied, "Of course I am happy, as happiness goes, for a woman who has so many memories and lives the lonely life of an actress. It is restricted, as all artistic life necessarily must be. I've often put in as many as forty weeks on the stage in a single year, so you might say I've had precious little opportunity to brood or feel sorry for myself. I've sometimes been accused of lacking sentimentality, a quality I haven't been able to afford, and I think that is all to the good. The sentimentalist ages far more quickly than the person who loves his work and enjoys new challenges."

In 1907, General Sir Henry P. de Bathe, Hugo's father, died. Hugo inherited his title. Lillie was now Lady de Bathe. The title meant little to her, and she continued acting under her own name, telling Richard Le Gallienne, the English poet and critic, "Everything is precisely as it was. I'm still supporting my dear husband."

When in May, 1910, King Edward died, Lillie immediately went into seclusion, refusing to give interviews, and making no public appearances. When next seen a Boston reporter said to her that she looked like a young girl, Lillie replied, "What rubbish! I am 57 years of age, and I don't care who knows it. I don't look in the least young, as you and I well know. There isn't a woman in this world who doesn't look every day and every minute her age. We can't be younger than we are, and we can't look younger than we are. The most any woman of my age can do is hope she's well preserved."

For the next few years Lillie did some acting, and even made a movie, called *His Neighbor's Wife*, which received decent reviews.

In 1913, Hugo went off to war once again, and Lillie once again went on tour, traveling back and forth across the Atlantic. Her two leading men at the time were Lionel Atwill and Alfred Lunt.

When she was 63, she met Somerset Maugham on a transatlantic crossing. He had already achieved international renown as an author. He wrote of her then: "She still had a fine figure and a noble carriage, and if you were walking behind her you might have taken her for a young woman."

Jeanne was now the mother of three sons and a daughter, but Lillie never saw them. Circumstances had created an estrangement between daughter and mother.

Lillie was now tired of working. Still Hugo was content to let her support him while he led his own life. Lillie moved to Monaco. Her house was located on a steep mountainside overlooking the Riviera. There she plunged into the social whirl with the Riviera's permanent residents.

Somehow—no one knows who made the first overture—Lillie and her daughter were reconciled. Lillie now became acquainted with her three grandsons and grandaughter. Soon, photographs of the four grandchildren filled Lillie's bedroom.

Lillie, however, was not about to permit age to get the better of her. She followed the style of the times by shortening her skirts. She imitated Irene Castle and bobbed her hair. When it began to turn gray, she dyed it an auburn shade. Her husband's escapades caused her some embarrassment. He was now in his fifties and was still chasing girls with the same fervor that he had displayed in his younger days.

It was autumn of 1928. Lillie was now 75. She suffered from bronchitis, complicated by pleurisy. At the time she lived in London, but she soon returned to the Riviera. But even there, she rarely left her home.

In Feburary of 1929, Lillie fell ill again, this time with influenza. On the morning of February 12, the young girl who had made up her mind to electrify the world, and who succeeded at it, closed her eyes forever.

She was buried in the churchyard of St. Saviour's on the Isle of Jersey. Jeanne, and only her eldest son, were present. Hugo was not to be seen.

Edna St. Vincent Millay described Lillie's life in these words:

> Down, down, down into the darkness of the
> grave
> Gently they go, the beautiful, the tender, the
> kind;
> Quietly they go, the intelligent, the witty, the
> brave.
> I know. But I do not approve. And I am not
> resigned.

2

Voltaire
and his Exalted Mistress

Voltaire immortalized and chastised his mistress in the same breath. "Emilie," he said, "in truth is the divine mistress, endowed with beauty, wit, compassion and all of the other womanly virtues. Yet, I frequently wish she were less learned and her mind less sharp, that her appetites for the making of love were less voracious, and more than all else, that she would acquire both the ability and desire to hold her tongue on occasion."

The love affair between Voltaire and the Marquise du Châtelet (Emilie), was not an ordinary love affair. It couldn't be—Voltaire and Emilie were not ordinary people. Frederick the Great of Prussia, in a letter to both of them, wrote: "What admirable and unique people you both are! The wonder of all who know you increases day by day."

Voltaire, in his personal memoirs, noted that meeting Emilie was the turning point in his life. "I found, in 1733, a young woman who thought as I did, and decided to spend several years in the country cultivating her mind."

Emilie didn't stop at that. She went further. She declared that she was planning to spend the rest of her life with him.

The lovers were not romantic, passion-driven, sex-hungry teenagers. Voltaire was 39; Emilie 27. She had been married eight years, and was the mother of three children, one of whom was only several months old. She was a woman who went to excesses in every way, including love-making.

Emilie was born on December 17, 1706 of wealthy parents. Her father, Louis-Nicholas, Baron de Breteuil, was a nobleman in the court of Louis XIV. Her mother, Alexandra-Elizabeth de Froulay, was the impoverished younger sister of the Baron's mistress. By today's standards the family's yearly income was the equivalent of at least $150,000. They enjoyed every luxury, and for Emilie, the youngest and her father's favorite, nothing was too good.

When Emilie was seven years old, it appeared as if she had not inherited her mother's good looks. Her father, with unusual frankness, wrote in his diary: "My youngest is an odd creature, destined to become the homeliest of women. Were it not for the low opinion I hold of bishops, I would prepare her for a religious life, and let her hide in a convent. She stands as tall as a girl twice her years, she has prodigious strength, like that of a wood-cutter, and is clumsy beyond belief. Her feet are huge, but one forgets them the moment one notices her enormous hands. Her skin, alas, is as rough as a nutmeg grater, and altogether she is as ugly as a Cascon peasant recruit in the regiment of royal foot-guards."

Louis-Nicholas realized that something had to be done for Emilie if she were to get anywhere in the social world; and he spared no expense. From the age of six he surrounded her with tutors of exceptional talent. And tutored she was! She became fluent in Latin, Italian, English, and German. Tasso and Milton were as familiar to her as Virgil. She translated *The Aeneid*, and could recite long passages from Horace by heart. She studied the works of Cicero, and was at home in Virgil and Lucretius. She was able to translate Aristotle's *Politics and Aesthetics* from the original Greek, and had a healthy aptitude for metaphysics and mathematics. If this ugly duckling was to lead the life of a spins-ter, she would be the most cultured and educated woman around.

A fine wardrobe was selected for her and, by the time she reached maturity, she had developed a fine taste for interesting and varied styles of dress. "No queen owns a larger wardrobe," Voltaire wrote, "and no one but a queen could afford so many gowns, shoes, wigs, and other fripperies."

Emilie's father left nothing to chance. She was taught how to fence and ride. She became so adept at fencing, in fact, that a good swordsman feared crossing swords with her. How would it look to be beaten by a woman!

At 14, the ugly duckling began to change into a beautiful swan. It was as if someone had waved a magic wand. The family was delighted. At 16, she was presented at court. She was tall, but her figure was in perfect proportion. Her tiny waist and full bosom provided great sexual appeal. She had blonde hair and gray eyes. Her face was oval-shaped with lips that were provoca-tively sensual. She carried herself with the vigor of an outdoor girl. She exuded sex. No sooner did she make her debut at court than wagers were made as to who would be the first to seduce her.

There was no urgent need for Louis-Nicholas to protect his daughter's virginity from those who lusted after her. She made clear her own ability to do this by donning fencing clothes for a contest with Colonel Jacques de Brun, commander of the Royal Guard. Though she lost the bout, she gave so remarkable a per-formance as to put second thoughts into the heads of those who entertained ideas of bedding her down. Who wanted to run the risk of being challenged to a duel by a woman, and an expert swordsman to boot!

When Emilie was 19, she married the 30-year-old Marquis Chatelet, colonel of a regiment and head of one of the great families. His grandfather was a marshal of France. However, for all his titles, he was far from rich. This was not too important, since Emilie came with a generous dowry.

Two children, a boy and a girl, were born during the first years of their marriage. However, the father, whose great interest was the army, was seldom at home. Emilie and the children were left to their own devices.

It wasn't long before Emilie plunged into amorous relationships. Evidently, there was something of the whore in her, if we are to believe the words of W. C. Hazlitt:

Wanton look and twinkling,
Laughing and tickling,
Open breast and singing,
These without lying
Are tokens of whoring.

On a particular occasion, a footman was summoned to Emilie's bedroom one morning. While giving orders, she took off her nightdress and stood absolutely naked before him. On another occasion she rang for him asking that he bring a kettle of hot water for her bath which was getting cold. As she did not use bath salts, the water was clear and her naked body could be seen without any difficulty. Without the slightest hesitation she separated her legs so that he could pour the water between them. What effect this had on the footman was never indicated, but can well be imagined.

"The wench is formidable," the Duc de Richelieu wrote years later, when their famous affair was beginning to wane. "No man can resist her natural beauty, but no man has the courage to admit that she exhausts him. She rides and wields a sword like a hussar, and she becomes so ferocious when a lover vexes her that she would not hesitate to run him through. I hope to arrange the termination of our relationship in such a way that Emilie, not I, will be responsibile for our parting. I have no desire to cross swords with her, for I am convinced that her blade would be as deadly as her tongue."

Emilie's first lover was the Marquis de Guebriant. After a while he took up with another lover, not something that Emilie could easily accept. When she realized that he was not going to return to her, she asked for a final interview. During that meeting, Emilie made her former lover pour her a cup of soup which she drank; they then said farewell. Before he left the house, Emilie had placed a final note in his pocket. Luckily, he read it at once. It said that the soup was poisoned and she was now dying at the hands of her beloved. The Marquis immediately proved he was practical. He lost no time in rushing to her side. Quickly, he obtained an antidote which he forced her to swallow. Though it made her violently ill, it did serve to remove the poison from her system.

Emilie's marriage did not differ from those of other French aristocratic women. She had breakfast in bed at mid-morning, spent several hours getting ready for an afternoon of conversation. Two chambermaids helped her dress, handed her the various tubes, bottles, and vials of cosmetics she used, and then drenched her with quantities of perfumes.

Her second lover (she didn't wait too long to find one) was the Comte Pierre de Vincennes, a middle-aged former abbe who had given up the religious life because it was too confining. They were soon sleeping together. However, the former abbe was someone she could talk with. In fact, when the wits of high society asked one another, "What do you suppose they do together?" the reply, which caused much laughter, was, "They talk each other to death."

By this time, Emilie's personality was fully formed. She seemed to take her beauty for granted. She always needed an audience. When displeased, she lost her temper; she was known to be an expert at temper tantrums. She gambled, and did not know the meaning of self-discipline.

Louis Francois Armand du Plessis, Duc de Richelieu, had bedded some of the most beautiful women in France. He selected his mistresses because of their beauty. In fact, to be selected by Richelieu as a bed partner was a sign of success.

He came from an illustrious family. His granduncle had been the renowned Cardinal Richelieu, the famous patriot statesman. Richelieu was charming, quick-witted, wealthy, and dressed in the latest of fashion.

He knew women, and he had the knack of making each of his mistresses feel that he was devoting himself to her alone. Though some of his enemies called him a debaucher, he had the reputation of never seducing a virgin.

With all women practically at his feet, Richelieu exercised great care in selecting his mistresses. He loved and appreciated physical beauty. Voltaire wrote of him: "He seeks only perfection of face and form, and any blemish, however slight, is enough to turn him aside from a conquest. He has no other need in a mistress. If he wishes to exercise his mind, he converses with his friends or reads a book. If he seeks adventure, he leads his troops into a new campaign, and, if he yearns for solace, his Duchess is at hand to give it to him, always ready to interrupt her own activities for his sake. Venus adores him because he worships so devoutly at her shrine."

At the start, Richelieu and Emilie were attracted to one another on an intellectual basis. Emilie, who read every book of consequence and saw every play, was one of the very few .persons of either sex who could converse with him on his level. In the autumn of 1730 they became lovers. Though she wrote to him at least once a week until the end of her days, there is little known about their love affair. Emilie, who was never reluctant to discuss her affairs, was totally discreet about her romance with Richelieu.

Emilie and Richelieu continued to live in separate dwellings —within walking distance from one another. Richelieu was a busy man, and he did not spend all of his waking and sleeping time in bed with his mistress. Emilie accepted this behavior. It also matured her, gave her opportunities for further growth. She advanced several mathematical theorems of her own, and took advanced studies in physics and mathematics from professors at the Sorbonne.

The affair lasted one year. Few people, at the time, realized that Richelieu was fond of Emilie and enjoyed her company in a salon, at the dinner table as well as in bed. However, a year later, Richelieu tired of the relationship and sought a new mistress. Emilie was not too disappointed; she had expected this outcome all along.

François Arouet used the pen name of Voltaire. He was probably the most versatile writer in the history of French literature. Born in Paris on November 21, 1694, he enjoyed hinting that he was illegitimate. Voltaire's father, a prosperous notary, wanted François to follow his or some other honorable profession.

Voltaire was a philosopher, metaphysician, mathematician, and physicist—and was hailed as a genius. He was also a professional historian, and writer. He considered himself a poet. *Candide* is regarded as the best of his works. Among his other writings are at least 60 plays, comedies and tragedies. His energy seemed limitless.

Blessed with a healthy ego, Voltaire was intolerant of stupidity. His high self-opinion made him rash. He believed his work was "stunning," and could never resist reading it aloud. His relations with other French authors of the age were turbulent, and on one occasion he remarked, "If there is an author in this country with whom I have not quarreled, his work isn't worth reading."

At the age of 10, Voltaire was sent by the Abbé to the Collège Louis-le-Grand, a Jesuit school. When he left the Collège at the age of 17, he was probably one of the best educated youngsters in France.

Voltaire's star continued to rise. At the age of 30, his fame as a writer had been established. His love affairs had also developed at a lively pace. With success came improved health. No longer did he suffer from the nervous indigestion which had plagued him earlier. He knew his own body, and, when ill, he took to bed and starved himself.

An argument with the jealous Chevalier de Rohan, a man who loved Voltaire's mistress, had serious consequences. Rohan, to take revenge, hired thugs to beat up Voltaire. Voltaire challenged him to a duel—which was illegal. As a consequence, Voltaire was imprisoned in the Bastille.

Not wishing to remain in jail, Voltaire went into exile in England where he remained for more than three years. He loved England, especially its tradition of free speech. When he returned to Paris, it was 1729, and it was at this point that he wrote and produced his own plays successfully, becoming a millionaire in the process.

From then on, everything Voltaire touched turned to gold. He won an enormous state lottery, his investments prospered, and his books sold better than ever. But, in spite of all this prosperity, he was unhappy. "My misery embitters me and makes me shy," he told Thieriot.

It is not surprising that the Marquise du Chatelet (Emilie) and Voltaire were attracted to one another. He had returned to France fascinated with the scientific discoveries of Newton, and swayed by the philosophical teachings of Locke. In Paris, he searched for people with whom he could carry on interesting intellectual conversations. But there were few around. Emilie, with her young, brilliant, scientific mind understood him. This pleased him immensely. Her rank, and her influence at Court, were also sources of gratification. He liked the idea that a woman so intelligent and so important should become his mistress.

Voltaire loved feminine company. "The only difference between men and women," he said, "is that women are more amiable." Falling in love with Emilie inspired him to work hard, and was also an inspiration to her to pursue her own interests with enthusiasm. One result of this was that in only three weeks she learned to speak English.

Voltaire spent a great deal of time at the Cafe Gradot. Moreau de Maupertuis, a flamboyant explorer, astronomer and physicist who had achieved a great reputation, was starring there. Very few cafes admitted women diners and the better cafes did not serve women under any circumstances.

Emilie thought this regulation stupid, and decided to challenge it. One day she arrived in her carriage in men's attire. This put the Cafe management in a dilemma. They decided to pretend that she was a male, and served her like any other male patron. And so, the ban was broken, and Emilie became a regular at Gradot. It was here that Emilie and Voltaire met.

What started as friendship grew into love. Voltaire wrote soon after one of his early visits with Emilie: "Everything about her is noble—her countenance, her tastes, the style of her letters, her discourses, her politeness. . . If books were written as well as she speaks, love of reading would be the virtue of the world." Though Voltaire was in the habit of sleeping with any lady who made herself available—and many did—this time it was different. Overnight, he became the romantic schoolboy.

Exactly when Emilie du Châtelet and Voltaire first slept together is not recorded in the annals of romantic history. However, by mid-summer of 1733 their affair was in full bloom. Voltaire was almost 40 years of age and in poor health. Emilie was in superb health, and could function well on as little as two to four hours sleep.

It is interesting to point out that Du Châtelet, Emilie's husband, accepted Voltaire into his home. In fact, the two men became quite fond of one another. It is related that Châtelet once caught Voltaire escorting another lady and reproached him for not being faithful to Emilie. Du Châtelet was proud of his wife, but was entirely able to do without her company much of the time. He was a practical man: Since his wife made no objection to his affairs, how could he interfere in hers? Besides, Voltaire was a very wealthy man, and it was pleasing to Du Châtelet to associate with men of means.

Voltaire and Emilie made their home in the Château de Cirey. The house was owned by her husband but had been permitted to fall into disrepair. It was a huge, rambling structure, which, rebuilt by Emilie and Voltaire, still stands today. It is located at the eastern edge of Champagne, a short ride from the Lorraine border. Voltaire arrived there several months before Emilie, and he planned to convert the neglected place into a comfortable home. In three months, he accomplished a near miracle, but not without some dissent from Emilie who had her own ideas.

Alone in the Château at the beginning, Voltaire missed his mistress. Why Emilie elected to remain in Paris for another three months is a mystery. It is known that she went about her usual business absorbing the wisdom of Maupertuis and other scientists, paying social calls on friends, playing cards, and even spending a little time with her otherwise neglected children.

The time came when Emilie decided to join Voltaire. Her caravan consisted of five large carriages, and her party included her children, her personal maids, her principal cook, and several other servants. She made arrangements before leaving Paris for additional carriages to be filled with her clothing, and to be sent the following week. One of the additional carriages was stuffed with books. She did not concern herself with pots, pans, dishes or other household appliances.

It wasn't long before Voltaire and Emilie differed on how to design and decorate the house. Complained Voltaire: "Mme du Châtelet is going to put windows where I have put doors. She is changing staircases into chimneys and chimneys into staircases. Where I have instructed the workmen to construct a library, she tells them to place a salon. My salon she will make into a bath closet. She is going to plant lime trees where I have proposed to place elms, and where I have planted herbs and vegetables nothing will make her happy but a flower bed."

But Voltaire's tremendous love for her tempered his annoyance. He was not stingy with Emilie. He poured large sums of money into his mistress's hands, and she spared no expense to indulge her tastes. Living together strengtened the bond between them. They were at home with each other, and Emilie happily pursued her decorating and furnishing, while Voltaire returned to his writing desk. On occasion, they worked together, as when they collaborated on an exposition of the works of Sir Isaac Newton, which was entitled, *Newton*. Although, at the start, the couple was ridiculed, the study was hailed as a masterpiece by every scientist in France. The following year Emilie worked on her own and translated *The Aeneid* of *Virgil* into English.

In 1734, Emilie made several trips to Paris where she was promptly snubbed by a number of prominent ladies because of their disapproval of her extramarital affairs—not that these very same ladies were themselves above indulging in adulterous relations with gentlemen of prominence. However, the difference was that they were conducting their affairs with discretion—not so Emilie.

Although, both Voltaire and Emilie flouted convention, they were now afraid of how Emilie's husband, Florent-Claude du Châtelet, would react to this kind of widespread publicity. He had already made it clear that he did not object at all to his wife's affair with Voltaire, so there was no chance that he would challenge Voltaire to a duel. Thus, Voltaire had no reason for concern. But Emilie's situation was quite different. A husband who had been publicly humiliated by his wife could, in those days, place her in a convent for as long as he wished, or until *he* died.

Emilie, terribly disturbed, wrote to her former lover, Duc de

Richelieu: "The more I reflect on Voltaire's situation and on mine, the more I think the steps I have taken to preserve the situation are necessary. Firstly, I believe that all those who love passionately should live in the country together if that is possible for them, but I think still more that I cannot keep my hold on his imagination elsewhere. I should lose him sooner or later in Paris, or at least I should pass my days fearing to lose him and in having cause to lament over him.

"I love him enough, I confess it to you, to sacrifice all the pleasure and delight I might enjoy in Paris for the sake of the happiness of living with him without fears, and of the pleasure of protecting him, in spite of himself, from the effects of his own imprudence and fate. The only thing which causes me anxiety and which I shall have to manage carefully about, is the presence of M. du Châtelet. I count greatly on your conversations with him. A permanent peace would destroy all our hopes, although I cannot keep myself from longing for it on your account.

"My position is indeed embarrassing, although I take pains to conceal that embarrassment from all, particularly from Voltaire, whose discomfort in all matters is always greater than mine. But love changes all the thorns into flowers, as it always does among our mountains of Cirey, our terrestrial paradise. I cannot believe that I was born to be unhappy; I see only the delight of spending all the moments of my life in the company of the one I love."

The Duc de Richelieu did have a number of frank talks with the Marquis du Châtelet in which he pointed out that a wise husband would ignore the whispers and gossip that reached his ears. Evidently, du Châtelet took the advice, and difficulty was avoided.

After a year and a half of living at Cirey, Voltaire wanted to visit Paris. Emilie was not too happy to make the trip, fearing that she would surely lose him. They could not live together openly at the Hotel du Châtelet, so they parted upon reaching the city. Voltaire rented an inexpensive lodging. In Paris they were seldom seen together. Obviously, they were sensitive to gossip and criticism. As Alexander Pope so wisely wrote: "At every word a reputation dies."

When they left for Versailles, they traveled separately. There, Emilie plunged into her usual heavy social life. She spent money at her usual, reckless pace. Dressmakers visited her at the Hotel du Châtelet, as did booksellers. Soon she was sending convoys of carts to Cirey. There was a jeweler who was also a frequent caller, and in addition to such items as gold earrings and bracelets, she purchased a magnificent emerald ring and matching pendant.

Though Emilie was nervous and feared losing her lover, she

did not hold too tight a rein on him during their visit to Paris. They made no public appearances together—not even to the theater. In fact, there was speculation that the affair had ended.

It was at this time that Voltaire found himself in trouble with the Church for his publication of *La Pucelle,* a long poem that ridiculed French life. So, when early in July of 1735, Emilie closed her Paris house and left for Cirey, Voltaire stayed on. Voltaire feared that no one would visit them at Cirey should they incur Cardinal Fleury's wrath.

No sooner did Emilie arrive at Cirey that she wrote to Voltaire advising him that Fleury would not punish him for writing *La Pucelle,* nor would he take action against anyone visiting Cirey. Voltaire left for Cirey within 24 hours.

Emilie was delighted; their relationship had survived a Paris stay. Voltaire had been exposed to all the temptations and joys of Paris and had returned to her. He had indicated his loyalty to her by showing absolutely no interest in any other woman. Love had triumphed; their bonds were now stronger than ever.

Emilie now threw herself into her scientific studies. She turned the great hall into a mammoth physics laboratory. Voltaire was fascinated by all this. Emilie invited him to observe her tests; and he was forced to admit that her scientific thinking was sound.

In 1736, the Crown Prince Frederick of Prussia, later to be known as Frederick the Great, invited Voltaire to visit him at his hunting lodge. From the very moment Emilie heard of this, the idea displeased her. She and Voltaire were in love and were sharing a home. Though not married, their home had more warmth in it than the homes of many married couples. She had no desire to have anyone intrude upon their paradise, and she didn't want Voltaire to go to Prussia.

Prince Frederick was a homosexual, and although Emilie realized that no women except middle-aged servants ever set foot on his property, there was the possibility that Voltaire might become infatuated by one of the intelligent, creative, talented "creatures" who lived on the prince's estate. Added to this fear, Emilie had heard rumors in the past identifying Voltaire as a party to several homosexual affairs. And there was a lingering doubt that there might be some credence to these rumors and that her lover might have homosexual tendencies. She was determined to go to any lengths in order to stop him from going to Prussia; and she wrote lengthy letters to friends of Voltaire asking them to persuade him not to go.

At this very time, Voltaire's *Adam and Eve* appeared. It was a book of verses in which he ridiculed Church doctrine concerning the origin of man. Church officials were furious, and Voltaire's friends advised him to leave France. He took their advice, and, without advising Emilie, left Cirey and traveled to neighboring countries under an assumed name. Not until the last day of the year 1736 did frantic Emilie hear from him, and this only via a short note in which he complained that the translation of his *Alzire* into Dutch had been sloppy and unimaginative.

"My heart is breaking with anxiety and grief," she wrote back, pleading with him to write more often. But Voltaire decided not to respond to the love letters of his mistress. He felt that the secret police was opening his mail, and they might cause trouble. His notes to her were, therefore, brief and exceptionally formal. In them, he addressed her as "Madame."

So torn with grief was she over this turn of events that she wrote a letter to their mutual friend d'Argental. Stripped of all pride, she wrote:

"Persuade M. de Voltaire, I beg you, to return to Cirey at all costs. I am ill; I have had fever for two days; the violence of my feeling is capable of killing me in four more.

"Who is there could save him in spite of himself? I, at least, have nothing to reproach myself with, but that is a sad consolation. I am not born to be happy; my brain is dazed with grief."

It was some time later that Emilie learned that Voltaire had settled in Amsterdam on a semipermanent basis. Soon, she began to bombard him with letters. The unending stream of letters from Emilie on the one hand and the continued pressure from Prince Frederick on the other were beginning to have their effect and Voltaire felt himself weakening.

Suddenly, Voltaire made a totally unexpected visit to Cirey. Emilie was ecstatic. In order to return to France, Voltaire had to shake off the secret police who were still determined to find enough cause to jail him for his anti-Church views.

A few days later the Marquis du Châtelet made a brief visit to the Château. When he left for Paris, he carried with him a letter from Voltaire to d'Argental. It read:

"I confess to you that if I had not been recalled by a friendship stronger than all sentiments, I would willingly have spent the remainder of my days in a country where at least my enemies could not harm me. I have only to expect persecutions in France; that will be the whole of my reward. I should regard my presence in this country with horror if it were not that the tenderness and all the great qualities of the person who holds me here did not make me forget where I was.

"I have become a willing slave for the sake of living with the individual near whom all disagreeables disappear.

"I have always said that if my father, my brother, or my son were prime minister in a despotic state, I would leave tomorrow, but Mme. du Châtelet is more to me than father, brother or son. I ask nothing more than to live buried in the mountains of Cirey."

Love had conquered—at least for the moment. Prince Frederick of Prussia had lost the battle to Emilie.

On the last day of May 1740, Frederick of Prussia acceded to the throne, his father having died after a long illness. Within a week, King Frederick wrote to Voltaire and again asked him to come to Prussia. When Emilie learned of this invitation, she wrote directly to the king indicating her desire to accompany Voltaire on the visit.

The king was not at all interested in meeting with Emilie, and Voltaire was caught in the middle of the triangle. He knew that if he left without Emilie, she would make his life miserable. And so he delayed answering. In the meantime Emilie kept up a steady barrage of letters to the king telling him how eager she and Voltaire were to see him.

The king finally capitulated, and Emilie was elated. She had won a victory. But her victory was short-lived. The king followed with a letter saying that he had a fever and could not receive them, but that Voltaire could meet with him in Antwerp. Though Emilie was deeply anguished, she wrote the king: "I do not know what afflicts me most, to know that Your Majesty is ill, or to be disappointed in the hope I had of paying court to you."

Voltaire left to meet with King Frederick, who welcomed him with joy. Not even in England had Voltaire been greeted with such respect.

Back at home, Emilie brooded over his absence.

Voltaire kept a promise he had made to Emilie and left for The Hague within a few days. To keep him from returning to Prussia with Frederick, Emilie had arranged for Voltaire to be invited by King Louis, knowing that Voltaire would give up his Prussian visit for a visit to his own king.

Emilie was right. Voltaire was delighted, and their visit was at hand. At the palace, Emilie's conduct at Fontainebleau in France astonished the court. Her clothes, as always, were expensive, but she refrained from wearing the very low-cut gowns that almost completely exposed her bosom and had so shocked the court. Her gems were dazzling, but she wore only a selected few at any one time. She meant to impress the court with her good taste and maturity.

In 1741, Emilie and Voltaire traveled extensively, seldom remaining in any one place for more than a few weeks. Emilie was now devoting herself exclusively to Voltaire, even foresaking her own scientific experiments.

Voltaire kept up with his writing. They had no quarrels.

Both were subdued and managed to stay out of difficulties with the authorities. The year 1741 was a quiet one for the two lovers.

Voltaire's plays were meeting with success. *Merope,* one of his plays, was not only Voltaire's greatest success, but the biggest hit of the century. Audiences went wild, sometimes applauding for more than an hour after the final curtain fell. Voltaire's wallet bulged with francs.

Relations between Emilie and Voltaire were strained during the winter and early spring of 1744. Neither of them was very productive. In addition, the Marquis du Châtelet, enjoying his first long leave of absence from the army, had moved into Cirey together with his redheaded mistress. Neither Voltaire nor Emilie enjoyed the thought of spending months with that pair. And so they remained in Paris.

Voltaire sulked, but Emilie was quite happy. She visited friends, attended dinner parties, frequented the theater, and was a regular at the opera. And she gambled. Voltaire believed that Emilie was now punishing him for neglecting her during his months in Prussia. Emilie gambled for large stakes, and Voltaire paid the enormous debts she accrued (today's equivalent of about $40,000 a day).

Finally, she stopped gambling, and both returned to work. They returned to Cirey. Writing to d'Argental, Emilie said, "It's more charming than ever. Never have we known such tranquility, never has there been a more benign spring, never has the sun been brighter or warmer. Your friend appears enchanted to be here."

In the spring of 1744, Emilie finished her work, a long philosophical essay, *Trait dur le Bonheur.* Then she wasted no time in returning to her gambling. Gambling kept her young, she insisted. Gambling, she said, made one run the gamut—from extreme hope to extreme fear, and, consequently, the gambler stayed in good health.

In a philosophically reflective mood, she gave her recipe for human happiness:

> One must live virtuously.
> One must rigorously rid his being of all prejudices against persons and customs.
> One must retain the illusions one deemed important in childhood.
> One must live sensibly in order to enjoy the blessings of good health.
> One must cultivate strong tastes.
> One must develop strong passions.

Emilie often addressed women's groups, speaking about women's concerns. She reminded them that every woman, even the homeliest, loved pretty clothes. When a woman's spirits drooped, Emilie advised, she should lose no time in ordering a new gown; it should be a lovely gown, she insisted, rather than one that was merely practical.

For the most part, Emilie and Voltaire spent uneventful days in 1745 and 1746. Voltaire continued to provide funds for the household, and Emilie had learned caution in her spending habits. Emilie continued to make extensive notes for her new work on Newton; and Voltaire, thoughtful, considerate, and generous as ever, spent countless hours helping her with her studies.

In the spring of 1747, tensions in Paris increased. Voltaire had taken on a new burden and was writing *Semiramis*. To occupy her time, Emilie played cards. One day, Voltaire, wandering around at the Fontainebleu, came upon Emilie gambling at the queen's table.

"You're mad," he said to her, addressing her in English. "Don't you know you shouldn't be playing cards with these women? Every last one of them is a cheat!"

Calling Marie Catherine Sophie Felicite Leczinska, Queen of France, a cheat was something not easily to be forgiven. Voltaire was petrified and had reason to be. Emilie immediately asked to be excused from the table. Queen Marie smilingly granted permission.

There was no doubt that Voltaire was now in danger. A squad of Musketeers, bearing a royal warrant for his arrest, could be expected at any time. Voltaire was in a state of near hysteria, but Emilie kept her head. She knew that taking her lover to her home would make it easy for the police to apprehend him, so she took him to the castle of Mme. de Maine, a duchess who was afraid of no one.

Emilie returned to Paris by herself. What they had expected did not materialize. No action was taken against Voltaire, but they decided to be cautious. Emilie would not visit Voltaire, nor would she even risk writing him a letter. After a while, the incident was forgotten and Voltaire returned to Emilie.

It was during 1746 that Emilie realized that something was amiss. Someone else, not so involved with herself as Emilie, might have realized much sooner that Voltaire was not too well, and that he needed a period of tranquility. However, Emilie, instead of taking him to Cirey, went on a heavy gambling spree.

The love affair was in the doldrums. This was at least partly due to the presence of Emilie's husband who had come to Cirey for a stay. Emilie now found that she had two husbands on her hands. But she prevented Voltaire from taking a new younger mistress. Emilie would not permit Voltaire a younger substitute.

Jean François Marquis de Saint-Lambert, a respected nobleman, now entered Emilie's life. Although not too great a scholar, he had won election to the Academy in his middle years.

Saint-Lambert had one desire and that was to seduce the mistresses of other men. He had an affair with the Marquise de Foufflers for a time in 1747, but he bored her, and so she terminated the relationship. In later years he stole the mistress of Jean Jacques Rousseau. Saint-Lambert had a theory which he was determined to prove—and that was that there were no unseductible women, only inept men.

Emilie was 10 years older than Saint-Lambert, but still extremely attractive. They met in the court of King Stanislaus of Lorraine.

Saint-Lambert made no secret of his admiration for Emilie, and his advances were ostentatious. Here was a young, virile, and handsome man who desired her, and Emilie acted in accordance with her impulses. Overwhelmed by sexual desire, she fell into Saint-Lambert's arms and announced her intention of spending the rest of her life with him. She would now add Saint-Lambert to Voltaire and M. du Châtelet. As Confucious noted: "Rare are those who prefer virtue to the pleasures of sex." Soon Emilie had a key to a secret bedroom, and Saint-Lambert discovered quickly that his flirtation had blossomed into a full-dress love affair.

At age 42, it seemed odd, indeed, that Emilie, one of the most learned of women, a woman engaged in translating Newton, and the mother of two grown children, fathered by the greatest writer of the day, should be able to send letters to her new lover that read like those of a love-infatuated teenager.

Almost at once, Saint-Lambert fell ill in the little, secret room. He developed a fever, and his body was covered with a rash. Of course, Emilie took care of him, dosing him with all kinds of homemade remedies. She would go to the secret room and watch him as he slept. When she couldn't come, they would exchange letters. Saint-Lambert wrote: "It is very sweet to wake up and read your charming letters and to know the happiness of loving and being loved by you. I feel that I shall never be able to do without your letters which are the joy of my life. You have never been more tender, more loveable and more adored."

Emilie was not deluded. She knew that she loved him more than he loved her. He was waiting for her love to subside. All she asked was that he permit her to go on loving him. This he did, even postponing a journey to Italy when she begged him to do so.

Voltaire did not seem to mind Emilie's new-found joy. She never thought of her own selfishness, never thought at any time that she was behaving unfaithfully towards him. He no longer made love to her and, therefore, could not expect her to be loyal to him alone.

In May of 1748 Saint-Lambert rejoined his regiment. Voltaire and Emilie went to Paris. It was now clearly evident to Emilie that she was more in love with Saint-Lambert than he with her.

Emilie lived only to retrieve her lover, and soon she persuaded Voltaire, ill as he was, to go with her to Lorraine where Saint-Lambert was, or would soon be visiting. As usual, her wishes prevailed.

Life at the little court was cheerful and inane. One evening Voltaire wanted to have a word with Emilie before supper. There was no footman in her anteroom and he went straight into her boudoir, as he always did, without waiting to be announced. He found Emilie and Saint-Lambert in a position that demanded little of the imagination. Voltaire was shocked and insulted. He flew into a violent tantrum and upbraided them. Saint-Lambert formal and elegant, told Voltaire cooly that if he did not like what he saw, he could leave the room, leave the premises and meet him anywhere—with any weapons he chose.

Voltaire had no intention of dueling. He left the room, returned to his own rooms, and tried to hire a carriage to take him to France. Emilie, learning of this, made certain that no carriage would be available. She did not want Voltaire to leave under these circumstances.

The next morning Emilie entered Voltaire's room. She tried to reassure him, only to hear his reply: "Oh, you expect me to believe all this after seeing what I saw with my two eyes. I have sacrificed my whole life to you—health and fortune, and have lain at your feet, and this is my reward! Betrayal!"

"I still love you," she replied. "But you must admit that it is a long time now since you have been able to . . . I have no wish to kill you. Nobody is more concerned with your health than I. On the other hand, I have my own to consider. As you can do nothing for it any longer, it is not very reasonable of you to be so angry when I find one of your friends who can." Freud, years later, wrote: "The great question that has never been answered, and which I have not yet been able to answer despite my 30 years of research into the feminine soul, is 'What does woman want?' " Emilie could have given him the answer.

When Voltaire heard Emilie's explanation, he could not help but laugh. "Ah, Madame!" he said, "Of course you are in the right as usual. But you really should manage so that these things do not take place before my very eyes." Thus, Voltaire was calmed.

She then went to Saint-Lambert in order to soothe him as well. He was still ready to duel. Emilie gently pointed out that dueling with an old man, and a famous one at that, would not add to his laurels. She advised him to apologize to Voltaire—which he did.

Voltaire was mollified at once. "No, no, my child, I was wrong. You are still at the happy age when one can love and be loved. Make the most of it. An old, ill man like myself can no longer hope for these pleasures." Thus they resumed their relationship.

Some time later, in Cirey, Voltaire saw that Emilie was perterbed about something. She was worried and depressed. It wasn't long before she confessed that, at age 43, she was pregnant. How was she going to face her world? How would her husband react? Who could she claim was the father?

Voltaire behaved remarkably well. His concern was for Emilie. He bolstered her spirits, assuring her that everything would be all right. But Emilie was worried. She had not had sexual relations with her husband for a long time and could not claim that he was the father. Voltaire, with all his overt concern, had no intention of claiming fatherhood. Emilie faced the twin horrors of ridicule and disgrace.

Saint-Lambert was no longer in touch with Emilie, but when Voltaire wrote him to come at once, Saint-Lambert got on a horse and was in Cirey within a few hours. Together, the three of them pondered a course of action.

The important question was how to break the news to her husband, M. du Châtelet, the liberal mate who permitted her the same bed partner luxuries he took for himself. For the past 17 years she had had a platonic relationship with him. Who could she name as the father of the child? Voltaire cautiously suggested that it be classified as one of Emilie's miscellaneous works.

Emilie sent for her husband who came post haste. Never had he been granted so wonderful and warm a reception. Emilie greeted her husband tenderly. Voltaire and Saint-Lambert extended themselves to please him. His neighbors cheered him. He was wined and dined.

At supper, Emilie, in a low-cut gown, adorned with her many diamonds, sat next to her husband, plying him with food and drink, encouraging him to speak about his military campaigns. He was quite overcome by the good food, and by the loving looks which Emilie flashed at him over the tantalizingly exposed bosom.

At last, Châtelet begged Emilie's permission to pay her his homage as a husband. He wanted to take her to bed and his wants and desires were immediate and great. She pretended to be shocked and surprised; she blushed and refused. But, almost intoxicated by her perfumes and feminine assets, he insisted;

and she said she would think about it.

In due course, Emilie surrendered, and, begging to be excused, she and Chatelet retired. This was the beginning of a three week "honeymoon." It was then that Emilie told her husband that their union was once more to be blessed. Chatelet nearly fainted with joy. He announced the good news to all, far and wide.

During the months of her pregnancy, Emilie continued to work on finishing her book about Newton. She felt she was going to die, and she wanted, above all, to finish her book. At the same time, she continued writing torrid love letters to Saint-Lambert. His replies were cold.

Few women will believe how Emilie gave birth. On September 1, 1749, she was seated, as usual, at her writing table. She was very much absorbed in her work and did not realize that she was in the throes of childbirth. Suddenly she felt something strange: she had given birth while seated at her desk! Not knowing what to do with the infant until she could summon her maid, she placed it temporarily on a large mathematics textbook. Then, because it was expected of her, she retired to bed.

For several days, she recuperated nicely. But soon thereafter she began to feel feverish. She asked repeatedly for ice drinks make of almonds. Despite advice to the contrary, she drank copious amounts of this concoction and became very ill. A physician diagnosed her condition as an upset stomach.

On September 7th, Voltaire and Saint-Lambert were summoned to Emilie's apartment. She was in a coma. Suddenly, horrible sounds came from her bedroom. They entered. Emilie lay quite still. They tried to revive her, but to no avail. Emilie was dead.

Voltaire lost control. He wept; then dashing out of the apartment, he stumbled, lost his balance and tumbled down a flight of stairs. Badly shaken, he mourned to Saint-Lambert, "My friend, my death, too, lies at your door."

Grief overwhelmed him. He spent 24 hours alone in his chambers. Before leaving, Voltaire wrote to d'Argental: "I have not lost merely a mistress, I have lost the half of myself—a soul for which mine was made, a friend whom I saw born. The most tender father does not love his only daughter more truly."

Voltaire could not bear to stay at Cirey, and left the following day. Before leaving, he wrote to King Frederick:

"She was a great man whose only fault was in being a woman. A woman who translated and explained Newton, and who made a free translation of Virgil, without letting it appear in conversation that she had done these wonders; a woman who never spoke evil of anyone, and who never told a lie, a friend attentive and courageous in friendship—in one word, a very great woman whom ordinary women know only by diamonds— that is the one whom you cannot hinder me from mourning all of my life."

Life went on. Du Châtelet lived to be 70. Voltaire set up house with Mme. Denis and lived another 29 years. Saint-Lambert set up house with M. and Mme. d'Houdetot and lived another 54 years.

In the words of Seneca: "Why do you ask, 'How long did he live?' He still lives; at one step he has passed over into posterity and consigned himself to the guardianship of memory."

3
A Woman for a Throne

For the love of a woman, he gave up an empire.

Never in history, never before on screen or stage or within the covers of a book has a love affair so stirred the sympathies and imaginations of millions of men and women in every part of the world. With the words,

> "I have found it impossible to carry the heavy burden of responsibility and discharge my duties as king . . . without the help of the woman I love,"

did Edward abdicate his exalted position.

As king of England, he was a descendant of kings and queens. He was dashing and good-looking—an almost fairy tale Prince Charming. He could have had his pick from a bevy of acceptable and beautiful women. Instead, his heart had been captured by a divorcee, an American, a 40-year-old married woman.

This is the story of the Prince of Wales. He ascended the British throne on January 20, 1936, the day after the death of his father, King George V. England at the time was in a state of turmoil: Hitler's emerging Germany was a threat to England and the rest of the world. Yet, the new king seemed unconcerned with these ominous developments. He was deeply involved in a love affair with Wallis Warfield Simpson, and his mind was elsewhere.

Much of the press was critical of his behavior.

"She is his oxygen. He cannot breathe without her," declared *Le Journal* in France.

In the United States the newspaper headlines carried the following blazing headline: "The Yankee At King Edward's Court."

Who was Wallis Warfield Simpson? That depended on where you went for your information, and with whom you spoke.

Upton Sinclair, the novelist who was a cousin of Wallis, stated that her maternal grandfather was a direct lineal descendant of Chief Powhatan, Pocahontas' father. One genealogist claimed that she came from the blood of at least six English kings, and at least two Magna Carta barons.

Doubtful as many of the claims were, however, there is no

doubt that her family tree had many distinguished branches, particularly in Maryland and Virginia. Governor Edwin Warfield of Maryland was one of her father's ancestors and Governor Andrew Jackson Montague of Virginia was an antecedent of her mother.

Wallis' mother was a beautiful woman. A Baltimore newspaper referred to her as "one of the two beautiful Montague sisters." She was popular with men from the time she was 13 years of age and could have had her pick of suitors. But being ruled by her heart and not by her head, she picked Teackle Wallis Warfield, a postmaster, as her husband. He was neither handsome, healthy, nor wealthy; and since all of his brothers had become quite rich, he was considered the black sheep of the family.

Wallis' parents were married on November 19, 1895, and, exactly seven months later, on June 19, 1896, their daughter was born. They had wanted a son and so bestowed the rather masculine name, Wallis. Perhaps Dr. Allen was prophetic when, at her birth, he responded to the question of the mother: "Doctor, is the baby all right? Has she all her fingers and all her toes?" He said, "She's perfect. In fact, she's fit for a king."

There is no doubt that Bessiewallis—as she was called—was spoiled by her mother who was widowed at an early age.

At the age of 12, her mother remarried, much to the disappointment of Bessiewallis who wanted her mother only for herself. The account of the wedding described "the beautiful young daughter of the bride" who "wore a dainty gown of embroidered batiste laced with blue ribbons." The *Baltimore News* referred to her as "Miss Wallace Warfield." This delighted her; she had always hated the name of Bessie.

Wallis' first crush was on 17-year-old Lloyd Tabb. They would read to each other everything from Kipling and Robert Service to Monsieur Beaucaire. He described her as very feminine, never silly, not impulsive, very clever and at times shrewd.

At 16, she attended Oldfields, a school with very strict, traditional rules, which Wallis often broke. There was a rule that girls were not even permitted to correspond with boys, let alone see them. But Wallis managed to spend time with the opposite sex: Carter Osburn, for one, not handsome, but the owner of a car; Arthur Stump, tall, dark, and quiet, also the owner of a car; and Thomas Shryock, Jr. whose father was a general. She also did not forget her first boyfriend, Lloyd Tabb, whom she invited to join her at Oldfields. Wallis' friends all agreed that she preferred boys to books. How she managed so varied a social life in so strict a school as Oldfields is difficult to imagine.

At 18, Wallis was a young lady who had poise, manners,

style, and perfect taste in everything. Her schooling and social experiences had worked wonders on her. Basil Gordon, one of her cousins, said of her, "She attracted men the way molasses attracts flies."

Wallis knew herself well; she was aware of her assets as well as her liabilities. She was only five feet four, but was slender and straight. She had distinctively high cheekbones and a beautiful broad brow. Her hair was parted in the center, and was drawn off her face in soft waves. She neither wore nor needed any ornaments.

Her voice was low-pitched and she had mastered the art of using it to maximum effect. Her single most outstanding feature was her large, luminous, violet-blue eyes which were piercing and intense.

Her taste in clothing was excellent; she looked as though she had "stepped out of a bandbox." There was not a crease in her dress, nor a hair out of place. She was alive and exciting, and, when she spoke, she made one feel that he was absolutely the most important person in the world. She had so much charm that she was able to captivate almost anyone—especially men.

To Wallis and teenage girls everywhere, the Prince of Wales was the Prince Charming of the world. He had royal blood, royal mystery, royal titles. His life, she thought was exciting, full of love and adventure. He had everything—money, power, romance. Was it any wonder that she placed a picture of the Prince of Wales in her diary? Little did she know how lonely the prince really was. He was without meaningful relationships, and hungered for love. His father showed him little affection; and his mother was cold and rigid—a person who did not understand a child's mind or heart.

At most, his parents saw him at bedtime when they appeared to bid him goodnight. Queen Mary disliked the routine of childbearing and childrearing. In fact, she once wrote to her husband: "Of course it is a great bore for me and requires a great deal of patience to bear it, but this is alas the penalty of being a woman."

David (the name by which the prince was christened) was frightened by his father, who believed that children should be seen and not heard. With his very stern look, which was intensified by his formal-looking beard, he projected a frightening and fearful figure to his young son. To make matters worse, David's first nurse was a neurotic who often twisted his arm and made him cry. In short, the environment of his formative years contributed to making David a highly nervous child who fidgeted and was quick to cry.

David grew up in a royal atmosphere, knowing full well that

one day he would be king. The thought did not make him happy; the expression of his face often betrayed sadness.

When World War I came, as the Prince of Wales, he was annoyed at the time and money wasted in the state visits he was called upon to make. He was awarded many medals, and, though he wore them, they offered no satisfaction, because he had not earned them. Though he made frequent visits to the front and to hospitals, he was not permitted to assume a more important role in the war effort.

By the end of World War I, the prince (now 25) was advised by his father to associate more with other people. "You can mingle with them, but remember your position," cautioned the father.

The prince now became daring and reckless. He loved steeple-chasing. He bought a Daimler, and enjoyed driving it at very high speeds. He played polo and learned to fly his own plane. He then began a series of visits across the country. The more he traveled, the more popular he became. The world liked his sincerity, his love of pleasure, his youth, and his good looks.

David seemed tireless. He could dance all night, review troops, shake thousands of hands, make a speech, play golf, attend a luncheon, drive through the streets, make a second speech, shake more hands—all in a single day. For six years he toured the world as the public relations man of the British Empire.

When he visited America, one of the headlines read:
HERE HE IS GIRLS—THE MOST ELIGIBLE
BACHELOR YET UNCAUGHT!

There was no shortage of available women to the prince; he just wasn't ready for marriage. He did have relationships with women. One involved Winifred Birkin, the wife of the Right Honorable Dudley Ward, a man 20 years his wife's senior, and a liberal member of Parliament. She was called Frieda by her friends, and was pretty, bright and petite. She had a nice figure and a glowing face. Wherever Frieda invited him, the prince went. When he was away, he cabled her often. When he could manage it, he would spend time at a college at Le Touquet in France.

This relationship lasted 10 years.

"I know he was in love with her, because he told me so," confided Lord Brownlow, one of the prince's closest friends. He did propose marriage to her, a proposal she refused, knowing full well that he could not marry her because of the royal rules concerning divorce.

The prince found another true love in Thelma Furness. Thelma had much beauty, but few brains. She was gay and friendly, but had no sense of humor. She described their romance in these words: "His arms around me were the only reality; his words of love my only bridge to life. Borne along on the mounting tide of his ardour, I felt myself being inexorably swept from the accustomed moorings of caution . . . Each night, I felt more completely possessed by our love, carried even more swiftly into uncharted seas of feeling, content to let the prince chart the course, heedless where the voyage would end."

Then David met Wallis Simpson. At the time, she was married to Ernest Simpson. The prince adored her. He stimulated her mind, made her alive, kept her interested. They enjoyed reading and going to the theater. He was handsome. His intellect captivated her and her respect for him was deep. He was brave and courageous. He was well-read. She liked him for all these qualities. The prince loved her for her laugh, her wit, her ability to be a hostess, her good taste. And he indulged her with clothes, jewels, and antiques. He wanted to please her.

Her good friend, Thelma Furness, suggested that Wallis be presented at court. By this time Wallis Warfield Simpson had already been divorced from her first husband. The problem was: how could a divorced woman be presented at court? Somehow, this difficulty was overcome, and Wallis was to be presented.

The presentation went well. The Prince of Wales complimented Wallis on the dress she was wearing and offered to drive her home.

Some time later, she was invited to spend a weekend at Fort Belvedere, the prince's private home, 25 miles from London. There was more than one weekend at The Fort, as the hideaway was called. Wallis was elated and told her intimate friends that she was now a member of the Prince of Wales' set. She was delighted; she had made it on her own.

The prince took warmly to Wallis. She was, he claimed, the only woman who had ever shown interest in his work. Friends of the prince offered other reasons for his feelings about her. One stated that she made him feel worthwhile. A much closer friend of the prince said, "Her hold over him must have been sex. She must have given him something in bed that no other woman ever had. She made him feel more vital, more masculine, more satisfying."

The truth is that the prince had never known true fulfillment. He had been in love with Frieda, but it was not reciprocated. His love for Thelma Furness was purely physical. Thelma, on the other hand, complained that he was a most inadequate lover and was guilty of premature ejaculation. What actually happened in the bedroom between Wallis and the prince is, of course, open to conjecture.

Wallis mothered him, advised him on his diet, made sure he was dressed warmly enough when it was cold, persuaded him to cut down his smoking, and even limited his drinking.

At first, friends of the prince thought Wallis to be just another woman in his life. Their opinions changed when he soon began to acknowledge her publicly in important places.

Wallis had remarried and her husband was now Ernest Simpson. They made their home in England. Simpson was aware of the relationship between his wife and the prince and understood that the prince was not making nightly calls at his home to discuss business. As the number of telephone calls from His Royal Highness increased, Simpson found himself in a most difficult position. He could not confront Wallis, she who was living blindly in a romantic world; nor could he confront the prince.

The prince and Wallis were living together quite openly, and this caused even greater tension between Wallis and her husband. Comments about Ernest Simpson were cruel. One story told that Simpson was going to write a play called, *The Unimportance of Being Ernest*, in which the hero cries out, "My only regret is that I have but one wife to lay down for my king."

Now Wallis became the Hostess at The Fort. Her husband no longer appeared even on weekends, as he had at the outset of the relationship.

Early in 1936, King George V died, and the Prince of Wales was named King Edward. Edward sincerely wished to be a modern king, in touch with his people. The coronation ceremony was scheduled for May 1937, more than a year away. Edward had become king at a moment of increasing national problems. Germany was rearming at a frantic rate; the British were worried. But Edward VIII was less concerned with the possible outbreak of war than he was with his personal future. He had scheduled his first formal dinner at York House, and he told Wallis that he wanted her there because, "Sooner or later, my Prime Minister Stanley Baldwin must meet my future wife."

This was the dinner that caused great controversy. Prime Minister Stanley Baldwin and his wife were the guests of honor. Also present were Mr. and Mrs. Charles Lindberg; Alfred Duff Cooper and his wife, Lady Diana; Lady Cunard; Commander Lord Louis and Lady Mountbatten; and several other guests, including Mr. and Mrs. Ernest Simpson.

Many of the invited guests as well as many other important Englishmen were angry and offended at this intrusion. The Baldwins resented the forced meeting. The thought of Mrs. Simpson being the king's mistress was an affront to the puritanical Mrs. Baldwin. But there was little recourse. Wallis was now socially important, and no one in British society would dare stay away because of her presence alone.

The prince no longer hid his feelings. For one thing, he took Wallis on yachting trips, although no real secrecy was involved. After all, his yacht was escorted by two British destroyers manned with sailors. As they cruised along the coast, Wallis and the king would leave the yacht to go rowing together, and would often spend time in a quiet cove. Many times, they walked, unnoticed, to a remote village.

Daily, the prince sent his mistress long-stemmed roses. A beautiful Buick driven by the prince's own chauffeur was at her service. Edward phoned her several times a day, and was her nightly guest. He presented her with the most beautiful jewels—emeralds usually—the kind he knew she liked. The time soon came when the king's closest friends, as well as British and other leaders, deferred to her. There was no doubt that she felt she could be a queen.

The king's family resented her, resented the fact that the royal bedroom, formerly occupied by King George and Queen Mary, was now the bedroom of Wallis Simpson. They resented her because she was an outsider, because she was an interloper, and because she was stealing their king. She was not one of them, nor could she ever be, no matter what the king did!

There were several meetings between Ernest Simpson and the king. One evening when Wallis wasn't present, the king, obviously agitated, confronted Simpson saying, "I must have her!" On another occasion, Simpson told the king that Wallis would have to decide which man she would live with. He demanded to know if the king would marry her. His answer to Simpson made history: "Do you really think that I would be crowned without Wallis by my side?"

Nor did it take long for Wallis to announce her selection. Her husband moved out of their home and the king was now ready to hire legal advisors to begin a divorce action for Wallis.

The love affair had already reached the point where Wallis could no longer think of living without her king. His way of life had become hers. A royal wish was like a command, and she was royalty. Living with him was like having an ever ready magic wand. She made a wish and, instantly it was fulfilled.

The king was happy. He smiled and laughed a great deal. He danced with Wallis into the early morning hours. It was reported that one evening Wallis was wearing a dinner jacket made of spun glass, a single glittering diamond in her hair. Another report mentioned a $750,000 emerald and diamond necklace.

The divorce action itself was now set into motion. In the United States, the headlines were larger than ever:

YANKEE AT KING EDWARD'S COURT
MOST ENVIED WOMAN IN THE BRITISH EM-
PIRE

Wallis did not believe the king would ever marry her. "What absolute nonsense all this is about marriage," she told a friend. "How could English people be so silly? There is no question of marriage."

But the king saw this as his hour. He had both courage and obstinacy. Queen Mary knew that she could not talk with her son, although she sincerely desired to. She did not want to give her son the impression that she was interfering in his private life. The queen also knew that to oppose him was to make him even more determined.

The British Constitution did not prevent a king from marrying anyone he wanted—unless she were a Roman Catholic. To marry a Catholic, a king would have to surrender the throne to the next Protestant heir in line. In addition, there was no prohibition about marrying a divorced woman.

The night before the divorce Wallis did not sleep much. She paced the floor of her room. The international press waited at the courthouse in great numbers. More than two dozen photographers parked themselves on nearby rooftops waiting for Wallis' arrival at the courthouse.

It was the first case scheduled that afternoon. Wallis wore a navy blue woolen suit, a blue and white polka-dot scarf, a single ring on her left hand.

The presiding judge was His Lordship Justice Sir John Hawke.

Wallis was called to the witness box. Most observers agreed that her voice was clear and firm. She answered the usual routine questions, indicating that her husband had abandoned her for weekends. She asserted that instead of going on business trips, as he claimed, he went to hotels with female company. After 19 minutes of court time, the divorce was granted.

That evening she entertained the king at her home. They dined alone. He confessed that he had been very lonely without her.

The American press gave the Simpson divorce enormous play. The *New York Journal* stated, "Primarily, the king's transcendent reason for marrying Mrs. Simpson is that he ardently loves her, and does not see why a king should be denied the privilege of marrying the lady he loves."

The king had not yet decided that if there was no marriage, there would be no coronation. The king and Wallis were playing their own game and making their own rules. Both were living in a romantic, dream world—politically immature. The king's lack of patience didn't help any. He counted too much on his popularity with the masses, many of whom were still totally ignorant of the fact that there was a Mrs. Simpson.

But the majority did know what was transpiring, and people of prominence became more and more incensed at the unheard-of relationship between their king and a twice-divorced woman.

The king hoped for a miracle, but began to experience reality. "I told him it was too heavy a load for me to carry," said Wallis. "I told him that the British people were absolutely right about not wanting a divorced woman for a queen. I told him I didn't want to be queen. All that formality and responsibility. And I told him that if he abdicated, every woman in the world would hate me, and everybody in Great Britain would feel he had deserted them. I told him that if he stayed on as king, it wouldn't be the end for us. I could still come and see him, and he could still come and see me. We had terrible arguments about it. But he was a mule. He said he didn't want to be king without me, that if I left him, he would follow me wherever I went. What could I do? What could I do?"

"They can't stop me," said the king. "On the throne or off, I'm going to marry you."

Wallis tried to convince him of the hopelessness of their position. The king answered that he was going to confront Baldwin the next day. "I'm going to tell him, if the country won't approve our marrying, I am ready to go."

The king and Baldwin did meet on November 16, 1936 at Buckingham Palace. The king came to the point very quickly: "I intend to marry Mrs. Simpson as soon as she is free to marry." If he could marry her as king, he added, then it would make him a better king. If, however, the government opposed the marriage, then he was prepared to abdicate.

Prime Minister Baldwin knew that there was nothing in the British Constitution that prevented the king from marrying a commoner and making her his queen. He decided that he would leave the king with the threat that the government would resign should the marriage take place.

King Edward was concerned. How was he to break the news to his brothers? If he abdicated, his brother Bertie would succeed him as king, and Bertie was shy; he stammered; and he was unsure of himself.

There was some talk about a *morganatic* marriage. This was a legal marriage between a male member of a royal house, and a woman who was not. The wife does not take the husband's rank, and their children do not succeed to his titles. To make it legal, a specific act of Parliament would be required.

The more Wallis thought of a morganatic marriage, the more

she liked it. She never did like the formality and stiffness of royalty anyhow. She was a natural woman wo enjoyed her freedom. The king, however, felt that the whole concept was "strange and almost inhuman."

Baldwin now succeeded in isolating the king. Clement Attlee had assured him that "despite the sympathy felt for King Edward, and the affection his visits to the depressed areas had created, he would object to a morganatic marriage."

Soon, everyone in the government became involved. Both the king and Wallis were under a tremendous strain—he, in his determination to make her queen; she in her desire to please him and everyone else. It seemed as though the two of them were challenging the rest of the world.

In America things were different. In New York, for example, Helen Hayes played the part of Queen Victoria in *Victoria Regina*, and, in an opening scene, she said, "British kings have married commoners in the past, and they better do it again." The audience greeted this with sustained applause.

All the doors seemed to be closing in on Edward. One day, Wallis suggested that the king emulate Franklin D. Roosevelt's successful "fireside chats." After all, the king came off very well on the radio. He thought well of the idea. It might succeed, and he could get the English people on his side. But he delayed action.

It was unfortunate that the elderly, but still vigorous Lloyd George was out of England when the storm broke. He did send a telegram wich read: "A nation has a right to choose its queen, but the king also has a right to choose his own life; if Baldwin is against them, I am against Baldwin."

Threats began to reach Wallis, which included her life. For her, this period was a time of great loneliness and fear. She worried about her safety and she worried that, under pressure, Edward might abandon her in favor of the Crown. Both of them, she felt, were no more than pawns in a series of events that might overwhelm them.

The king began to count more and more on the proposed radio speech. The written speech described how long it had taken him to find the wife he wanted, and how much he wanted to marry her. And he added, "Neither Mrs. Simpson nor I have ever sought to insist that she should be queen. All we desired was that our married happiness should carry with it a proper title and dignity for her, befitting my wife."

Ignoring his advisors, the king gave a copy of his proposed speech to Baldwin. Later, Winston Churchill, a man with tremendous influence, discussed the king's speech with Lord Beaverbrook, a powerful member of the government. Churchill urged the king to have patience; but patience was one thing the king in love did not possess.

Churchill spoke out for the king in Parliament, but he did not win support. Baldwin emerged stronger than ever. Wallis was now ready to give up the king. She issued a statement which rang out in newspaper headlines on every street in England. When the king became aware of the action Wallis had taken, he exploded, "You're ruining my plans. You're making me look like a fool."

However, he did not tell her of his own plans.

When Wallis discovered that the king planned to abdicate, she was filled with worry. She had been told that if she let him abdicate, and married him, she would be the "most hated white woman in the world." All her life she had wanted people to like her, and now, suddenly, there was hate—more hate than she had ever known.

The king had made up his mind. He signed seven copies of the instrument of abdication, and eight of the King's Message to the Parliaments of the Empire. Then, as his brothers signed their names, the king stepped outside to the garden. After having served 325 days, 13 hours, and 57 minutes, he was no longer king.

When, later he called Wallis and told her that he had abdicated the throne, she was numb. She told him that he was a fool.

News of the abdication was broadcast to the largest radio audience the world had known to date. The ex-king said:

> At long last I am able to say a few words of my own. I have never wanted to withhold anything, but until now it has not been constitutionally possible for me to speak.

> A few hours ago I discharged my last duty as king and emperor, and now that I have been succeeded by my brother, the Duke of York, my first words must be to declare my allegiance to him. This I do with all my heart.

> You all know the reasons which have impelled me to renounce the throne, but I want you to understand that in making up my mind I did not forget the country or the Empire, which, as Prince of Wales and lately as king, I have for 25 years tried to serve.

> But you must believe me when I tell you that I

have found it impossible to carry the heavy burden of responsibility and to discharge my duties as king, as I wish to do, without the help and support of the woman I love; and I want you to know that the decision I have made has been mine, and mine alone. This was a thing I had to judge for myself. The other person most nearly concerned has tried, up to the last, to persuade me to take a different course. I have made this, the most serious decision of my life, only upon the single thought of what would in the end be best for all.

The decision has been made less difficult to me by the sure knowledge that my brother, with his long training in the public affairs of the country, and with his fine qualities, will be able to take my place forthwith without interruption or injury to the life and progress of the empire, and he has one matchless blessing, enjoyed by so many of you, and not bestowed on me, a happy home with his wife and children. During these hard days I have been comforted by my mother and by my family.

The ministers of the Crown, and in particular Mr. Baldwin, the prime minister, have always treated me with full consideration. There has never been any constitutional difference between me and them and between me and Parliament. Bred in the constitutional tradition by my father, I should never have allowed any such issue to arise.

Ever since I was Prince of Wales, and later on, when I occupied the throne, I have been treated with the greatest kindness by all classes wherever I have lived or journeyed throughout the empire. For that I am very grateful.

I now quit altogether public affairs, and I lay down my burden. It may be some time before I return to my native land, and I shall always follow the fortunes of the British race and empire with profound interest, and if, any time in the future, I can be found of service to His Majesty in a private station, I shall not fail.

And now we all have a new king.

I wish Him, and you, His people, happiness
and prosperity with all my heart.

God bless you all.

God save the king.

When the speech was over, Wallis, who had been listening
in Cannes, was sobbing uncontrollably.

The king was bidding his mother, Queen Mary, adieu. As
the *HMS Fury* slipped away with the former king aboard, he
stood on the deck staring at his beloved England. Later he said,
"I knew now that I was irretrievably on my own, the draw-
bridges were going up behind me. But of one thing I was certain:
so far as I was concerned, love had triumphed."

Thousands and thousands of letters now poured in on Wallis, many filled with hate. One of them was from her former
husband. It read;". . . And would your life have ever been the
same if you had broken it off? I mean, could you possibly have
settled down in the old life and forgotten the fairyland through
which you had passed? My child I do not think so."

Now that the king had abdicated, the question was: Would
he marry her and would she marry him?

The answer came from the newly-titled Duke of Windsor. He
sang in his bathtub, his mood brightened. He played golf. New
questions arose. Where could they live? What should he do?
Where were they going? Now with peace and quiet settling in,
Wallis began to get her bearings once again. She was 41, waiting
for her divorce decree to become absolute. It arrived on May 3,
1937. She was now free to marry, and she *would* marry. She called
the duke and told him, "Hurry up!"

The wedding would be simple, with only a few friends and
relatives. The royal family set the pattern by refusing to attend
the wedding, and the aristocracy followed suit. In no way would
the royal family give its blessing to this marriage!

But the wedding did take place. It was an unusual wedding
for a man who only six months before had been the king of
England and the emperor of India; the ruler of 500 million people
living on 13 million square miles of the earth. The total number
of people attending the wedding was 161.

The world now awaited the answer to a simmering question:
"Will they be happy?"

The answer was not long in coming. The duke and the duchess would, indeed, be slaves to each other. Their togetherness was like a pair of shears, cutting anyone who came between them. Theirs was a marriage that could not fail. The price had been too high to so much as consider failure.

The duke was happier than he had been in his whole life. At first, the couple lived in hotels. She had her bedroom, and he had his. They breakfasted separately. They stayed apart in the mornings. However, she felt that a hotel was not a home, and set about looking for one.

There was much searching and much deliberating. Finally, she found a house in Versailles that suited the duke. It was luxuriously furnished with tennis courts, a golf course and a swimming pool. Later they took a 10-year lease on La Croe—the villa that Wallis had originally chosen for the marriage ceremony.

During World War II, Wallis opened her house to the allied war effort. Meetings and get-togethers were held there. In addition, she joined the French Red Cross. She was assigned the job of delivering blood plasma and bandages to hospitals behind the Maginot Line. Edward was at loose ends and resentment was building. On one occasion he made a quick trip to London, desperately looking for a significant assignment. He wanted to do his part, but received no encouragement. He returned to Paris more resentful than ever.

As the war went on, the duke and duchess moved from one country to another. It was difficult for both of them. Wallis once said, "I am well aware that there are still some people in the world who go on hoping our marriage will break up. And to them I say, 'Give up hope,' because David [she always called him David, not Edward] and I are happy . . . And that's the way it will continue to be."

They were deeply in love. Once, the duke was asked, "Sir, if you had to do it all over again, would you do it?" The duke's voice was firm and he replied, "Yes, I would do it again." And when asked how they wanted to spend the rest of their lives, he quickly answered, "Together."

That's how it was, throughout the years. They aged together, entertained regally together, and were entertained together.

One such highlight was the party given by President and Mrs. Richard Nixon at the White House on April 4, 1970. The 75-year-old duke tapped with his cane at the music, but did not dance. He complained of his arthritic condition.

And then the expected shock came. He took ill. It was diagnosed as throat cancer. The Duke of Windsor was as stoic about death as he was about life. What concerned him most was his wife. He did not wish to be separated from her even in death.

With this in mind, he had purchased two plots at Green Mount Cemetery in Baltimore. He felt sure that the British would refuse to bury his wife alongside him—if he died first. He need not have worried. It was agreed after some deliberation that he and the duchess would be buried in royal grounds in England. The duke left Wallis financially secure. He knew how much she loved life and wanted her to enjoy her remaining years.

On May 28, 1972 the Duke of Windsor died at his home in Paris at 2:25 A.M. In Sydney, Australia, the *Sun* declared, "The great love story has ended."

Wallis had lost much in her lifetime but she had won much more. She might have been queen of England, or at least the woman behind the king. As it turned out, to history she was a footnote, but in the history of romance, she had made a significant mark. When before in history had a king given up his throne for the woman he loved?

After the duke's death, there remained on Wallis' dressing room table a photograph of her David, with this message inscribed on royal stationery:

> My friend, with thee to live alone
> Me thinks were better than to own
> A crown, a scepter, and a throne.

4
William and Marion

This is the complicated, pathetic, intimate story of William Randolph Hearst and Marion Davies. He was the greatest newspaper executive of his era. She was a former Fifth Avenue clothing model. He was a spoiled child—the only son of a millionaire; she was one of the four daughters of her lawyer father. Theirs is the story of an enduring, romantic, unselfish, immoral love affair.

At first glance it would appear that William Randolph Hearst had everything necessary for eternal happiness, and that she—Marion Davies—would succeed in using her charm, beauty, and vivacity to ensure a full and exciting life.

Hearst had wealth, power, prestige, fame and the love of the woman whom he had sought and won in marriage. In his wife Millicent, Randolph had a woman who embraced idealism, tenderness, loyalty and absolute dedication to her husband. But he discovered before long that he was not fulfilled.

Molière once wrote that "Love is often a fruit of marriage." But this was not the case with William Randolph Hearst. Nor were the words of George Eliot applicable to the lives of William and his wife. Eliot wrote: "What greater thing is there for two human souls than to feel that they are joined for life—to strengthen each other in all labor, to rest on each other in all sorrow, to minister to each other in all pain, to be one with each other in silent, unspeakable memories at the moment of the last parting."

Millicent and William did enjoy such solid feelings as described by Eliot. Each gave of their all to one another, But theirs was more a union of two minds than two hearts and two bodies.

Hearst had a great need to love and make love. He was probably no different from most men, married or single, who secretly dream of themselves as great lovers capable of overpowering all women. To each, Don Juan is but a pale portrait of potency.

In the case of William Randolph Hearst, his wish was no secret. And when there appeared in his life a beautiful woman filled with feminine exuberance and warmth, he succumbed to her charms. Marion Davies was such a woman. She provoked his masculinity; she gave his ego a giant boost. With Marion he could be himself; he could remove his mask of pretense and permit his primitive impulses to take over.

Marion Davies had all the attributes of a movie queen plus youth. She came; he saw; and the result is a chapter in illicit love that has made history. Like others who have found themselves in similar situations, Hearst realized that there was a route that had to be taken and a price that had to be paid. He had to make a choice, and, having made it, he could not help regretting that he had to give up something important to him.

On the surface, Hearst was able to maintain two relationships—the approved one with his wife and family, and the other with Marion. If he did actually suffer from guilt, doubts, regrets, frustrations and disappointments they were quite private. These were feelings that he never shared with either wife or mistress.

It is rare in human history to find a man of such unexcelled, brilliant, diversified talents like those possessed by William Randolph Hearst. He loved to build empires and he built them; he loved big business, and finally owned and operated the largest publishing corporation on earth. He not only assumed leadership, but dominated his chosen field. And he accomplished these goals with inventive ingenuity, with daring imagination, and with undisguised audacity.

Such adjectives as brash, adventurous, imaginative, enthusiastic, insatiably curious and doubtlessly self-confident have been used to describe Hearst. He was all this and much more.

He was a dreamer and a doer; he was chauvinistic, flag-waving, boastful and chivalrous; not overly scrupulous, yet warmhearted, generous to a fault, courageous, quick to resent and to avenge injustice. One of his friends remarked: "Hearst lived and died an eternal juvenile." In his mode of living, he was probably one of the disciples of Henry Ward Beecher. "No man is sane who does not know how to be insane on proper occasions," said Beecher. Perhaps Hearst took that advice too literally, for his genius often bordered on insanity.

William Hearst grew up in San Francisco. In 1863, the year of his birth, San Francisco was gay, vigorous, and stimulating. All his life, he remembered his home town with fondness. As a youngster, he loved the theater and could often be found at the California Theater on Bush Street, or attending a performance of Booth's *Hamlet* or Jefferson's *Rip Van Winkle*. He was so smitten with Adelaide Neilson's Juliet that when she died in Paris in 1877, he could not sleep for two nights. While he was capable of experiencing such grief, he could also roar at the antics of Billy Emerson's Minstrels, who also appeared at the Bush Street Theater.

Willie was stage-struck, and he decided that acting would be his career. When this bit of news reached his mother, she was horrified. Acting was a vulgar profession and she had no intention of permitting her son to waste himself in such shallowness. Despite his mother's objections, Willie and his friends built a theater in a stable and presented ministrel shows and dramatic productions. The audience consisted mostly of relatives and friends. The glamour of the stage gripped Willie like a fever, and throughout his life he felt close to it.

During his college years, Hearst did not wait to be selected for leadership; he assumed it. His allowance was unlimited and this coupled with his generosity enabled him to offer his classmates frequent parties and good times. He led and they followed. No one was in a position to compete with young Hearst for leadership. He ruled those around him, and so it continued throughout his later years. He led his young pack with his money, his personality and his charisma. Hearst always lived high and he took along those who would follow, indulging them and himself with reckless abandon.

He was given more money than was good for any college man. His father, who handed out twenty-dollar gold pieces, bet thousands at the poker table, and gave thousands more to the Democratic party, was not going to be stingy with his only son. One of the gags at Harvard was that William Hearst regularly received a fist-sized gold nugget from his father's mines.

William was not a dedicated student. His forte was not in the arts but in the field of practical jokes. He dropped courses he didn't enjoy, and, whenever possible, he was at the theater. However, in his second year at college, he indicated that he could be enthusiastic about other interesting projects if they really challenged him. It was this interest that made him take over the college magazine, *Lampoon*, which was in financial difficulty.

Hearst took over the job of business manager and attacked the problem with energy and ingenuity. He went to all the retail stores in the area and solicited ads. He wrote to Harvard graduates asking for contributions and subscriptions. He launched a circulation drive and before very long the *Lampoon* began to show a profit.

This motivated him to learn about other newspapers, especially the *San Francisco Examiner* and the *New York World*. It opened a new world for him, and it lessened his interest in his college studies. This led to his eventual expulsion from Harvard. He could have been a good student, but was simply not interested. In fact, he made his wishes clear to his parents: "I want the *San Francisco Examiner*," he said. On the same day that his father was sworn in for a full Senate term, William, not yet twenty-four years old, stayed up all night to publish his first issue.

The rest of Hearst's newspaper enterprise is history. He went on to buy the *Journal* and other papers and magazines both here and in Europe. Hearst was a man with an insatiable appetite for adventure, power and success. His newspapers and magazines were reaching a large percentage of the world's population. To compete with Pulitizer's *Evening World*, Hearst put out the *Evening Journal*. To compete with the *Daily News*, he put out the *Daily Mirror*.

Whatever Hearst wanted to do, he did! It has been said that Hearst not only reported news, he made it. If he wanted a particular writer on his staff, it didn't matter that he was employed at another newspaper. Hearst would buy him, doubling his salary if necessary. And if Hearst wanted to report a war, it is said, he started one.

In the strictest sense, the Hearst papers were not newspapers at all, but printed entertainment. In fact Hearst once stated: "Putting out a newspaper without promotion is like winking at a girl in the dark—well-intentioned but ineffective."

The wealthy William Hearst was a monumental spender who purchased whatever he wanted. If he so desired, he could buy a tenth century Spanish cloister for $40,000, have it dismantled stone by stone, placed into 10,700 crates and then kept in storage. Whatever his eyes told his heart he wanted, he purchased. Price was never an issue. When he decided that he would own a genuine English castle, he bought one, asking Alice Head, his manager in England, to shop for one. Later, sight unseen, relying completely on her decision, he bought St. Donat's Castle for $120,000. The number of castles he finally owned and why he so indulged himself could fill a chapter in a psychological text on man's habits of self-indulgence.

The two Hearst New York warehouses were the repositories of millions of dollars worth of art. The five-story buildings contained objects that quite often represented Hearst's instant desire for ownership. He saw, was pleased, and bought. A staff of 30 men worked in the warehouses, cataloguing each incoming piece and photographing it for the master file kept by Hearst. Here were stored thousands of items ranging from paintings, statuary, entire English rooms, thousands of rare books, and a variety of sundry items.

On one occasion, out of curiosity, Millicent visited her husband's warehouse. She shook her head and remarked, "How could one man buy all these things?" But Hearst *loved* things and he accumulated them with relish and satisfaction.

When he purchased St. Donat's Castle for $120,000, he modernized it at a cost of $1,370,000. He used it for approximately four months. Simple arithmetic indicates that it cost him a rent of

$11,400 per day. There was method to Hearst's madness, a sort of cool-headed method which led to a well-defined goal. Hearst occupied about half his waking hours making money, and the other half spending it! His need for money was endless; his anguish when he did not have it was painful.

In Hearst's best of all possible worlds, people were expected to do his bidding, accede to his whims, indulge his desires. When one of his friends in Egypt was concerned about eating Egyptian food, Hearst wired his representative in the Pulitzer Building in New York, RUSH DOZEN CANS BOSTON BEANS/ DOZEN CANS CLAM CHOWDER/TWO CODFISH ALEXAN-DRIA EGYPT. At first, there was confusion in the office. Nobody could decide which code Hearst was using, and they wired him asking that he identify the code being used. He wired back: *No Code. Just send it.* And so it was done.

Hearst was a puzzle to many people. Though he ran the most unrepressed, sensational newspapers, he personally bordered on the shy side. To many acquaintances, the external Hearst was a fraud, not real, a deception. To them, his shyness, modesty, courtesy and high-pitched voice were affected traits. These were signs of a man who was indecisive, timid and retiring. Underneath they were sure that Hearst was a Caesar, a Charlemagne, a Napoleon, all combined into one.

Hearst was at the same time the most megalomaniac of men. He revered greatness and felt a kinship with the great. His sympathies were quickly aroused. He was emotionally unstable. What he wanted to believe, he believed, abandoning reality when he wanted to accept his own fantasies as facts. Caution was not a word to be found in his vocabulary. Like Schiller, he, too, believed that "he that is over-cautious will accomplish little." In the case of Hearst, the comment of one biographer was absolutely on target: "To many, fame comes too late; to him, too early."

To William Randolph Hearst the image projected by his father was something to emulate. The older Hearst was a tall, bearded man with a rough sense of humor and generosity to match. He would give his son a twenty-dollar gold piece when all the boy asked for was ice-cream money. George Hearst was equally generous with his wife and friends.

Born in 1820 in Missouri, George Hearst was brought up on his parents' small plantation. He worked along with four slaves and received barely two years of schooling. His home life was not the happiest, for his father was interested in another woman.

Though a slow reader, he did manage to plow through several books on geology and digest them thoroughly. Mining had interested him from a young age. Whenever possible, he talked with lead miners and was able to impress people with his knowledge of the earth.

In 1849, George Hearst, like thousands, caught the gold fever and went to California. With his strength, courage and ingenuity and his rudimentary knowledge of mining, he began mining with pick and shovel. He spent nine lean years trying his luck in a dozen places, and finally returned to Missouri when his mother took ill.

He was 40 years old when George fell in love with eighteen-year-old Phoebe, the town schoolteacher. He was good-natured and kind but was uncouth in appearance and manner. He could curse with a vengeance. He drank, chewed tobacco, and was quite loud. With all this he wooed Phoebe, pretty as a doll, and young enough to be his daughter.

Swanberg, in his book, *Citizen Hearst*, writes: "One of the more fabulous might-have-beens of history arises from conjecture at what might not have happened had George failed in his suit. For then William Randolph Hearst would never have been born, the United States might not have gone to war with Spain, Theodore Roosevelt might have remained a frustrated minor politician, and the name of Dewey might never have risen out of obscurity. Without William Randolph Hearst, the Presidency would have eluded Franklin Delano Roosevelt, sweeping social changes now accepted might never have been consummated, the newspapers might still be preoccupied with the mere gathering of news, and California would have lost a castle."

On June 15, 1862, George and Phoebe eloped and were married.

For all his coarseness, George Hearst was a warm-hearted person who liked to fill his pockets with twenty-dollar gold pieces and stroll down Market Street, quietly distributing them to those in need. He liked to play poker for pots as high at $10,000. In 1865, he began to purchase large tracts of land and, between land and mines, he extended himself precariously.

George Hearst, the gambler, made out well on his investments. His land deals were profitable; his gold mines were rich with minerals. When he died he wisely left his fortune of $18,000,000 to his wife. She had good business sense, and the fortune continued to grow.

Phoebe Hearst, the mother of William, was a very loving woman. He admired her and felt the closeness that only children can feel for a mother they adore. She was a lover of the arts, and this love and knowledge she passed on to her son. She exposed him to the cultural aspects of opera, though his taste in music remained consistently low-brow throughout her life. She also had the foresight to take her young son on a tour of Europe so that he might get acquainted with the museums and art galleries, and see the work of the world's masters.

Cherchez la Femme—find the woman. Hearst needed one and he was a good finder and picker. Early in his life he was attracted to Sybil Sanderson, the daughter of a Supreme Court Justice in California. Hearst met her at the Hotel del Monte, in Monterey. He adored her beautiful figure, was fascinated by her dark eyes, and enraptured by her beautiful soprano voice. Hand in hand they would stroll under the Monterey moon. They rode horseback, swam and spent many wonderful hours together. Before long they became engaged.

Hearst had found heaven on earth. But this first love came to an early end. Sybil wanted to devote herself to her musical career, and so, together with her mother, she left for Paris to study. Young Hearst, heartbroken, returned to Harvard to continue his studies. He missed Sybil desperately. He truly loved her and never really recovered from the tremendous disappointment of not winning her heart.

Hearst's heart was won a second time when he met Eleanor Calhoun, one of the young beauties who was a frequent visitor at his mother's house. Again, taken in by sheer beauty, Hearst fell in love.

It seemed like a perfect match. Eleanor aspired to be an actress. Her ambition, she confided to William, was to be the finest Shakespearean actress in the world. Both of them loved the theater, and William wooed her with great zeal. It was not long before they announced their engagement.

This time it was mother, Phoebe who objected. She did not feel an actress worthy of inclusion in her family. Tactfully, but firmly, she suggested that the marriage be delayed until William finished Harvard, and that Eleanor pursue her dramatic studies in England. Both agreed, not realizing that the distance would dull the attraction.

In London, Eleanor was succeeding on the stage, and, in what appeared to be a dream world, she met such famous men as Robert Browning, Bernard Shaw, Oscar Wilde, Henry James and Whistler to mention but a few. William faded from her life as she became more and more involved with artists, writers, actors and stage impresarios. She eventually married a Serbian prince.

For William, it was no easy matter to forget Eleanor. His score with women was not what he had hoped for. He had loved two girls and had lost them both.

When Hearst met Millicent Wilson, a dancer in *The Girl From Paris*, he fell in love for the third time. She was tall and beautiful, but was neither frivolous nor shallow. She had genuine values which were similar to his, and which he appreciated. He was no longer the starry-eyed young man he had been.

Again he pursued and wooed his new *find*, and, one day just before reaching his fortieth birthday, they were married. His mother's approval was not forthcoming. She did not attend her only son's wedding, claiming that she was ill. Only after the honeymoon did she see fit to send the bride a gift of a beautiful brooch.

For the 15 years following her marriage, Millicent was a devoted wife and mother. She gave birth to their five sons. She was hostess at William's glamorous parties. She counseled him when he was in need of comfort or guidance. But with it all, Millicent was part of the triangle that became the talk of the world.

Being married brought few changes to Hearst. His bedtime hours were abnormal; he seldom went to sleep before three in the morning. He took in every single Broadway show, time permitting. Hearst felt that he had the world on a string, and he was aiming for the presidency.

In the meantime, he sought new worlds to conquer and it wasn't strange to find him suddenly involved in the motion picture industry.

Whatever Hearst did, he did with gusto, and with an open hand. One of the early classics in which he invested money was the serial called *The Perils Of Pauline*, starring Pearl White. Young and old, in those days, waited anxiously for Pauline to be saved from being crushed to death by an oncoming train, or being drowned in a dungeon filling up with water.

In time, his motion picture company acquired a new star. She was a petite girl, who had some time earlier been introduced to Hearst when she was a performer in the *Ziegfeld Follies*. Her stage name was Marion Davies. She had been born Marion Cecilia Douras, one of four daughters of a Brooklyn lawyer. Her blond hair, her blue eyes, her cute stammer, and her tremendous enthusiasm made her very exciting.

When Hearst entered this new industry, he was 55 years old and at the height of his power. Here, in the making of movies, he could permit his creative talents to find their worth. Here he could have his every dream enacted on the screen. And here, into this exciting new life walked the exciting Marion Davies.

Marion wanted to become a great actress. Hearst accepted her ambition as his challenge. He was most eager to be the instrument through which this simple, young, attractive girl would find her sought after career. And at this point he began a love affair that lasted for 32 years. It ended only when William Randolph Hearst closed his eyes for the last time at 88 years of age.

Generally, his brother-in-law is credited with having introduced Marion to Hearst. Another version states that Millicent herself introduced her subsequent rival into their home.

Millicent, a former entertainer, understood the hardships of women aspiring to make a career on the stage. One day, she brought Marion home and introduced her to her husband, hoping that he would give her a part in one of the movie epics he was financing.

Hedda Hopper, a friend of Marion's, claims that the meeting occurred when Hearst happened to drop in at the *Follies* one night, saw her, and returned nightly for the next four weeks. One night, he invited Marion to supper after the show. She consented, and thus began the long attachment.

Marion Davies tells a completely different story. She explains that she was in a flop movie called *Runaway Romany*. By some chance Mr. Hearst saw it, and told his film company to sign her up at $500 a week, an unbelievable sum in those days.

Whichever version is correct, it all happened when Hearst was 55 and Marion was a mere 21. And although he was the owner of a newspaper chain, a man to be reckoned with by famous men all over the world, and although Marion was grateful to him, she refused to be cowed by him. In later years, when there were pitched verbal battles between them, Marion did not hesitate to slug it out—with Hearst admitting his error and apologizing.

Marion's first starring role under Hearst's direction was in a movie called *Cecilia of the Pink Roses*. Though it wasn't a great movie, the Hearst newspapers treated it as though it was international news and praised it lavishly.

Louella Parsons, motion picture editor of the *Morning Telegraph*, in her autobiography, *The Gay Illiterate*, described Marion as follows:

> She had received so much publicity, I expected to find a haughty star, affected and sure of herself, waiting for me. But, instead, I found a golden-haired girl, little more than a child, who was dressed in a simple blue suit that a schoolgirl might have worn, and who spoke with a delightful and confused stammer. It is impossible for anyone to meet Marion Davies and not like her. Even when she was very young she was never an ingenue type. She didn't inherit that strong, determined chin for nothing. And while she looked like an angel, she had great wit and charm and poise. I liked her from the beginning. She had no false illusions about herself, and kidded Cecilia with disarming frank-

ness. And I was pleased that she seemed to like me, for she asked me to lunch with her soon again at the studio.

Subsequently, Marion starred in *Little Old New York*, *The Floradora Girl*, *Blondie of the Follies*, *Peg O' My Heart*, *White Shadows in the South Seas*, *The Big House*, *Operation Thirteen*, *Gabriel Over the White House*, and the first sound musical, *The Broadway Melody*. Hearst loved to see his beautiful star dressed in elegant clothing, and, consequently, in most of her pictures he exercised final approval of her costumes.

There is no doubt that Hearst helped launch Marion Davies on the path to stardom. With money, and with every type of publicity that Hearst could muster, Marion was acclaimed as the leading actress of her day. Although he attempted to be discreet at first, Hearst was seen with her both on and off the set. But by August of 1924, his association with Marion became a "wide-open secret." When Millicent became aware of the relationship between her husband and Marion, she was neither indignant nor distraught. She did decide not to share the same house with William, though she refused to divorce him. She could not understand her husband and sometimes even doubted his sanity.

Hearst had two great loves throughout his lifetime. One was power, the second was Marion. The entire world knew of his love for power and control. When Hearst wanted a war with Spain, he manufactured one. When Hearst wanted talent, he bought it. What Hearst wanted, Hearst got.

In the affair with Marion, however, Hearst adopted a policy of caution. He felt himself to be a presidential or gubernatorial aspirant, and so he had to maintain an image of being a middle-aged conservative. He was careful not to give Marion any occasion to create adverse publicity for him.

While at Palm Beach, Marion was kept in seclusion while Hearst partook of activities that would improve his prospects of becoming a candidate for high, public office. The overpowering yearning of his entire lifetime was the presidency. This ambition was so intense in fact, that it led to a general loss of perspective.

In 1913, he was only 50 and had his eye on the governorship. He wanted to depose Boss Murphy as state Democratic leader. He attacked President Wilson for his pro-British stand. He would destroy anyone who stood in his way of achieving his goal. As time passed, it became less important to Hearst to keep Miss Davies *sub rosa*. He spent millions on her pictures, had the entire Hearst press declare her the super-screen star of the super-screen movies. Once, upon being told that there was money in the movies, he responded, "Yes, mine."

The Hearst-Davies affair was a painful one; he was torn by indecision. While he respected his wife Millicent, and in a way had an affection for her, he could in no way give up the love of his beautiful Marion who was almost 35 years his junior.

Marion, again and again, wanted to legalize their love and pleaded with him to obtain a divorce. It was reported that for almost a year Hearst had detectives trailing his wife, hoping to find her guilty of some indiscretion, but with no success. Millicent's private life was as impeccable as Hearst's own mother's had always been. Hearst was confused and frustrated.

This unresolved problem undoubtedly influenced Hearst's future actions. He gave Marion the world, granted her every wish —except marriage. Friends reported that Marion's greatest love scenes were portrayed in their home; she was never nearly as good on the screen. She pleaded, cried, loved, did everything she could think of but her married lover was adamant and a divorce action was never begun.

The triangle was now firmly established. William could privately do whatever he wished. When it became necessary for Millie to be at her husband's side, she was there. At affairs of State, at social functions, and at family gatherings, Millicent and William could be found together. With the passing of time, strange as it may seem, the bond between Hearst and his family seemed to grow stronger. Even on bad days, he managed to summon strength enough for a chat on the telephone with his wife or one of their sons.

Marion became an accepted fact in the lives of friends and relatives. When Millicent was at San Simeon, Marion was elsewhere. When Marion was there, Millicent was elsewhere. Friends were expected to show no surprise when either Millicent or Marion was the hostess at a gathering. Though it is true that Hearst never married Marion, he did make the great and the near-great accept her openly and willingly as his good friend.

Marion had become the fairy godmother of the studio. She was generous and openhearted. When an office boy developed an eye ailment, she paid for the operation. She sent a newsboy to military school for four years. If anyone was in need, she would help them with sympathy, understanding, and money. She was one of the most generous and kindhearted women alive.

Minor disagreements were bound to arise. Marion, who was a clearheaded business woman, had from time to time adivised Hearst on business matters involving the *New York Mirror.* Just as often, Millicent offered suggestions, although hers were on a different level. Sometimes, the suggestions of Millicent were followed, but more often the practical suggestions of Marion were put to use. Both women received ample coverage in the Hearst newspapers. Millicent had her charities publicized and praised. Marion had her friends rewarded and her enemies punished in the columns of the Hearst press.

The marriage was obviously no more than pretense, with the entire world joining in the game of marital charades. Yet, something amounting to real affection did exist between Millicent and William. When they were together they enjoyed each other's company. Up to the time of his death, Mrs. Hearst spoke of him affectionately as "Willie." Difficult though it may be to believe, he called her on the telephone nearly every day of his life.

How did Hearst explain his relationship with Marion? "I'm not saying it's *right*," he said, "Im saying it *is*." He could not be persuaded to give it up.

Marion adored her William, though they did quarrel from time to time. Hearst did much for Marion. His wealth and power skyrocketed her to both fame and fortune. He helped her family, seeing to it that her father became a magistrate. Her brother-in-law was an executive in the Hearst film corporation. Her sister, Reine Douras, was a well-paid supporting actress at the Hearst movie lot.

Marion did a great deal for her middle-aged lover. She helped him to become a mature adult, taught him to enjoy genuine human relationships, gave him pleasure he could not obtain elsewhere. In addition, she gave him loyalty, affection and devotion— rare commodities even in good marriages.

Marion was not a passing fancy for Hearst. He wanted to marry her and she wanted to marry him. Millicent stood in the way by refusing to grant him a divorce. Elsa Maxwell, a good friend of Millicent's, wrote indignantly of the blow suffered by her friend, the mother of Hearst's five sons, when she was asked to step aside in favor of Marion. She was still beautiful and accomplished, the object of admiring glances wherever she went. She had her own firm principles. According to Elsa Maxwell, Millicent showed only one flash of anger, indulging it by going to Tiffany's, buying a pearl necklace priced in six figures and saying, "Send the bill to my husband's office."

Four years before his death, on August 14, 1951, William Randolph Hearst came out of seclusion from his mountain paradise, Wyntoon Castle on the McCloud River in northern California, and settled in the Beverly Hills home of Marion Davies. Some say he came home to die.

The house where he would end his days was a fabulous palace. Number 1007 Beverly Drive was a rambling, three-story, stucco structure set amid beautiful lawns and gardens. The building housed a fortune. Valuable paintings of the masters adorned the walls. The only modern art in evidence were the four life-size portraits depicting Marion in various roles. Two special guards constantly patrolled the property.

During his illness, Marion was William's devoted companion. She planned her days so as to be available to take care of his needs. Her personal pleasures were few, especially toward the end of Hearst's life. During the day, she would often shop in Beverly Hills. Alone with Hearst at night, she sat in his room reading and sewing while he was busy with his papers. Occasionally, she would attend a party given by friends. The pace of life was much slower than it had been for both of them at San Simeon. Thinking about those days, she said, "Oh, it was gay, let me tell you. We were riding and swimming and playing tennis and Mr. Hearst was very active. We were always running, always doing something, always with people and always having fun."

This slower life, the result of being confined with a sick, old man waiting to die, would have depressed some women, but not Marion. She loved William with a love that was deep and sincere. She was his protector, his adoring and faithful friend. She once told a reporter: "I don't care what you say about me, but don't hurt him. He is a wonderful, wonderful man."

Marion was always at his bidding. When he wanted to talk, she would talk. When he wanted to be read to, she would read to him. When he was able to manage it, and wanted to walk, she would walk with him through the gardens. And when he just wanted company, she was there.

Did he appreciate her? Did he love her? Often, when he awoke from a fitful slumber, he would dash off a tender note to her and slip it under the door. In fact, he did it so often that she eventually had a collection of hundreds of them.

One of Marion's friends said, "He gave her everything in life except something to live for—everything, except his name." That he could not give her. At his bedside was Marion's photograph, inscribed, "To W. R. from Marion," to which he had added lines from *Romeo and Juliet*:

> My bounty is as boundless as the sea,
> My love as deep;
> The more I give thee, the more I have,
> For both are infinite.

The devotion between these two, triumphing over illness, and then the specter of death, made people and even friends marvel.

On the day of his death, Marion had been sitting by William's side. Early in the morning, when she had left the room, a nurse recalled, "Mr. Hearst puckered up his lips like he always did to kiss her good night. That was the last thing he did."

How apt the words of Bayard Taylor:
> I love thee, I love but thee
> With a love that shall not die
> Till the sun grows cold,
> And the stars are old
> And the leaves of the Judgment Book unfold!

Marion stood vigil to the end. One of the doctors gave her a sedative; she had scarcely slept for forty-eight hours. The house was quiet. The nurses hovered near the dying man's bed, listening to his irregular breathing as it rose and fell. On the morning of August 14, 1951, Hearst, at the age of 88, was dead. Neither of the women he loved were at his bedside at the moment of death.

When Marion awoke, the body of Hearst had already been taken away by a Beverly Hills undertaker. "I asked where he was," she said later, "and the nurse said he was dead. His body was gone, whoosh, like that! Old W. R. was gone, the boys were gone. I was alone. Do you realize what they did? They stole a possession of mine. He belonged to me. I loved him for 32 years and now he was gone. I couldn't even say good-bye."

On the day of the funeral, the cathedral was crowded with many hundreds of mourners, many of them standing. The street, outside, was likewise mobbed.

Mrs. Hearst was accompanied by her five sons. The mourners included men and women of distinction from every field. The honorary pallbearers were headed by California's Governor Earl Warren. Also present were Herbert Hoover, Bernard Baruch, Arthur Hays Sulzberger, General Douglas MacArthur and others.

William Randolph Hearst's will set up three trusts. The first was for his wife. It consisted of $6,000,000 worth of Hearst Corporation preferred stock, with an additional outright bequest of $1,500,000 in cash to cover taxes which would be due on the stock.

The beneficiaries of the second trust were the Hearst sons.

The third trust, residuary, was for the benefit of the customary "charitable, scientific, educational and public purposes."

Marion Davies, the woman he had loved for over three decades, was not named as a direct beneficiary in the will. She had been provided for earlier.

Just two months later, on October 31, 1951, in Las Vegas, Marion Davies married Horace G. Brown, Jr. a skipper in the Merchant Marine.

5

George Washington
& Sally Fairfax

George Washington has always been a hero, a father figure, to the citizens of the United States. Gladstone described Washington as "the purest figure in history." Byron said of him: "He is next to Divinity." And Thackeray wrote about him as having "a life without stain; a frame without a flaw."

Statues and oil paintings of George Washington can be found in every town and hamlet in America. And many of us do not even notice that American coins, dollar bills and stamps bear his likeness.

On the canopy of the United States Capitol, within a six thousand square feet area, one gazes up at Brumidi's mural, *The Apotheosis Of Washington*. It boldly represents the father of our country, flanked by Liberty and Justice, and thirteen female forms representing the thirteen original states and their personifications of war, agriculture, commerce, mechanics, the arts and sciences.

Early in our schooling, we are given a taste of the personality and character of Washington. Here was a man very much unlike other men. That he could not tell a lie is the legend we are taught very early in our lives. The boy grew into a fearless soldier, and the father of this great democracy—a leader who presided over it wisely.

The famous American writer, Nathaniel Hawthorne, with tongue in cheek, wondered whether anyone had ever seen Washington in the nude. He concluded: "It is inconceivable. He had no nakedness, but was born with his clothes on, and his hair powdered, and made a stately bow on his first appearance in the world."

Did this heroic figure possess any flaws? Is it possible that this man of virtue and truth could be married, and yet seek the love of a friend's wife?

Attempts to discredit Washington that began during his lifetime, continued after his death. He was accused of philandering. There was talk that he had fathered a son. Rumors existed that a member of his cabinet was his illegitimate son and that he had a Tory mistress.

Although nobody told *farmer daughter* stories about Washington, they did tell Mary Gibbon stories. Supposedly, Mary lived in New Jersey, and Washington himself had been rowed across the Hudson at night by a devoted aide-de-camp to visit her in the suburbs. Another variation of the story claims that it was the Passaic River that he crossed. The fact that the story was improbable did not stop the gossip-mongers. There were those anxious to destroy the reputation and popularity of Washington. They did not stop to consider that to cross the Hudson at night in a small boat—often while British warships were patrolling the river—would have been an incredible feat.

Washington was maliciously slandered when he was accused of fathering Alexander Hamilton. The allegation gained credibility because it was common knowledge that Hamilton was an illegitimate child, and that Washington, during the war with the British, referred to his favorite lieutenant colonel and private secretary as "my son."

As Washington's popularity and influence increased, so did manufactured rumors. One rumor had it that he was unduly attracted to the beautiful spouse of one of his officers. Another had him dancing with Kitty Greene at a party in Middlebrook, New Jersey in March 1779.

Although there did not seem to be a particle of evidence that Washington was anything but faithful to his wife, stories kept cropping up throughout much of his life. They would subside for a while, only to break out once again. Eighty years after his death, new and unfounded stories kept surfacing.

Washington scholars have probed many aspects of the first President's life.

Was he soft on civil rights, as ownership of 212 slaves might indicate?

Was he guilty of using profanity? It was suggested that at the height of battle he addressed General Charles Lee, with these words: "Get your fat ass out to the battlefield!"

Did he marry Martha Curtis only for her money, her land-holdings, her slaves?

Did he carry on an affair with the wife of his next-door neighbor?

A most persistent rumor concerned Washington's depraved use of slave women. George Washington's personal life suggested that the almanac in which he kept his diary indicated that he was intimate with slaves. His custom of listing his female properties with circles, dots, checks and curves around some of the names was interpreted by some writers as possible evidence that he had immorally used the women thus designated. The truth is that if all the printed or spoken rumors about Washington's illegitimate children could be substantiated, he would be the most prolific progenitor in our history, and the title, "father of our country," would be more than a mere figure of speech.

Washington wasn't born with a silver spoon in his mouth. He had to make his own way, to fight against social and economic forces which tended to drag him down. As a 13-year-old, while his friends, the children of Colonel Fairfax, rode to the hounds, he was forced to learn a trade as a surveyor. There were no child labor laws in those days, and Washington struggled to accumulate whatever assets he had—bit by bit.

Historians are not clear about the extent of George Washington's formal schooling, but we can safely assume that he was in the classroom between the ages of seven and eleven, and that he did not go, like many of the other political leaders of Virginia to the College of William and Mary. He was one of the very few Presidents of the United States whose formal studies came to an end at the elementary school level. He did, however, in 1776, receive an LL.B from Harvard, making him a Doctor of Law.

George lost his father when he was 11, and his mother, Mary, did not remarry. History—perhaps to protect the mother of our first President—describes her as a stoic who wanted to raise a son who would be completely independent, but it appears more likely that she was an extremely self-centered person. She did her best to stop George whenever he did anything that was not to her immediate advantage. She never swelled with pride over his rise to greatness. On the contrary, she resented it. She was worried that his successes might make him neglect her. Though she lived into George's second presidential term, she never budged from home to participate in any of his triumphs. On the contrary, she had a habit of belittling her son's achievements. In fact, once, during the Revolution, she complained that the Commander-in-Chief (who actually was providing for her quite well) was allowing her to starve.

Washington did not enjoy a happy childhood. He felt rejected by his mother and was eager to escape from her home as quickly as possible. One of George's childhood playmates remembered Mrs. Washington with these words: "I was ten times more afraid of her than I was of my own parents." The effect of his mother on his later life—on his attitude towards women, love and marriage—is open to debate.

Washington has been described as a man of ill humor, cold, unfriendly and unable to show affection. He seemed to be distant and remote, unable to accept criticism. At the same time, he has been written of as a wise, good, and great man. All of these adjectives probably have some basis in truth. George Washington was an extremely human individual.

He was a man of flesh and blood, a man who craved great

wealth; a man who could covet his neighbor's wife; a man who could (unsuccessfully) court two heiresses before he married the richest widow in Virginia.

No doubt, Washington was a status-seeker, and a big spender. His desire for a very elaborate home, for fine food and expensive recreational activity brought him to the brink of bankruptcy in the prewar and postwar years.

As a man who occupied high public office, his life was exposed to public scrutiny and his every action was minutely examined. As President of the United States, his life was an open book.

As Washington's fame and power increased, so did the number of jealous men eager to tarnish the reputation of the hero of the Revolution.

During his teenage years, George was not very successful with girls. He was interested in them, but they were not interested in him. He was very big, almost in a frightening way. He towered over them, and was not graceful in movement. His speech came slowly, and he often found it difficult to sustain a conversation. The fact that he had the largest hands and feet in the State of Virginia hardly made him appealing to the opposite sex, and the romance he sought was denied him.

At an early age, he fell in love with Betsy Fauntleroy, the marriageable daughter of a rich Virginian. At almost sixteen, Betsy was a petite brunette, whose turned-up nose, small, round face, light brown eyes and smiling lips reminded one of a high-spirited minx. Her father, who was about to send to London for a six-horse chariot on which his coat of arms was to be emblazoned, did not envision George Washington riding beside him. Washington, whose mother was a permanent squatter on a second-rate farm, was no catch for his daughter. He also thought of George as a sickly person, probably as sick as George's brother.

When Washington wrote to Betsy's father, apprising him of his intentions "to wait on Miss Betsy in hopes of revocation of my former cruel sentence, and see if I can meet any alteration in my favor," the response from Betsy's father was negative. How could he, a wealthy man, who lived on such a grand scale, think of Washington as a promising suitor for his rich and beautiful daughter? The colonel did not even take the time to answer him. And when Washington was 22 and proposed marriage to Betsy, she immediately rejected him.

Whenever George was rejected by a woman, he went to his desk and wrote poetry about love, romance, and passion, and his lack of success with women. On one occasion, George composed this adolescent plea for love and romance:

Oh, ye Gods, why should my poor resistless
   heart
Stand to oppose thy might and power
At last surrender to Cupid's feather'd dart
And now lays bleeding every hour
For her that's pitiless of my grief and woes
And will not on me pity take
I'll sleep amongst my most inveterate foes
And with gladness wish to wake.
In deluding sleepings let my eyelids close
That in an enraptured dream I may
In a soft lulling sleep and gentle repose
Possess those joys denied by day.

George, who had little or no affection at home, had not yet developed protection against such hurts. He felt an aching, stinging emptiness. He suffered from the loss of his own dignity. His search for feminine acceptance led to repeated failure. He could find no peace of mind.

Being a natural at mathematics, at the age of nineteen George decided to become a surveyor. His first opportunity was given him by the Fairfaxes. The job was that of assistant to a surveyor who at the time was laying out a town at the head of the Potomac. The town was called Alexandria and, being only a few dozen miles from Mount Vernon, was to become an important center of activity in future years.

George was a frequent visitor at the mansion William Fairfax had built overlooking the Potomac. Needless to say, the Fairfaxes had a great influence on young George. William Fairfax introduced George to a world from which the young man was eventually to draw strength for revolutionary ends. William Fairfax came to love George Washington like a son, perhaps because his own son, George William Fairfax, was so unexciting. And it was in the Fairfax home that George fell in love with Sally—William's wife. This was a love that conquered both time and space, a love that lasted a lifetime.

Sally was a coquette, full of charming vanities. She knew how to baffle and disturb her not very secretive suitor, getting him to advance or retreat, increase or decrease his attentions, as it suited her. Sally was able to speak French, which added to her charm and grace. She had everything a young, uneducated, and heretofore rejected man might seek. No doubt she wanted George, and she was annoyed when other women got more of his attention than she. At the time, Washington was 16 years of age, and Sally a mature 18. In Virginia, she was considered a mature woman; George was but a teenage, auburn-haired boy. Sally brought to Belvoir, that provincial outpost of English aristocratic life, the best in culture and education.

At first it seemed that George was attracted to Sally's younger sister, Mary, who had come from England for a lengthy stay with her sister. However, Washington longed for Sally, who was two years his senior. In her he had discovered depth and richness. In her he found a thrill comparable to no other. She taught him the social graces. She read to him, taught him to dance, advised him how to dress, and even induced him to perform with her in amateur theatricals.

Did Washington think of love as did the knights of old who worshipped their ladies from afar, seeing them only as superior creatures who did not acknowledge the ordinary aspects of existence? Was he imagining her to be a fairy princess instead of a woman of flesh and blood? Was his attraction to her sexually stimulated?

To "Dear friend Robin," George, nineteen years of age, wrote that he was staying at Lord Fairfax's hunting lodge, "here I might, was my heart disengaged, pass my time very pleasantly, as there's a very agreeable young lady lives in the same house . . . but as that's only adding fuel to the fire, revives my former passion for your Low Land Beauty, whereas was I to live more retired from young women, I might in some measure alleviate my sorrows by burying that chaste and troublesome passion in the grave of oblivion or eternal forgetfulness."

George Washington was now ready for the love of a woman. He wanted to settle down in his own home, away from his mother's coldness. This, he knew, would bring him contentment and happiness.

If love and acceptance were what he needed, he was determined to find them. Fortunate for him, there was a neighbor who was interested in him, and in that neighbor's home, there was a beautiful, cultured, appealing girl who could fill his days with meaning. Most of all, in that home he was accepted by a woman.

When life treated George badly, he would readily turn to Sally for comfort. He had learned to dance well, and dress well, and was very attractive. Sally continued to love her handsome and understanding husband, and merely thought of George as a distraction. She enjoyed teasing him and keeping him at her beck and call. It strengthened her female ego to have him at her side whenever it so pleased her. Evidently, her husband was good-naturedly tolerant of George, and considered Washington a young romantic whose involvement with a sophisticated older woman was no threat.

In 1752, Washington was appointed adjutant of the smallest and most distant section of Virginia. He was 20 at the time he got the berth he wanted, the adjutancy of the Northern Neck. Later, in an order dated October 30, Washington was commanded to proceed into the wilderness; to make contact with friendly Indians and obtain information as to where the French forces had posted themselves. Years later, Washington wondered about this mission with these words: "It was deemed by some an extraordinary circumstance that so young and inexperienced a person should have been employed on a negotiation with which subjects of the greatest importance were involved."

The report he submitted showed his success. By present day standards, young Washington was hardly mature and rather cocky. There is no hint that he ever felt he had come up against anything he could not understand and could not handle. He moved forward without hesitation, accomplished what he had set out to, and returned triumphantly.

Washington was soon promoted to lieutenant colonel. He led a small Virginia task force to fortify the Forks which was soon to be attacked by a huge French war party. On March 15, 1754, he was ordered to march to the Ohio River and take up defensive positions. However, a real series of battles developed; Washington emerged victorious. In later battles, although Washington was not victorious, he inflicted such great losses on the enemy that at 22 years of age he had become an international figure. He had fought against the French, and had made errors. Although he knew little of military science, his army fought bravely against superior numbers. He became a hero to his neighbors, a person to be reckoned with in foreign capitals.

As Washington rode to join General Braddock at Frederick, his thoughts were with Sally Fairfax. Stopping at his Bullskin Plantation, he wrote her, urging that she lighten the campaign by writing to him. "None of my friends," he wrote, "are able to convey more real delight than you can, to whom I stand indebted for so many obligations."

Although he had been ordered by Braddock to proceed as quickly as possible to the seacoast and bring back 4,000 pounds needed by the paymaster, Washington took a roundabout route that permitted him to spend a night at Mount Vernon and see Sally Fairfax. She loaned him a horse so that he could continue his journey; then enticed him by saying that she hoped he would inform her of his "safe arrival at camp." Unfortunately, she dampened the romantic fire by insisting that he not write to her directly, but send the news through a mutual friend.

When his mission was accomplished, he wrote to her, "I took as a gentle rebuke your polite manner of forbidding me to correspond with you, and conceive this opinion not illy founded when I sifted it thus. I have hitherto found it impracticable to engage one moment of your attention. If I am right in this, I hope you will excuse my present presumption and lay the imputation to lateness at my successful arrival. If, on the contrary, these are fearful apprehensions only, how easy is it to remove my suspicions, enliven . . . [here Washington, in reading the letter after the Revolution, erased a word] . . . and make me happier than the day is long by honoring me with a correspondence which you did once partly promise me."

At the death of Braddock, Washington, who was the most active of his aides, took command of a shattered group of fighting men. No doubt General Braddock had been defeated. Washington, his mind full of the horrors of war he had experienced, made his way slowly to Mount Vernon.

Once again he was greeted with a letter from William Fairfax and a postscript in Sally's handwriting: "Dear Sir: After thanking heaven for your safe return, I must accuse you of great unkindness in refusing us the pleasure of seeing you this night. I do assure you that nothing but our being satisfied that your company would be disagreeable should prevent us from trying if our legs would not carry us to Mount Vernon, but if you will not come to us tomorrow morning very early, we shall be at Mount Vernon."

Politics now entered the picture with Washington requesting a commission under threat of resigning from the army. He traveled to Philadelphia to meet men of importance. Washington, although an international figure, had until this time never visited a major city. It was just a few days prior to his twenty-fourth birthday that he arrived in Philadelphia.

The time had now come for Washington to find the woman he would marry. He wanted to free himself of his involvement with his friend's wife. And so, after four or five days in Philadelphia, he went to New York where he met Speaker Robinson's son. More important, he met Polly, Robinson's wife's sister.

Polly was a statuesque brunette with delicate features. Her full mouth was both sensuous and firm. She was beautiful, rich, and an heiress to one of New York's baronial families.

George took her to see *Microcosm or the World in Miniature*, a kind of pre-movie movie. He also escorted her to a dance. During the week they travelled through the city. He then had to leave for Boston but, returning several days later, he spent an additional four days with the 26-year-old beauty. But all his ardor was in vain; Polly was in love with Lieutenant Colonel Roger Morris, whom she married two years later.

It was in 1758 that Washington found himself a wife. George had heard that Martha Dandridge Custis had become a widow. She was a petite and pretty woman. Going out of his way, Washington stopped to offer his condolences to the widow.

At that time, Martha was twenty-six and the mother of two children. She had an estate of 15,000 acres in and around Williamsburg, a beautiful residence in Williamsburg proper, a country place called the White House, twenty thousand pounds, and more than 200 slaves. Her estate was tentatively appraised at 23,632 pounds.

Martha was described as a good-humored woman with dark hair, beautiful teeth, hazel eyes, and a figure that could be said to be agreeably plump. She wore elegant clothes with a lack of self-consciousness.

The 26-year-old Washington who entered Martha's parlor was described as "straight as an Indian, measuring six feet two inches in his stockings and weighing 175 pounds . . . His frame is padded with well-developed muscles, indicating great strength. His bones and joints are large, as are his hands and feet. He is wide-shouldered but has not a deep or round chest; is neat waisted, but is broad across the hips, and has rather long legs and arms. His head is well-shaped, though not large, but is gracefully poised on a superb neck. A large and straight rather than a prominent nose; blue-gray penetrating eyes which are widely separated and overhung by a heavy brow. His face is long rather than broad, with high round cheek bones, and terminates in a good firm chin. He has a clear though colorless pale skin which burns with the sun. His movements are graceful, his walk majestic, and he is a splendid horseman."

Martha must have encouraged the colonel since when he returned to Williamsburg after spending the night, it was with the understanding that he would soon return. It took hardly a week for him to do so, and, on each visit, he presented wonderful gifts to Martha's servants. Of greater importance was the way he pleased Martha's children, John and Martha. The two-year-old girl could be cooed at and dangled under the eyes of her adoring mother, and the boy, almost four, was impressed with Washington's uniform. Washington took the children seriously, feeling that were he to marry Martha, the responsibility of raising the children would be his, and this was not a matter to be taken lightly.

Washington courted her steadily and swiftly. Within a few weeks, Martha and George were serious in their intentions. On May 4, Washington ordered a ring from Philadelphia, costing two pounds sixteen shillings. He also undertook the rebuilding of his home at Mount Vernon, engaging George William Fairfax to do the construction. (No doubt, William kept Sally informed about what was going on at Mount Vernon.)

Finally, Washington wrote a letter to Sally saying, "I have always considered marriage as the most interesting event in one's life, the foundation of misery or happiness."

How did Sally reply? It is not known because Washington, later, as was his practice, destroyed her letter. However, his reply to her gives us clues as to what her response must have been.

"Tis true, I profess myself a votary of love," he wrote. "I acknowledge that a lady is in the case, and further confess that this lady is known to you . . . Yes, Madam, as well as she is to one who is too sensible to her charms to deny the Power whose influence he feels and must ever submit to . . . Misconstrue not my meaning; doubt it not, nor expose it. The world has no business to know the object of love declared in this manner to you, when I want to conceal it . . . But adieu till happier times, if ever I shall see them. I dare believe they are as happy as you say. I wish I were happy also."

Once again her answer did not satisfy Washington. This time he wrote:

"Do we still understand the true meaning of each other's letters? I think it must appear so, though I would feign hope the contrary as I cannot speak plainer—but I'll say no more and leave you to guess the rest . . . *Adieu*, dear Madam, you possibly will hear something of me or from me before we shall meet."

Sally wrote a coy reply to him in which she told of playing the amorous young heroine in an amateur production of Addison's *Cato*. To which Washington replied, but did not refer to his own coming marriage, nor did he even mention Martha.

In his correspondence, Washington referred to his feelings for Sally. It is difficult to fit them into the pattern of Washington's life. He wanted marriage, cared for Martha, knew that his marriage would give him strength. Possibly, with marriage imminent, he experienced a renewed wave of emotion for an old love, which he would be leaving behind.

George remained a favorite of Sally's father-in-law and became an even closer friend to her husband. Evidently, although both admired the same woman, George William Fairfax remained convinced that his wife and Washington never overstepped the bounds of morality.

After his marriage to Martha, he wrote, "I am now I believe, fixed in this seat with an agreeable consort for life." However, he continued his association with Sally Fairfax, and even Martha was brought into the friendship. History records that though his love for Sally was never consummated, it was surely the most passionate experience George Washington ever had with a woman. History does not record any scandal in this relationship.

Years later, Washington wrote: "I feel the force of her amiable beauties in the recollection of a thousand tender passages that I could wish to obliterate till I am bid revive them."

It is certain that Washington's love for Sally was no passing fascination. It extended across years and was woven into the existence at Belvoir which had been, even before Sally had set foot there, a shining part of his life.

Many years later, Washington rode his horse along the road to what had been Belvoir. He described how in February of 1785 he came across the ruins. "When I viewed them," he wrote, "when I considered that the happiest moments of my life had been spent there; when I could not trace a room in the house [now all rubbish] that did not bring to my mind the recollection of pleasing scenes, I was obliged to fly from them." With tears in his eyes—for the general was not ashamed to weep—Washington rode home "with painful sensations and sorrowing for the contrast."

That Washington fell in love and remained in love with the wife of his friend and neighbor cannot be denied. On the very eve of his marriage to Martha, he declared in writing his love for Sally; and as an old man, separated from his love by more than twenty-five years, he wrote her that all the events of the Revolution and his presidency had not "been able to eradicate from my mind those happy moments, the happiest of my life, which I have enjoyed in your company."

There was a time when he wrote to the Fairfaxes to return and rebuild Belvoir, and recreate those old times. This request was made after he had married Martha and the heat of his passion for Sally had abated and the two families had been intimate neighbors. He begged "that you consider Mount Vernon as your home until you could build with convenience, in which request Mrs. Washington joins very sincerely."

Washington's continuing love for Sally in no way lessened the satisfaction he received from his own marriage. In writing to others he praised marriage.

Martha, in what seems to have been an act of possessiveness after having been forced to share her husband so relentlessly with the world, burnt their correspondence when her husband was dead. This raised whispers that there were rifts in the marriage which she desired to hide. This is untrue. Martha (except for her failure to bear him a child) satisfactorily fulfilled Washington's needs.

She brought him relaxation; she was a creator of comfort. If Martha lacked the variety and ability to keep her husband continually interested, her greatest gift made up for the lack. Her greatest gift was a social sense—the ability to get on with all kinds of people.

How did Sally feel, spending most of her mature years in England, about the George Washington who had become one of

the heroes of the human race? Did she think that she had indi-
rectly made a contribution to the emerging greatness of the
United States?

When Sally Fairfax died in England in 1811, the letters she
had received from Washington were sent to relatives in America.
They guarded them from public knowledge until 1877, when two
letters appeared in the *New York Herald Tribune*. One, written
from Fort Cumberland on September 12, 1857, was an avowal of
love. At that time he was already engaged to Martha Custis. A
second letter, written approximately four months before his marriage, reiterated his romantic interest in Sally. In 1886, 81 additional letters to Sally were published. Unfortunately, a complete
picture of this romance is not available because none of the letters she had written him were preserved.

But a romance it was, ending only with her death. Despite
his shortcomings, including his tremendous yearning for his
friend's wife, George Washington dominates early American history, and his name comes through as one who saw his magnificent and grandest dreams come true.

6

A President Lusts for Love

Sex, love and marriage—most men and women crave all three. They seek the thrill and excitement of passionate love-making; they want to love and be loved; to marry and stay married. In many cases, the lifelong desire for an amorous relationship remains unfulfilled. Such was the story of Warren G. Harding, the 29th President of the United States.

Warren's formative years were spent in Blooming Grove, a small village in Ohio. His life, in its rural self-sufficiency, was typical of Ohio at the time. Children were expected to help in the fields from the time they reached school age.

The village school which Warren attended was built by his grandfather. It was a rectangular one-room building with two front-door entrances, one for girls and one for boys. Inside, there were rows of double desks. In this way, the school policy of the separation of the sexes was implemented. By the summer of 1873, Warren had already finished his first term in school. He had read Parson Weems's account of George Washington and the cherry tree in McGuffey's *Second Reader*.

George Tryon Harding, father of the future President, was a born gambler. He was born on June 12, 1844, in the log cabin built by his great-grandfather, Amos. Although it was expected at the time that Tryon would continue to farm, he was neither by nature nor inclination a farmer.

In 1858, at the age of fourteen, Tryon entered Iberia College. In 1860, he received his bachelor's degree. Commencing in the autumn, he taught for two terms at a rural school, four miles north of Mount Gilead. He then tried his luck in a number of different fields of endeavor, always seeking to make his fortune overnight, but without much success. After many years of trying and speculating, he finally put his mind to the field of medicine, and, after a few years of concentrated study, earned an M.D. degree.

He joined Doctor McFarland's travels around the countryside, in his buggy. It was after two years of apprenticeship with Doctor McFarland that Tryon went on to Cleveland where he spent a term at Doctor McFarland's old medical college. After one session, during which he registered with Doctor Hamilton Biggar, Tryon was admitted to practice with a certificate issued by the Northwest Medical Society. Two sessions at the Homeopathic Hospital were required before a student was allowed to put an M.D. after his name. Tryon was not able to return for his final session until the spring of 1873. However, even as a doctor, he found that prosperity was not quickly won. His practice was not lucrative, and very often his small fee was paid in butter and eggs instead of dollars.

From the day he arrived in Caledonia, Ohio, he was always in debt. There was a time when he decided to buy odd lots, and then mortgage them. With the mortgage money, he purchased additional lots. But this excessive speculation and mortgaging led to the failure of the entire venture. It ended in near bankruptcy.

For many years, it was Warren's mother, Phoebe, who helped meet the family budget. While her husband was studying, she learned the skills of a midwife. It is doubtful that her husband could have supported the family with his meager medical fees.

The Hardings arrived in Caledonia from Blooming Grove early in 1873. For their son, Warren, born in 1865, Caledonia was a large and glittering new world. Yet all was not favorable to the Hardings. The rumor that there was Negro blood in their veins preceded them. In any quarrel at school, the jeering cry would go up: "You Hardings are part nigger!" This feeling of a lack of identity with any one group was to always haunt Warren.

Warren loved to read and to recite. He was always ready to take part in the Friday afternoon declamation contests, reciting Patrick Henry's "Give Me Liberty or Give Me Death," "The Boy Stood on the Burning Deck," and "Horatius." Many years earlier, dressed in Kentucky trousers and a gingham shirt, as a preschool child Warren had stood up before mother and aunts and recited:

> You'd scarce expect one of my age
> To speak in public on the stage;
> And if I chance to fall below
> Demosthenes or Cicero,
> Don't view me with a critic's eye,
> But pass my imperfections by.
> Large streams from little fountains flow,
> Tall oaks from little acorns grow.

This was written by David Everett and had been recited the first time at a New Hampshire school declamation contest.

When Warren was about ten years old, his father brought home a cornet. This became Warren's most precious possession; and in a few months he was able to join a band and toot his B-flat cornet.

During Warren Harding's early years, there was no indication that he was destined for political leadership. He curried horses, milked cows, moulded bricks, made brooms, helped with the painting of the barn. He was part of a group of boys his own age; he made money playing the cornet in a band.

In the autumn of 1880, he entered the Ohio Central College. Tuition was seven dollars a term; and there were three men on the faculty. Harding was 14 years old at the time.

His years at school were not outstanding, although in his last year he became president of the Philomathic Literary Society. It was at this time that he developed an interest in newspaper work. Together with a fellow student, he put out the *Iberia Spectator*, a college newspaper. It was published fortnightly. At graduation, Harding gave the commencement address; there were three graduates.

The Hardings now resided in Marion, Ohio. Here Warren took his first teaching job, one that paid $20 a month and twice that during the winter months when he had to light the fires and sweep the floors. At the same time, he joined the Huber Silver Band. At the time he did his best to look a bit older and more mature since several of his students were older than himself. That he preferred playing with the band to teaching school is a certainty.

Harding's father was determined to make something of his son, so he went out and purchased a secondhand set of law books. Warren tried to interest himself in the writings of Blackstone (the English jurist and legal historian), but with little success. He was more interested in serving as local agent for several insurance companies. However, this interest did not last either. He had inherited his father's restlessness, and he soon dropped insurance to take over the Marion newspaper. This led to his fascination with politics.

Harding met his future wife, Florence M. Kling, when he was twenty-five. She was the only daughter of three children of Amos Kling. There were many times that her father wished that she had been a boy. She was born the year before the outbreak of the Civil War. Her father was a determined, self-made man who wanted to be the absolute head of the house. From the very start of her childhood days, her father found her as headstrong as himself. Whenever they saw one another, they seemed to quarrel.

However, Florence's father gave her what he believed to be appropriate: piano and riding lessons, several years at a good school, and whatever leisure-time activities money could buy.

Flossie had already been married to Peter DeWolfe, who had no purpose other than to amuse himself. Pete was two years older than Flossie and the story went that he had to marry her. Six months after their marriage, their son Eugene was born.

Flossie did not help Pete become more settled. In fact, she so dominated him that he turned to drink. He was incapable of making the effort to earn a living, was resentful of his wife and indifferent to his child. Flossie's father did not help voluntarily, nor would Flossie ask him for the assistance she needed. Instead, she borrowed a piano and began giving music lessons.

In September of 1884 Flossie obtained a legal separation from her husband. Their child was now four. Her petition for divorce was granted in May 1886, on the grounds of gross neglect. She continued giving piano lessons at fifty cents per hour.

One of Flossie's pupils was Harding's sister Chat, and it was while giving her a piano lesson that Flossie met Harding.

There was unfortunately nothing feminine looking about Florence. She had a gawky face and an ungraceful gait. She was the type of woman who never elicited a glance from a male.

It was in Tryon Harding's parlor, at the old upright piano, that she first met Warren, the editor of the *Star*. This was not sheer accident. Under her unlikely exterior, Flossie was still a woman with a warm female heart. From her upstairs window she had noticed this handsome young man. Silently, and within her own mind and heart, she marked him down as hers.

Harding had developed a lock of gray hair above his forehead, and a dusting of white at his temples. The effect further refined his good looks. He looked much older than his age and girls were drawn to his attractive, virile appearance. His response was generally casual. Though crudely experienced in the flesh, he never had been emotionally involved with a woman. To him, making love had been more important than loving.

Flossie flirted with Warren with a calculated tenacity. His lack of response only increased her determination. She had made up her mind not to let him *"escape."* She spread rumors about their close relationship and soon it was whispered that they were keeping company.

Once, upon returning from a visit to an old girl friend in Caledonia, Warren found Flossie waiting for him at the station. Harding was flattered by her constant attention. He was just starting out in life, and the prospect of being married to Flossie, the daughter of a rich man, gave him the assurance he needed. Through her he could forsee the acceptance that had been denied him. The realization that he did not really love her escaped him.

Flossie's father was against the match. He did not appreciate a poor, hapless son-in-law, a newspaper upstart who, it was said was tainted with Negro blood. But strongheaded, determined Flossie ignored her father's sullen threats. She had made up her mind to marry Warren, and parental protest would not stand in her way.

Her father protested loudly. When he once met Harding in the courthouse, he cursed him at the top of his voice, called him a "nigger," and threatened to blow off his head. When Kling realized that he could not stop his strongwilled daughter, he filed suits against Warren's father for outstanding debts, and prohibited his own wife from having anything to do with their daughter. For seven years, Kling could not manage to nod his head to his daughter when they met on the street.

The wedding was ignored by Flossie's parents. But just before the ceremony, Louisa Kling slipped in the side door unobserved, leaving immediately afterward, before even her daughter knew she had been present.

Warren and Flossie mailed out their own wedding invitations, and were married in the front hall of the house on Mount Vernon Avenue that they themselves designed and had built by their friend, Captain Jacob Apt. Approximately 100 guests were present, and a harpist from Dayton played the "Wedding March." Mrs. Kling had secretly given her daughter money for the furniture.

Flossie Harding loved her husband, a love that was hardly returned in kind. Harding was a promiscuous husband who sought affection and sex from several women, with Nan Britton topping the list. His wife, now called "Duchess" by Harding, a name conferred upon her because of her domineering personality, was neither warm nor affectionate. She was hard and brash, and her lack of tact was considerable. She not only inherited her father's business ability; she inherited his bluntness as well.

After his marriage, Harding began his pursuit of elected office. Any Republican meeting in the country found him among those present. He began to develop fame as an orator. People liked his friendliness, his resonant voice and the words at his command. Harding found himself elected to several offices. He served in the Ohio State Senate, was lieutenant governor, and served an obscure six years in the United States Senate. Had it not been for the chance meeting with Harry Daugherty, he might never have become President, nor would he have been involved in a scandal, the magnitude of Tea Pot Dome.

Harding met Daugherty at a Union County Republican rally. They spent the night before the rally at the Globe Hotel. Daugherty was to be the principal speaker at the evening's rally. Harding knew that Daugherty was the former chairman of the Republican State Committee, the man who had nominated McKinley for governor six years earlier. He was a power behind conventions. The two men met in the morning and, with rain continuing all day, Harding and Daugherty became better acquainted. Daugherty warmed up to Harding and, before the day was over, suggested that Harding make the first speech of the evening. The audience was large and he delivered an impromptu speech. It was at this meeting that Harding became recognized as an excellent public speaker.

With six hundred boosters gathered in Marion's bunting-festooned Grand Opera House to welcome their home town candidate for governor, the second woman in the life of Warren G. Harding, and the one most responsible for the destruction of Harding's posthumous reputation, appeared on the scene.

Nan Britton was only fourteen at the time, but she had already developed rounded, firm breasts and provocative hips. Her plump half-pouting face was pretty and sensual. No doubt, she already possessed a keen awareness of men. The man she selected for herself was Warren Harding who was many years her senior. Going to and from high school daily, Nan had seen Harding's picture in all store fronts, and had proclaimed to friends and family alike that she was in love with him.

In her textbooks, she would scribble, "Warren Gamaliel Harding—He's a darling." She would call his home, hoping to hear his voice answer the telephone. Her mother urged her daughter to calm down. Until her preoccupation with Harding, Nan had had daydreams of being a famous actress or a brilliant writer, extravagant dreams that were never entirely eclipsed, even in later life. It is interesting to point out that her senior high school oratorical piece bore the title "What Every Woman Wants." Whether Nan really got what she wanted is open to question. That she became the mistress of the President of the United States is a well-established fact.

In the small, quaint town of Marion, Nan soon became the subject of vulgar gossip. In desperation, her father discussed his daughter's infatuation with Harding himself. Harding, aware of her feelings, was certainly not impervious to her premature charm, to her face, her figure, her sexual motivation. Once he happened to meet her alone on the street as she was returning from an errand. This was their first meeting; he a married man, she a teenager. He felt drawn to her; everything about her excited him. She was everything his wife was not. Harding later confessed that during this first encounter, he entertained the strongest urge to possess her.

In her confessional account of their affair, in a book called *The President's Daughter*, Nan admitted that she had become Harding's mistress when she was 20. Unadmittedly, she received surreptitious letters from him when she was 16 or 17. Even at the time of Nan's thirteenth birthday, both Harding and his wife were aware of her persistent infatuation.

When the Brittons broke up their Marion home, Nan went to Cleveland where she lived at the YWCA and worked as a salesgirl for six dollars a week. Before moving, she dropped into the Harding home to congratulate the then senator-elect.

The Duchess answered the bell and her stiffness became more pronounced as she looked at the impish, blonde schoolgirl. The sexuality of this pretty girl was apparent; and the Duchess could feel the threat that was posed by this youthful competitor, who openly talked of her love for the Duchess's husband. Well aware of Warren's weakness for women, the Duchess had good reason to resent the presence of Nan.

Harding was in the library alcove playing poker with his regulars. He came out into the brown hall, thanked Nan, and held her hand just a little too long and a little too tightly, until the Duchess bluntly reminded him that others were waiting for him. He snapped to attention. In no way did he wish to anger the Duchess.

In June 1913, Doctor Samuel Britton died, leaving his wife and family penniless. Mary Britton, the doctor's wife, turned to Harding for help and advice. Harding was eager to be of assistance and found her a position as a substitute teacher. At the same time he asked about Nan, the girl who had been so infatuated with him years ago. Inwardly hoping that it would motivate the girl to contact him, Harding offered to be of help to Nan as well.

Nan never permitted him to forget that promise. Although she did not appear to be unnecessarily demanding, she had a way of ensuring that she was well supplied with comfort and luxury; and Harding never stinted in giving her the funds she needed.

During the summer of 1914, Harding began a correspondence with Nan. At that time the affair had gone no further than an emotional exchange of letters. Nan's classmates at the time used to slip down to the post office and bring back the letters in their fat blue envelopes to prevent Nan's mother from learning about them. Harding had not, as far as is known, had any rendezvous with Nan.

During Harding's term in the Senate, he was not always vitally interested in the on-going debates. There were times when discussions on the Senate floor involved critical national and international issues, but Harding was busy scribbling 40 or 50 page letters.

While Harding was busy writing love letters to his darling, sweet Nan, the Duchess was busily running to clairvoyants for a summary of her husband's character. One such person was a Madame Marcia, who professed that given the date and the time of birth of any person, she could produce a character profile. How the Madame came to her conclusions is not known; but she did come up with this analysis of Warren Harding: "Sympathetic, kindly, intuitive, free with promises and trustful of friends; enthusiastic, impulsive. Perplexed over financial affairs. Many clandestine love affairs; inclined to recurrent moods of melancholia." All this she supposedly derived from Harding's birthday, November 2, 1865.

During his early senatorial years, Harding received a letter from Nan Britton written with feigned impersonality, knowing that it might be seen by secretaries. It read:

"I wonder if you will remember me; my father was Dr. Britton, of Marion, Ohio.

I have been away from Marion for about two years, and up until last November, have been working. But it was work which promised no future.

I have been reading of the imperative demand for stenographers and typists throughout the country, and the apparent scarcity, and it has occurred to me that you are in a position to help me along this line if there is an opening. . .

Any suggestions or help you might give me would be greatly appreciated, I assure you, and it would please me so to hear from you."

She wrote this letter from New York.

Nan was forever the schoolgirl who felt that it was the obligation of men to look after her. It was not that she was avaricious or mercenary. It was rather that she felt she needed the male of her choice to supply her with money and attention. At first her request was polite, but later she asked for money with much more buoyant ingenuity, taking for granted that she would be given what she asked for. She usually was!

When Harding received the letter, his male instinct grasped at the key phrase "it would please me so." In the midst of a very important debate on the Senate floor, he scribbled her a note. Nan received it several days later and read it while sitting on the window sill of her third-floor bedroom.

"You may be sure I remember you, and I remember you most agreeably, too." He indicated that though he had no position available in his office, he would do all he could to help her and would be willing to "go personally to the War and Navy Department to urge your appointment."

At the same time he indicated that there was every probability that he would be in New York the following week and if he could reach her by telephone or "becomingly" look her up, he would do so and would "take pleasure in doing it . . . You see, I do remember you," he concluded.

She lost no time in replying:

"It is good to know that you remembered me; and I appreciate your kind interest and prompt response . . .

"I am hoping that you will be in New York next week and that I can talk with you; I am inclined to believe that an hour's talk would be much more satisfactory. There is so much I want to tell you; and I am sure that I could give you a better idea of my ability—or rather the extent of my ability, for it is limited—and you could judge for yourself as to the sort of position I could competently fill . . . In case you are able to see me for an hour it would please me immensely to make an appointment—provided it does not interfere with your own plans."

Before she could reply to his answer (which came four days later), he telephoned her from Manhattan that he had arrived in New York and asked her to meet him as soon as possible at his hotel. Trembling with excitement, she was on her way within minutes. He was standing on the steps waiting for her and smiling. Arm in arm they went inside to the reception room and, sitting together on the settee, they talked intimately of the old days in Marion. At this time she confessed her school girl feelings for him. He suggested they go up to his room so they could talk in private.

Later, in her book, she wrote: "He had scarcely closed the door behind us when we shared our first kiss. The bed, which we did not disturb, stood upon a dais, and the furnishings were in keeping with the general refinement of atmosphere. I shall never, never forget how Mr. Harding kept saying, after each kiss, 'God! . . . God, Nan!' in high diminuendo, nor how he pleaded in a tense voice, 'Oh, dearie, tell me it isn't hateful to you to have me kiss you! And as I kissed him back I thought that he surpassed even my gladdest dreams of him."

During moments of affection and passion, Harding admitted that his only reason for coming to New York was to see her. He needed a woman. His wife was no match for the dimpled charm of Nan's youth, the charm of novelty that he had never been able to resist. But though he urged her to explore the "lovely mystery" of sex, she claimed she was still a virgin and was not yet ready to give in to his urgings.

They spent the full day together, and while returning in the taxi he asked her how fast she could take dictation. He suggested trying her out on a letter which he was about to dictate. Putting his arm around her, he dictated, "My darling Nan, I love you more than the world and I want you to belong to me. Could you belong to me, dearie? I want you . . . and I need you so."

Later, she wrote that the letter did not run too long because she silenced him with the kisses he pleaded for. "My sitting next to him made him tremble and this evidence of his need for me I adored."

Harding secured a position for her with the United States Steel Corporation, and then they both returned to the hotel. Back in his suite, she cuddled into his lap in the big armchair. He kept fondling her and telling her: "We were made for each other . . . I'd like to make you my bride, Nan darling." There were no other intimacies at that time, so the story goes. Before departing, he gave Nan $30, telling her he was sorry he had no more money with him at the time.

He visited her in New York once more before she left for Chicago. It was later than Nan received her first love letter from him—a rambling letter of forty incoherent pages, scribbled on scratch-pad paper and enclosing a snapshot of him standing on the Capitol steps. In her answer to him, she politely indicated she needed money. He sent her $42, an amount that could be explained later as payment for some work done.

Within a week, she received another letter asking her to meet him in Indianapolis where he had been asked to speak. When she arrived, he was waiting for her at the iron gate. When she took his hand, she noticed that it was trembling. All the way to the hotel, they held hands. He registered her as his niece with the name Harding. They had separate rooms but spent most of the night together. During the few days they spent there, Nan coyly withheld *love's sweetest intimacy.*

All the way to the station, he kept whispering over and over again, "Dearie, 'r y' going t' sleep with me? Look at me, Nan: goin' to sleep with me, dearie?" He had reserved a section in the train and they spent the night in each other's arms. She let him explore her entire body, but no more, When they finally arrived in Englewood Station, she told him that he looked tired. "God, sweetheart!" he almost shouted, "What do you expect? I'm a man, you know." In Chicago, for the first time, they registered at a hotel as man and wife. Under his breath, the room clerk muttered that if Harding could prove he was really married to the young lady, he could have the room for nothing!

It was not until the end of July that she and Harding reached their "climactic intimacy," and this makes for a story by itself. Harding had arrived in New York from Washington unexpectedly and immediately had taken her to the Imperial, a second-rate hotel on Lower Broadway. Nan looked even more youthful than usual. She wore a pink linen dress and could be taken for a teenager. A bellhop led them to their room, and then left them alone. In her diary, Nan wrote; "I became Mr. Harding's bride that day."

Their intimacy was soon interrupted by a telephone call which Harding answered with, "You've got the wrong party." No sooner had he said that when a sharp rap was heard on the door, which was quickly unlocked from the outside. Two detectives strode in and demanded to know Nan's name and address. She turned to Harding, who was completely frightened. "Tell them the truth," he said, "they've got us."

Never did a middle-age lover look more disconsolate. He sat on the edge of the bed with his naked feet dangling just above the floor. He begged them to let him go. "Tell your story to the judge," one of the detectives answered. However, when one of the detectives became aware that the man they were questioning was Senator Warren G. Harding, they became calm and respectful and withdrew quickly.

Passion gone, Nan and Harding dressed and packed and, with the detectives leading the way, slipped out a back exit. He handed one of the detectives a $20 bill, telling Nan later, that he thought it would cost him at least one thousand dollars to get out of this mess.

Many meetings between Nan and Harding followed. About the dinners she had with her lover, Nan wrote: "I used to love those dinners. They were so sweetly intimate and it was a joy just to sit and look at him. The way he used his hands; the adorable way he used to put the choice bits of meat from his own plate on mine; the way he would say with a sort of tense nervousness: 'That's a very becoming hat, Nan,' or 'God, Nan, you're pretty!' used to go to my head like wine and make food seem for the moment the least needful thing in the world.

Harding now sent gifts of candy, jewelry, and cash. While in the Senate chamber, he wrote her 30 and 40 and even 60 page letters, scribbling them in pencil on a memo pad, pages such as he had written to a former lover—Carrie. He wrote with the same mixture of banal tenderness and crude longing for flesh. Harding related that nowhere except in French had he ever read such love letters as those Nan sent him.

A period now began where Nan visited Harding regularly. She would register at his hotel as Elizabeth Christian, go to her room first and then to his. He greeted her in his pajamas, took her in his arms, whispered, "I'm so glad t' see you!" And then he quickly took her.

When his wife became ill with a kidney ailment that had plagued her for years, Harding began to escort Nan around Washington with extraordinary indiscretion. With this dazzling young lady at his side, Harding threw caution to the winds and strolled with her down Pennsylvania Avenue. There were times that he took her to his office in the Senate Office Building and made love to her. Because he thought that he would never be a father, he became careless about using contraceptives. It was there in the Senate atmosphere of law and order, late in January 1919, that Nan found herself pregnant.

Now Harding avoided seeing her. However, he continued to provide her with all the money she needed or might need later on. He kept sending 100 or 150 dollars at a time. Sometimes, the amount reached 300 or 400 dollars for her confinement and the baby's clothes.

Nan's pregnancy depressed him. He thought of his former lover, Carrie, and regretted not being with her. Carrie was a woman, not a young girl; she would never have led him into this predicament.

Early in the morning of October 22, 1919, Nan felt her first labor pains. And at two o'clock in the afternoon, "The President's Daughter" was born. Six weeks after the birth of Elizabeth, Nan left for New York. She immediately telephoned Harding in Washington. She sobbed on the telephone, telling him that she had to see him. Giving excuse after excuse, he indicated that this was the wrong time. She returned home.

The following June, the Republican Convention was to open in the Coliseum. Several times during this period, Harding slipped away to see Nan. Through all this time she could not persuade Harding to see his daughter.

The convention at that time heard such leaders as Henry Cabot Lodge, Chauncey Depew, Johnson, and Borah. Borah, at the time, insisted that he would riddle the League in the convention. It was an interesting convention with the wise insiders predicting the first ballot as follows: Wood, 249, Lowden, 232, Johnson 112, Butler 88, Sproul 76, Harding 58, and Coolidge 50. However, the Duchess did not foresee things this way at all.

Harding was not considered one of the promising dark horses. Reporters wrote that "Nobody is talking Harding." But a deadlock continued to tie up the convention.

The roll call of the ninth ballot started with the usual vote until the Connecticut delegation switched 13 of its 14 votes from Lowden to Harding. Later, Kansas cast its 20 votes for Harding. Kentucky followed for Harding. Suddenly, thousands of picture postcards of Harding were flung from the rafters. The march to Harding had begun. At 5:15 in the evening Harding learned that he had been elected with 692 1/5 votes.

Two women were at the convention specifically to see Harding nominated. One was the Duchess; the other was Nan, who had watched her lover's certain progress to the nomination. Before leaving Chicago, Harding managed to dodge photographers and reporters and make his way to Nan. She spoke to him about their daughter but he again refused to see Elizabeth. After their love-making, they walked together to the station.

Harding agreed to send Nan to Eagle Bay where she could regain some of her health. While there, Nan received a visit from a slight, soft-spoken stranger with a ruddy complexion. He handed her an envelope containing $800. The man was Jim Sloan, a secret service man who became Harding's trusted go-between.

When Harding was elected President, Nan Britton lay in an upper berth on the midnight train from Chicago to Marion, Ohio. At 6:30 she awoke and asked the porter who the new President was. "Harding's the man," he told her.

She arrived at the Union Depot at seven o'clock. Later, she registered at the Hotel Marion, called Jim Sloan and arranged to meet him that evening in front of the post office. Sloan was waiting for her in an official car and drove her to what had been used as a campaign center. It was empty. He led her into the sun parlor and in a few minutes Harding arrived. Sloan opened the door for the President-elect, then closed it; Harding and Nan were alone.

Later she described this moment with these words: "After affectionate greetings, I exclaimed softly, 'Oh, sweetheart, isn't it wonderful that you are President!' He held me close, kissing me over and over again. Our eyes were now becoming accustomed to the darkness and I could see his face dimly outlined. He looked at me some time before he answered. Then his 'Um . . . say, dearie, do you love me?' showed me that the glories of a victorious hero were submerged in the grander glories of a lover's delight in being with his woman. 'This is the best thing that's happened to me lately, dearie!' he murmured."

He was the first to leave, but not before giving her three 500 dollar bills.

Early in January, Nan's sister, Elizabeth Willits, went to Marion for a showdown talk with Harding. At this time, the President admitted his affair with her sister and assumed the responsibility of being the father of Elizabeth Ann. He agreed to provide for Nan and offered to pay the Willits $500 a month if they would adopt the baby legally. Harding was worried because the girl, without meaning to, could, in an indiscreet moment, bring ruin to his entire career. He was now the President of the United States of America.

Nan began to see Harding in the White House. Once, she came when the President was about to go to church. He was in his dark cutaway, but upon seeing Nan he immediately led her to the leather couch. In her diary, once again, she wrote:

"And there for a brief space of time—all too brief—we became oblivious to our surroundings, to his identity as President of the United States, and to all the world. 'Why don't you tell me you love me, Nan darling?' he coaxed, and I told him over and over again, as I had told him a thousand times, 'I love you, darling Warren Harding, I love you.' "

History records Warren G. Harding's administration as a catastrophe. He is remembered as a President who consorted with a mistress in the White House, who had a secret service agent stationed outside as he sought carnal pleasures with Nan on the floor of a closet, the only space where absolute privacy could be assured.

Harding had a weakness for feminine wiles and even in Marion there were some rumors about his sexual indiscretions. There is no doubt that his wife Flossie never satisfied him sexually. In fact, at the time of the marriage, acquaintances could not figure out why W. G. ever married Flossie. She was eight years older, a divorcee with a child, and, by any standard, no beauty. He never really loved her although she, a woman of principle and purpose, did her best to make the marriage work. It was Flossie, too, who turned his newspaper, the *Star*, into a profitable venture.

Harding's health was beginning to fail. He became despondent and ill. The Teapot Dome scandal had rocked the administration. He deteriorated quickly. Physicians diagnosed his malady as ptomaine poisoning from eating tainted crab. During periods of semiconsciousness, he repeatedly muttered something about "false friends." Questions about his unexpected and sudden death on August 2nd, 1923 grew. He was 58 years of age.

Mrs. Harding forbade an autopsy and the doctors finally signed a statement attesting to the fact that death resulted from a cerebral hemorrhage.

After Harding's death, scandals within his administration came to light. It was said then that had Harding not died he would have been impeached. His good friend, Harry Daugherty, defended by the famed lawyer, Max D. Steuer, left an impression that Harding's integrity was at stake. Many questions were left unanswered. As for missing ledger sheets, there remained the question, "Was there something in Harding's private life that might have been revealed by the ledger sheets?"

Before moving out of the White House, Mrs. Harding rounded up all correspondence of her late husband. She later burned all his official and personal letters with the excuse that the contents might be misconstrued to his discredit.

The public was now willing to believe almost anything about Warren G. Harding. In 1927, when Nan Britton authored a book entitled *The President's Daughter,* she made public what had only been rumored—that she had been his mistress from 1917 until 1923 and that he had fathered an illegitimate daughter.

At first, booksellers refused to handle the book and responsible reviewers were hesitant to pass judgment on it. However, within the following month, it became the second best seller in the country. The frontispiece featured a photograph of a six-year-old girl, The dedication was: "With understanding and love to all unwed mothers and to their innocent children whose fathers are not usually known to the world."

The contents of the book were sensational. It revealed that Nan Britton, 30 years younger than Harding, romantically doted on him when she was still a teenager. Her obsession with her ideal man existed without his knowledge until he entered the Senate. The rest of the story has already been stated.

Reasons for Harding's actions were quickly forthcoming. From a White House maid: "Mrs. Harding was always quarreling with her husband and that's why she never shed a tear at his death." Another referred to her as "a nagger" who continually attempted to dominate him.

In November 1931, Nan sued for a share of Harding's estate. The court found "no cause for action." When she instituted a libel suit to clear her character, the court again found "no cause for action."

Many questions are still unanswered, questions brought up in a book, entitled *The Strange Death of President Harding,* written by Gaston B. Means in collaboration with May Dixon Thacker.

Within the pages of the book, which had an enormous circulation, Means brings up many perplexing questions. Why was Harding the only one poisoned by crab meat when it was served to everybody in his party? Why had Mrs. Harding refused an autopsy? Why was she so singularly composed at the funeral? Why did she destroy Harding's correspondence? With these unanswered questions, the book hints that Mrs. Harding's insane jealousy led her to poison her husband.

Francis Russel, in his book, *The Shadow Of Blooming Grove—Warren G. Harding In His Times,* observed:

> The letters if they can be considered shocking—
> and some of them can—are more so because
> they were written by the President of the
> United States, than through the tumescence of
> their content. When I first read them, I felt a
> sense of pity for the lonely Harding, for Carrie

Phillips was clearly the love of his life, and he
was more loving than loved.

These letters are concealed in the Library of Congress and
will not be available for persual until July 29, 2014. What these
letters can reveal about Harding's search for love will only be
known in time.

7

Woodrow Wilson and his Many Women

Woodrow Wilson was the kind of man who danced to horn-pipes on station platforms while campaigning for the presidency, and did jigs in the White House after his election. He greatly admired Gilbert & Sullivan, appreciated limericks, and wrote some good ones himself. He was one of the best storytellers of his time and a mimic of rare talent. He doubled as a successful football coach at two universities while serving as professor, and led the cheering at Princeton-Yale baseball games. He became president of Princeton, governor of New Jersey, and President of the United States.

Wilson was also the kind of man who enjoyed the company of women. He was assailed in whispering campaigns from coast to coast as a rake and libertine. Often, he wrote letters to his women friends, but at the same time he was an affectionate husband and father.

Woodrow Wilson lived during the pre-Civil War to post-World War I era. History honors him for the role he played in guiding the United States of America to world power status. And, had the League of Nations—his dream for world peace—begun its operations during his administration, his place in American history might have been placed on a par with that of Abraham Lincoln.

Students of Wilson have described him as one who was austere, humorless, stern, even arrogant; as a person who would tolerate no disagreement; as one whose refusal to accept any compromises in his position with the League of Nations, led to its defeat in the Senate. He has also been criticized as having married much too soon after the untimely death of his devoted wife.

Woodrow Wilson was truly a study in contradictions. He was neither ruthless and opinionated nor cold and unfeeling. He could be lighthearted, "the life of the party," although he abhorred stupidity. He held definite opinions, but his mind was not closed to new ideas.

Physically thin, weak and unattractive, what he considered his ugliness obsessed him. His face was not well-proportioned: there was too much skin below his eyeglasses, too little above. He had a beaked nose, protuberant ears, a sagging jaw and loose, meaty lips.

In later years he poked fun at himself, joked about his appearance, considered himself "horse-faced." He sometimes was fond of reciting the limerick which has come to be associated with his name:

> For beauty I am not a star,
> There are others more handsome, by far.
> But my face—I don't mind it,
> For I am behind it,
> It's the people in front that I jar.

As a child, Woodrow was surrounded by women—his sisters and his mother. Marion was six years older than he; Anne two years older. They and his mother protected him from the outside world.

His father was a Presbyterian minister of such distinction that it was in his house that the Southern Presbyterian Church was organized during the Civil War period. His mother was the daughter of a Presbyterian minister, in Carlisle, England.

Woodrow liked to play with well-brought up girls rather than with boys, especially with his sisters and cousins. Above all, he enjoyed being with a little girl cousin, younger than he, who was named after his mother: Jessie Woodrow Bones.

He did poorly at school, considerably worse than the average boy. This was not due to a lack of brightness; rather it was due to a lack of interest.

Woodrow Wilson grew up during the great debate over the nature of the Union, and was influenced by the towering figures of Calhoun and Webster. Although his father was a fervent southern sympathizer and, for a time, served as a chaplain in the Confederate Army, Woodrow did not seem to be affected by the Southern loss. No war scars were left on him.

Wilson's elementary and undergraduate schooling were under Presbyterian influences: Davidson College in North Carolina, and Princeton University in New Jersey. He was graduated from Princeton University in 1879; studied law at the University of Virginia; tried the practice of law in Atlanta, and failed; and then went on to earn a Ph.D. from Johns Hopkins University.

He began his professorial career at Bryn Mawr, and then went on to teach history and political science at Wesleyan University. Large classes flocked to his lectures. They applauded his presentations, and were pleased with his insights about life and truth. His manner of presentation was appealing to his students. He possessed the power to stimulate and persuade the intellect. His development of ideas was always clear and orderly; and they came to life with his bland humor and tingling wit.

His first love, when barely out of his teens, was his cousin

Harriet. She was a lovely girl, with many talents. When she played the piano in concert, he applauded her loudly. They had met at family reunions, and, throughout the fifteen months of his illness in Wilmington, he wrote to her and she replied.

He sought opportunities to see her. He sent her a volume of Longfellow's poems and inscribed it "with the warmest love of Cousin Tommie." He took long walks with her over mountain roads. He wrote her often,, addressing her as "My Sweet Rosalind." He warned her against insincere suitors.

One night, he wrote to her, begging her to marry him, complaining that he could not sleep, grasping for the one thing that might save him from the terror of despair. But, although Harriet was fond of him, she did not love him. It took one or two final meetings for her to make him understand that she loved him only as a cousin; that she could never consider marrying him. Wilson gave her up; and at the same time abandoned his law practice.

Then, he had a stroke of luck. He went to Rome, Georgia to visit his uncle James Bones, father of Jessie Woodrow Bones. There, he met Ellen Louise Axson, daughter of the minister of the First Presbyterian Church.

Ellen was a small girl who resembled Wilson's favorite sister, Anne. Her life, like Wilson's, had been completely Presbyterian. Her grandfather had even been a minister of the Presbyterian Church in Savannah, Georgia. She had bright cheeks, a charming way about her, great kindness and common sense. She knew poetry, enjoyed literature, painted pictures and hoped to have a career as an artist.

That April of 1883, Woodrow Wilson fell in love with her. "I fell in love with her," he later said, "for her beauty and gentleness; because she was irresistibly loveable. Why she fell in love with me must always remain an impenetrable mystery."

In September 1883, they became engaged. They did not marry for two years because the practice of law in Atlanta, Georgia was so financially unrewarding that it offered him no way of earning a living and supporting a family.

Wilson had now found an emotional security that was as durable as the love of his own mother. He could relax in Ellen's presence, rest on her shoulder. He trusted her absolutely, and never, in the slightest degree, did she betray that trust. She proffered him the most sustaining love, and at the most critical moments of his life advised him wisely. With her, he could be completely frank. Not a day passed, when they were apart, that he did not write her a love letter.

". . . you are the only person in the world—except the dear ones at home—with whom I do not have to act a part, to whom

I do not have to deal out confidences cautiously; and you are the only person in the world—without any exception—to whom I can tell all that my heart contains." He wrote these words when they were engaged, and they applied to the 29 years of their marriage.

Though many remember Wilson as a prudish, rather rigid person, he could be completely different when the spirit moved him. He was once guest of honor at a dinner. The host and hostess, impressed with the stature of their guest—the President of Princeton University—planned the kind of formal evening they believed would impress a college president. Wilson, bored with all the formality, asked if he could recite an original limerick. When the host agreed, Wilson recited:

> There was a young monk of Siberia
> Whose existence grew drearier and drearier,
> Till he burst from his cell
> With a hell of a yell
> And eloped with the Mother Superior.

The response was enthusiastic, although the host and hostess were stunned at a view of this unexpected facet in the personality of their guest.

In 1885, just a few months before he married Ellen, he wrote her the following letter:

> It may shock you—it ought to—but I'm
> afraid it will not, to learn that I have a reputa-
> tion (?) amongst most of my kind and certain of
> my friends of being irrepressible, in select cir-
> cles, as a maker of grotesque addresses from the
> precarious elevation of chair seats, as a wearer
> of all varieties of comic grimaces, as a stimula-
> tor of sundry unnatural, burlesque styles of
> voice and speech, as a lover of farces—even as
> a dancer of the cancan!

They were married in Rome, Georgia on June 24, 1885.

Although happily married, Wilson liked the company of other women, liked to air his literary fancies before them. When he discovered feminine charm, he would tell Ellen about it. Like his father, he, too, enjoyed playing the lion with women.

Ellen Wilson encouraged and shared her husband's friendships with brilliant ladies. They kept their covenant, made before their marriage, to be quite open with each other in everything. All their treasures were held in common: books, money, pleasures, and friends, both men and women.

Ellen Wilson McAdoo, Wilson's married daughter, wrote about her father's fondness for women in *The Woodrow Wilsons*:

> Father enjoyed the society of women, especially
> if they were what he called "charming and con-

versable". . . . He had several deep and lasting
friendships with women, writing them long letters and spending hours in their company.
These friendships he shared with Mother, and I
never saw her show a trace of jealousy.

At another time, she stated that her father had said, "No
man has ever been a success without having been surrounded by
admiring females."

Ellen Ascon Wilson was a wife who understood her husband
and his needs. She was not only a lovely and talented person, but
at crucial points in his career gave him excellent advice. Wilson's
affection even extended to his wife's family, as evidenced by the
fact that for many years he contributed, from his meager means,
towards the support of Mrs. Wilson's sister.

Wilson enjoyed his evenings with the members of his
family. He once told his wife that he had gained confidence in
himself for the first time when he was convinced that she loved
him, and he repeated this affirmation to his wife frequently
throughout their life together.

Ellen was never too happy about the public part she had to
play as Woodrow's wife, but in her own quiet way she sustained
her husband through many crises and problems which he had to
face at Princeton, in Trenton, and during the early days in the
White House. She was completely devoted to her husband and
family and made a home that was a source of comfort and pleasure to all its members. Though they lived on a modest income,
Ellen kept her family happy.

Wilson was deeply devoted to his wife. That devotion expressed itself in many ways. In a letter to his friend Dabney, in
1888, he wrote: "Marriage has been the making of me both intellectually and morally."

Wilson declared that he felt the same adoration for his wife
more than a quarter of a century later when she died in the White
House. At that time he said, "She was the most radiant creature
I have ever known. Something like an aura of light always surrounded her."

In 1902, he was elected president of Princeton University by
a unanimous vote of the trustees. As president, Wilson raised the
image of Princeton throughout the educational world. Professor
Link, writing about Wilson's influence at Princeton, said, "Never
has so much new life and vigor been injected at one stroke into
an established faculty."

Within a few months, Wilson assembled a remarkable group
of young, competent and enthusiastic teachers to be the first
preceptors under his new plan of adding "practice to precept."
The "fifth guys to make us wise" celebrated year after year in the

faculty song of successive years, indicated how the students felt about their president. It was an extraordinary feat that has never been surpassed in any one college. It was his leadership and the men he chose to work at Princeton that has made it the great institution it is today.

Wilson resigned this office when he was nominated for governor of New Jersey in 1910. His popularity at Princeton, however, never decreased because, when he returned briefly following his election to the Presidency of the United States, he was given such an ovation by the students that the tears ran down his cheeks.

Wilson was plagued with illness during most of his life. It was during his presidency at Princeton that he was advised by his doctor to take a vacation. A winter vacation with wife and daughters was out of the question; it was much too expensive. Late in January, 1907, his physician and Mrs. Wilson urged him to go to Bermuda alone. They believed that a place far removed from family responsibilities and academic worries would help restore his health and raise his sagging spirits.

It was in Bermuda that he met Mary Allen Hulbert Peck. Her first husband had been killed in an accident and she was estranged from her second, Thomas D. Peck. She usually wintered in Bermuda, where her home became a gathering place for celebrated visitors. Her reputation was that of hostess to everybody worth knowing who visited the island.

Mrs. Peck was a beautiful woman, a successful hostess who could bring out the best in her guests. She had the ability to make them shine in brilliant repartee. She was at home in cosmopolitan society, could gracefully fence with both swords and words, and knew how to listen to men who had something worthwhile to say.

Wilson met her at a dinner party and was immediately attracted. Her wit stirred him. He loved to walk with her along the shore and read from the *Oxford Book of Verse*. When she danced, he would look on full of admiration, holding her scarf for her.

Mrs. Peck, who loved intellectual stimulation, arranged a party for Woodrow in her house. He held the men spellbound with good after-dinner talk. Soon thereafter, Wilson and Mrs. Peck were seen together quite often. Gossip began to link their names. Wilson protested, but his protests were often made in jest. And he laughed when his fondness for Mary Peck led him into situations that could set tongues wagging.

When he was preparing to leave Bermuda, he wrote his first of several letters to Mrs. Peck. Her prompt reply, and the interchange that followed, was the cause of a great deal of gossip during upcoming presidential campaigns. All in all, Wilson wrote her more that 200 letters. And although it was surely unwise for him, a public figure, to carry on so extensive a correspondence with any woman other than his wife, he did it with his wife's approval. She approved because she felt that she herself was "too grave" and that "since he married a wife who is not gay, I must provide for him friends who are."

He left Bermuda for home, but he returned soon again, at the urging of his wife and doctor. He was not in good health. He had lost the sight of one eye. He had survived a serious operation although his recurrent attacks of neuritis continued to torment him. His physician ordered him to retire but he refused. Both the doctor and Mrs. Wilson remembered how much good Bermuda had done for him . . . and so , he heeded their advice. And once again he was drawn to Mrs. Peck.

The social therapy helped him, and, after a brief second vacation, he returned to Princeton, refreshed and full of plans for his wife to meet the charming Mrs. Peck. The women met, and hit it off immediately. Mutual visiting resulted. Through all his remaining years at Princeton, and throughout his term as Governor of New Jersey, he wrote regularly to Mrs. Peck.

Wilson became governor-elect in November, 1910. The aim of his office: "No man is great who thinks himself so, and no man is good who does not strive to secure the happiness and comfort of others." He put his beliefs into practice. He cared for the people and they loved him. He appealed to the simple man, the everyday, hard-working citizen. In one of his speeches, he stated, "Communities are not distinguished by the average of their citizenship. I often think of the poor man when he goes to vote: a moral unit in his lonely dignity."

Wilson was nominated for the presidency in 1912. It was at this time that a whispering campaign began about his supposed extra-marital relationship with Mrs. Peck, "that woman in Bermuda." Gossips had managed to find out her name, learned about their correspondence, and even hinted that the Peck divorce was an outcome of the Wilson—Peck triangle. The Pecks had divorced in 1911.

The New York paper, *Town Topics*, sparked much of the gossip with such items as:

> Pittsfield, Mass. is now devouring with great
> glee the contents of little notes which Thomas
> D. Peck has been sending out to tradespeople,
> carrying information that he made Mrs. Peck a
> liberal allowance and hereafter she will pay all
> bills which she may contract.

All the gossip, however, did not prevent Woodrow Wilson from being elected President. The gossip now quieted down as Wilson demonstrated how effective a leader he could be.

He was the first Democrat to take the oath of office since Grover Cleveland in 1893. He was the first native Virginian to repeat the solemn obligation since Zachary Taylor; the first southerner since Andrew Johnson. He was the first scholar, student of government, and intellectual since Thomas Jefferson.

The average citizen looked to him with hope and affection. He set the keynote of his administration policy in his inaugural address, delivered on March 4, 1913. In it he said:

> This is not a day of triumph; it is a day of dedication. Here muster, not the forces of party, but the forces of humanity. Men's hearts wait upon us; men's lives hang in the balance; men's hopes call upon us to say what we will do. Who shall live up to the great trust? Who dares fail to try? I summon all honest men, all patriotic, all forward-looking men, to my side. God helping me, I will not fail them, if they will but counsel and sustain me.

When he stood to take the oath, he was so new to politics as to be relatively an unknown. Few Americans had followed his career at Princeton. His fight against "the bosses" in New Jersey and his campaign speeches had stirred the imaginations of those who were tired of the old Republican Party politics. Yet, there was no record by which the public and the politicians could judge the man who had become the 28th President of the United States.

In every person's history there are episodes that are deeply tragic. The illness of Ellen Wilson and her death almost destroyed Woodrow Wilson.

In March, 1914, she had slipped and fallen. The case was diagnosed as Bright's disease, and, with complications affecting both kidneys, her case was hopeless. In late July, her doctor took up residence in the room next to hers, and, as the month of August approached, it was apparent she could not live much longer.

Wilson, either did not understand or else blinded himself to his wife's imminent death. He was frightened when meals which were taken to her were returned untouched. Often, he would sink to his knees beside her bed and say, "Now please take this bite, dear. You will soon get well, darling, if you'll try to eat something." She, on the other hand, would ask her daughter, "Is your father looking well?"

During her illness, Wilson often worked by her bedside. His

secretary, Joseph Patrick Tumulty of Jersey City, New Jersey, stated that there by her bed he wrote his note offering to mediate the disputes of the Europeans, falling into the disaster called the Great War.

Towards the end, Wilson knew that his wife was dying, for she told him so herself, saying also that it was her wish that he marry again. Although he knew what was going to happen, he would not accept it. The next morning he wrote to a friend that he was hoping still.

Later that morning, the doctor told him that she would not live more than a few hours. All through that hot afternoon, not 48 hours after the first German troops crossed the frontier and met the defenders of Belgium, Wilson and his daughters sat with Ellen in her room decorated with flowered chintz and gay cushions and light-colored lamp shades. Dr. Grayson and two nurses were in attendance. In another room, the husbands of Wilson's married daughters waited with Joe Tumulty, who, not very much older than the girls, had loved Ellen Wilson like a mother. Dr. Grayson found himself alone for a few moments with Ellen, when she roused herself from a semi-stupor and took the doctor's hand to draw him to her. "Please take good care of Woodrow, Doctor," she whispered, uttering the last words of her life. A few minutes later, Grayson told the family it would be well if they came back into her room.

Darkness was approaching as they walked to her bed. The girls knelt beside it. Wilson took her hand and was still holding it when, a little later, just before evening, she died.

Wilson was controlled as he stared at the bed. "Is it all over?" he asked. Grayson nodded and Wilson straighted up to fold her hands over her breasts. She was 50 years old; they had been married 29 years. Exactly five months earlier she had become the First Lady of the land.

He walked to the window where he began to sob, "Oh my God, what am I going to do? What am I going to do?"

He did not want her to lie in a casket, so they placed her on a sofa in her room and he bent over to put a white silk shawl around her shoulders. For the rest of her time in the White House she was there, never alone at night, the President and one or more of the girls sitting by her, talking quietly. For two nights after her death, the President did not move from her deathbed. His world was shattered; the woman he loved was gone.

Monday morning, August 10, 1914 was the time set for the funeral service. At two o'clock in the afternoon the funeral train left Washington for Georgia and the hillside cemetery in Rome where Ellen's mother and father were buried.

Wilson accompanied the casket, rarely leaving its side. When they arrived in Georgia, they drove directly to the church where her father had been pastor, and a simple service was held. Though he had wanted a quiet funeral, almost the entire population turned out and stood by as her casket was lowered into the ground. When it rested in place, the President was told that now he could leave the cemetery. He refused, saying he would wait until the work was completely done. The crowds moved away and he and the girls were alone near a large oak tree. As the workmen began to pile earth on Ellen's casket, the President wept openly. His Ellen was gone.

As the train made its way back to Washington, the President thought of the now unbearably lonely White House. He pleaded with some of Ellen's relatives to stay with him for awhile. This they did and for many hours he talked with them, saying that it was his career and ambition that killed her. Wilson's depression was so deep that his personal physician became alarmed. Woodrow Wilson was indeed a sick man, and, he would be able to bear his deep grief only by burying himself in pressing affairs of state.

"I do not care a fig for anything that affects me," he wrote a friend. To another he indicated that it would be a blessing if someone would assassinate him. "If I hadn't gone into politics she would probably be alive now," he kept repeating.

Dr. Grayson could see the President declining before his eyes, and, he worked harder than ever to keep up the golfing and auto rides. In fact, there were many nights that the doctor remained in the White House, in case he was needed.

"God has stricken me almost beyond what I can bear," Wilson wrote a friend, and Assistant Secretary of the Navy Franklin D. Roosevelt confided to the secretary that he feared the President was about to have a breakdown.

To his daughter Jessie, Wilson wrote:

> My Darling Jessie,
>
> I am ashamed of myself when I think I have been so long in acknowledging the dear letter from you that made me so happy, and touched me so deeply. You cannot know, I fear, what it meant to me to have you say that I had in some sort taken your incomparable mother's place when you were here! Ah, how little I know how! and how impossible it was to do more than just let you feel as well as I knew how the infinite tenderness I felt and the longing that was at my heart to make up for what can never be made up for, either to you, my sweet daughter, nor to me nor to anyone who ever had a

chance to know how sweet and loving and infi-
nitely rewarding she was. I cannot yet trust myself to speak much of her, even in writing. My
heart has somehow been stricken dumb. . . .

On August 23, 1914, he wrote to Mrs. Peck:

I never understood before what a broken heart
meant, and did for a man. It just means that he
lives by compulsion of necessity and duty only
and has no other motive force. Business, the
business of a country that must be done and
cannot wait, the problems that it would be deep
unfaithfulness not to give my best powers to
because a great people have trusted me, have
been my salvation; but, oh how hard, how desperately hard, it has been to face them, and to
face them worthily! Every night finds me
exhausted,—dead in heart and body, weighed
down with a leaden indifference and despair (so
far as everything concerning myself is concerned). I am making a brave fight, the best I
know how to make, to work out into the light
and see my way. And I am not ungrateful: how
could I be when I had her so many happy,
happy years. God helping me, I shall regain command of myself and be fit for my duties again.
For a little while it must be only a matter of ex-
hausting will power.

In the spring of 1915, the Wilson daughters sought to bring
to their harassed father whatever relaxation they could. At about
the same time, Dr. Grayson, remembering his promise to Ellen
Wilson, came up with a practical way to bring the depressed 58-
year-old President back to normal. He decided to see to it that
Mr. Wilson became immersed in social activity.

One day, as Dr. Grayson and President Wilson were riding
in a White House limousine, they passed an automobile driven
by a woman. Grayson acknowledged the driver with a nod of his
head. Thereupon, Wilson asked, "Who is that beautiful lady?"
The beautiful woman, he was told, was Mrs. Norman Galt, the
42-year-old widow of a prosperous jeweler. She was a native of
Virginia and possessed a sympathetic and cheerful personality.
She had been traveling extensively in Europe since the death of
her husband.

Dr. Grayson had become acquainted with Mrs. Galt through
his courting of Alice Gertrude Gordon. Mrs. Galt was Alice's
guardian. Earlier, Dr. Grayson had promoted a friendship between Mrs. Galt and Wilson's cousin, Helen Bones. It was during

April 1915 that Miss Bones first introduced her to the President. Before this time, the only glimpse Mrs. Galt ever got of Wilson was from a distance. She had never before been invited to the White House. To Edith Galt, Wilson was just another man in the White House.

She recalled watching Governor Wilson reviewing New Jersey troops. "A thin man on a horse," she said. After he became President she saw him in a box at the theater. When her sister urged her to share an appointment to call on him, she replied: "Not if I know it. I have lived in Washington 17 years and never been inside the White House. Why should I bother a tired, busy man to shake hands with me? I would feel like an idiot going in there."

One day in March, however, at the suggestion of Dr. Grayson, Helen Bones asked her new friend to return to the White House for tea. When they stepped out of the elevator, they met two men coming in from the golf course. "I think you might invite us to tea," said Dr. Grayson, introducing Mrs. Galt to the President.

Edith Galt was a healthy, full-bosomed American woman of the upper middle class. She was plump, pretty and moderately rich, had abundant vitality, and a winning smile. At 42, she presented a picture of exciting femininity. She was the daughter of a circuit judge, a member of an esteemed Virginia family who could trace their ancestral line to Pocahontas and John Rolfe. She was not at all a pretentious individual. During her years in Washington, she had remained in the background, and now lived in a simple house at 20th Street and New Hampshire Avenue.

Wilson was captivated by her; so much so, in fact, that he could not see enough of her. Mrs. Galt became more important to him than the rest of the world. On April 28, 1915, Wilson wrote his first letter to Edith Galt. Two days later, he sent her a corsage of roses and an invitation to dinner at the White House. On May 3, she dined with him, dressed in white satin and creamy lace, with a deep square neck edged by green velvet. Turning his eyes directly upon her, he spoke quietly of love.

She was startled by the suddenness and simplicity of his declaration, and reminded him that he had been widowed less than a year.

"I know how you feel," he said to her, "but, little girl, in this place time is not measured by weeks, or months, or years, but by deep human experiences; and since her death I have lived a lifetime of loneliness and heartache. I was afraid, knowing you, I would shock you; but I would be less than a gentleman if I continued to make opportunities to see you without telling you what I have told my daughters and Helen: that I want you to be my wife. In the circumstances of the spotlight that is always on this house, and particularly on me as the head of the government, whoever comes here is immediately observed and discussed; and do what I can to protect you from gossip, it will inevitably begin. If you care for me as I do for you, we will have to brave this; but as I cannot come to your house without increasing the gossip, you, in your graciousness, will have to come here. . ."

Edith Galt didn't rush into marriage. She felt she had to make sure she loved Woodrow for himself, not because he was the President of the United States. But she indicated that she would like to see him frequently.

The President needed no further encouragement. He sent her the best purple orchids that could be purchased. He invited her to dinner often, took her for long drives, asked her to accompany him to New York on the *Mayflower*. The more she saw him, the more she felt a love for him. She wanted to help him bear his burdens.

Although he had received much sympathy when he was the grief-stricken widower, he now became the target of censure. Men and women alike felt that his involvement with a woman so soon after his wife's death smacked of coldness.

His new and sudden love affair stirred up a storm. Women were indignant at the swift faithlessness to his wife's memory. His courtship was called untimely, and old rumors about his excessive fondness for women were revived.

The dormant Peck-Wilson friendship was now once again revived with the ugliest of interpretations. There was much talk about Wilson's uncurbed sensuality, and, in July 1915, an attempt was made to drive him out of office on moral grounds.

A rumor existed that Mrs. Peck, now a resident of California, was quite angry that her long-time paramour was now involved in another love affair, and that she was all set to file a breach of promise suit based on Wilson's compromising letters to her. She claimed, it was said, that he had tried to buy her off with a payment of $7,500. Soon, from coast to coast, Woodrow Wilson was being called Peck's Bad Boy, with the worst of implications.

Secretary of the Treasury McAdoo, the President's son-in-law, was infuriated by the growing criticism. He was alarmed by the recurring whispers that Mrs. Peck was on the verge of selling her correspondence with Wilson. McAdoo claimed that he had received an anonymous letter stating that Mrs. Peck was telling everybody about the hush money from Wilson, and was consulting lawyers about a breach of promise suit. McAdoo further stated that he had sounded out newspaper reporters, and had found that they firmly believed she would sell the incriminating letters to the Republican Party the moment Wilson's engagement to Mrs. Galt was announced.

Wilson was shaken by these statements. He kept insisting that his letters contained nothing even remotely embarrassing, and that Ellen had known everything about his friendship and correspondence with Mrs. Peck. He stressed that the $7500 he had sent her was a loan to rescue her son from financial difficulty. It represented nothing more than assistance he would give any friend in need.

Mrs. Peck, now writing under the name of Mary Allen Hulbert, in her book, *The Story of Mrs. Peck*, recounts her ordeal stemming from a warm friendship that was never anything more. The book emphasizes that she and her second husband were estranged before she met Wilson, and that the rumored relationship, which led to so much later gossip, was unfounded. Her interest in Wilson was based solely on the brilliant man's accomplishments and aspirations. Yes, he had written to her: "You have a genius for friendship," and, "Your friendship gives me pleasure." She also cleared up the rumor about the $7,500 loan, which she said was to help her son, establishing that it was paid back in full.

Fron July 1915 on, Mrs. Peck was harassed. California news reporters hounded her. She was visited and grilled by a lawyer who said he was sent by "those boys in Washington," whom he identified as the President and Mr. McAdoo, to find out whether she planned to "make trouble" about his forthcoming marriage.

Anonymous messages poured in to Mrs. Peck with offensive questions about her letters from Wilson. Her California cottage was ransacked by unknown persons who were obviously searching for the correspondence.

Early in 1916, she was shadowed for weeks while visiting New York City. She was sought out and asked for her assistance in a movement to impeach the President. And she was offered substantial sums for her letters that could be used in the proceedings. She had received more than 200 letters from Wilson from February 1907 to October 1915.

Bernard Baruch did pay her $65,000 for her letters from Woodrow Wilson. He permitted her to retain them with the promise that she would not allow them to be published during the 1916 campaign. Today they are available and can be seen in the Library of Congress. In no way are they compromising. They talk about his visits to Bermuda, their long discussions, his daughters' romances and marriages, his worries about the war. Also, in them can be found innumerable references to his wife, Ellen. His concern about his wife's deteriorating health is repeatedly expressed. His letter after her death reads: "Of course you know what has happened to me; but I wanted you to know it direct from me. God has stricken me almost beyond what I can bear."

The wave of criticism soon swelled into a sea of allegations, most of them false, the most flagrant being that the President and "the Galt woman" were in love *before* Ellen Wilson's death, and that he had conspired with Dr. Grayson to dispose of her.

One fictitious story had it that the physician poisoned Ellen; another, that when Ellen threatened to divorce the President because of his new emotional attachment, he pushed her down the stairs, causing fatal internal hemorrhaging. Gossipers also pointed out that her unmarked grave was disgracefully neglected, overgrown with crabgrass, while the President was preoccupied with his latest love affair.

Wilson was furious at the uproar. He explained that the condition of his wife's grave was due to the caretaker's illness, of which he was not informed, and that the Carrara headstone he had ordered from Italy was delayed in shipment because of European conditions.

The Democratic party managers were distressed, and pleaded with the White House to down the rumors about his impending engagement, but Wilson refused. Director of the Mint, Robert W. Woolley, wrote: "The backstairs sewer gossips are doing deadly work among the women. I am sorry that the President has fallen in love at this time, for he will be criticized for not waiting longer after Mrs. Wilson's death."

On October 6, 1916, the engagement was made official by the White House, and the following morning the *New York Times* carried this front-page headline:

PRESIDENT TO WED MRS. NORMAN GALT,
INTIMATE FRIEND OF HIS DAUGHTERS:
ALSO COMES OUT FOR WOMEN'S
SUFFERAGE

Democratic leaders met in secret conference and agreed that someone had to convince Wilson that if he married Mrs. Galt before November, he might lose the election. Frank P. Glass, editor of the *Birmingham* (Ala.) *News*, and a friend of Wilson since their undergraduate days at Princeton, undertook the task. He told the President about all the gossip, especially about his involvement with Mrs. Peck. Tears came into Wilson's eyes as he said, "There is nothing in any letter I ever wrote that I am ashamed to have published."

Wilson was concerned that Mrs. Galt understand the entire situation. He asked Dr. Grayson to go to Mrs. Galt and tell her that he was releasing her from any promises. She later wrote to him that she was undeterred by rumors and threats, and would "stand by him" not for pity, not for honor—but for love . . . trusting, comprehensive love."

She waited three days for Wilson's answer. Finally, Grayson telephoned her that the President was ill and wanted to see her at the White House. There, they decided to be married before the end of the year.

On October 4, Wilson wrote the following letter to Mrs. Peck:

> Before the public announcement is made known, I want you to be the first to know of the good fortune that has come to me. I have not been at liberty to speak of it sooner. I am engaged to be married to Mrs. Norman Galt of this city, a woman I am sure you would admire and love as everyone does who knows her, and I feel a blessing greater than any I can measure in words has come to me . . . I am writing this in great haste, amid a pressure of clamorous engagements that cannot be gainsaid, but you will know in what spirit.
>
> Helen (Bones) joins me in an affectionate message.
>
> Your devoted friend,
> Woodrow Wilson

Woodrow Wilson and Edith Galt were married on December 18, 1915. Sigmund Freud, in his book, *Thomas Woodrow Wilson, A Psychological Study*, which he coauthored with William C. Bullitt, points out that Wilson constantly needed adoring women around him, needed a protecting mother figure. He offered this as the reason for Wilson's quick second marriage.

In November 1916, despite all the gossip, despite the dirtiest type of political campaigning, Wilson was elected to a second term of office. He was beset with grave responsibilities, including World War I.

In a message delivered before Congress on April 2, 1917, Wilson said:

> Right is more precious than peace, and we fight for the things which we have always carried nearest to our hearts, for democracy, for the right of those who submit to authority to have a voice in their own governments, for the rights and liberties of small nations, for a universal dominion of right by such a concert of free peoples as shall bring peace and safety to all nations and make the world at last free.

The years began to take their toll on a not-too-healthy executive. Wilson had lived through a war and was fighting with every bit of strength he possessed to establish the League of Nations, a body he hoped would avert future wars. The treaty, which he favored, had not been approved by Congress. Senator Lodge, a powerful leader, pleaded for modifications in the treaty, but no response was forthcoming from the White House. Even some of Wilson's closest advisors urged him to work toward a compromise, convinced that otherwise the treaty would never be ratified.

It was Wednesday, September 3, 1919, at 6:40 in the evening that Wilson, the First Lady, Dr. Grayson, Tumulty and two dozen reporters left the White House to go to Union Station. They were accompanied by eight secret service men, a corps of aides and a valet for him, a maid for her, and a double train crew. The train was seven cars long; the President's car was last in line. They were to travel 9,981 miles, almost to the Canadian border. The trip was going to last 27 days, with twenty-six major stops and at least ten rear-platform speeches a day. Though Wilson's wife complained that the trip was going to be too strenuous for him, and that rest stops should be included, he refused, saying, "This is a business trip, pure and simple." He was going to sell the League of Nations to his people.

The crowds were enormous and often uproarious as the President spoke about his dream of everlasting peace. The pace was killing. He did not have a minute's rest. When he tried to sleep, he could not. The First Lady was desperate, terrified of the way he looked and what still lay ahead. "Let's stop," she begged. "Let's go somewhere and rest. Only for a few days." "No," he said, "I have caught the imagination of the people. They are eager to hear what the League stands for. I should fail in my duty if I disappointed them."

Finally, the stops and speeches came to an end, and the Wilsons were on their way back to Washington. During the first night, when the First Lady was in her own room, she heard a knock on the door. It was 11:30 P.M. and she heard his voice: "Can you come to me, Edith? I'm terribly sick." He was sitting on the edge of his bed with his head resting on the back of a chair. "I can't sleep because of the pain. I'm afraid you'd better call Grayson."

Grayson could do very little to help his patient. After a while, the First Lady motioned Grayson to go to bed and she sat alone opposite her husband, breathing as quietly as she could for fear of awakening him. Wilson was rushed to the White House. He was too ill to receive any callers, and three days later he suffered a cerebral thrombosis that left him partially paralyzed.

Again, ugly rumor reared its head. Because the White House

was secret about his condition, it was said that he was stricken by paresis, resulting from the venereal disease that had intermittently incapacitated him since his years at Princeton.

The President's room was now filled with doctors and nurses. The First Lady did not leave his side for a minute. Grayson announced that "The President is a very sick man. His condition is less favorable today and he has remained in bed throughout the day."

All kinds of rumors developed. Suddenly people noticed that bars were in place on one window of the White House, and at once it was said that they were there because the President, insane, was trying to escape and run out into the street. Other rumors had him a prisoner, unconscious, sulking.

For days the bulletins were all the same: "The President had a very good night, and if there is any change in his condition it is favorable . . . The President had a restful and comfortable day. . ."

The truth was that one-half of his face had fallen and his arm and leg were paralyzed. Dr. Grayson knew that brain damage had been sustained. For a while, the President lay between life and death. Only a tiny group of people had access to his sickroom.

The President's desperate illness rendered him unable to make crucial decisions. Should he remain on as President? There was only one person who could speak in his name and make use of his powers as President. Only one person could decide whether or not he should continue in his job.

She made the decision. He was going to continue as President of the United States. No one could see him, no Cabinet officer, no senator, no visiting delegate—but he was still the President. And so it was until his death.

Wilson complained very little as he lay in bed. Never did a word of impatience come from his lips. He even preserved his sense of humor: a week after his severe bathroom fall, he held up a finger to halt the First Lady's attempt to hold a spoon to his lips and gestured that Grayson should come close. The doctor bent over and the patient whispered: "A wonderful bird is the pelican; his bill will hold more than his bellican. He can take in his beak enough food for a week. I wonder how in the hell-he-can."

New stories began to circulate that Wilson was not so much as attending to his mail, and that his wife was running the White House. When Wilson's correspondence was sent to the Library of Congress in 1952, several unopened letters from Colonel House were in the collection. One was an urgent plea for compromise on the League.

Edith Bolling Wilson, in her book, *My Memoir*, stressed that the barrier she set up around the President after his stroke was done on the advice of Dr. Francis K. Dercum who warned her that there was no hope for her husband's recovery unless he could be freed of the burdens of his office.

Wilson was now an invalid, and remained so until his death in 1924. He was not seen at all by the public for many months. Later, it was only on rare occasions that he went out for an automobile drive with his devoted wife.

Yet, even during his serious illness, when the Senate sent a delegation to confer with him, a spark of the old wit came to the surface. One of the group was Republican Senator Albert B. Fall, who said, "Mr. President, we have all been praying for you."

"Which way, Senator?" Wilson replied with a chuckle.

Edith Bolling Wilson was a source of tremendous strength to the President. She was aware of the time-consuming tasks that demanded so much of him. She related that during their engagement she was kept informed of affairs of state through daily communications from Wilson, and that she knew of his anxieties and responsibilities.

She was always at the side of her husband. She said, "Woodrow Wilson was first my beloved husband whose life I was trying to save, fighting with my back to the wall; after that he was the President of the United States."

Throughout the illness, Mrs. Wilson undertook to devote herself to matters that required presidential attention. With Dr. Grayson, she presented them to the President in digested form, whenever he was able to be attentive.

No doubt his fight for the League of Nations had eaten away at his health. His wife had urged him to compromise, but he gave her the answer that finally convinced her that such an action would be wrong. "Better a thousand times," said Wilson from his sickbed, "to go down fighting, than to dip your colors to dishonorable compromise."

When the vote came, the treaty was voted down: 39 "ayes" and 55 "nayes."

Wilson lived four years and four months after his September 1919 collapse. To a great extent, his second wife was the Nation's Chief Executive.

He had loved two women, had been infatuated with many more, carried on extensive correspondence with several others— and now it was over.

On Sunday, February 3, 1924, he died in his sleep.

8
Franklin - Eleanor - Lucy

The life of Franklin Delano Roosevelt reads like a television script. Theme: The story of a man who against all odds was instrumental in changing the history of the world. To describe his life, even such words as dramatic, exciting, romantic, adventurous are inadequate.

Roosevelt was born into one of the most illustrious families in America. He grew up on an estate that nestled on the beautiful Hudson River, with a mother young enough to be his sister. He was educated at one of the most exclusive preparatory schools in this country, and, as an undergraduate at Harvard, lived a life of spendor and luxury.

Later, for more than half a century, Roosevelt and his career were shaped and influenced by the world in which he lived: a world of Nazi growth and domination; a world of depression and bank failures; a world of war and misery and deep despair.

Here was a man who, at the height of his manhood, was struck down by polio; a man who waged the brave fight to overcome a crippling, terrifying illness. Yet, he became Assistant Secretary of the Navy under Woodrow Wilson, and a Democratic vice-presidential candidate before the age of 40.

Franklin Roosevelt, the cousin of the twenty-sixth President of the United States, Theodore Roosevelt, married a distant cousin whose family history was as distinguished as his own. But there was no joy in his marriage, and, to fill the void, he turned to other women.

Franklin's parents were opposites. His mother, Sara Delano was strongwilled and imperious. She had almost given up hope of marriage, when she met James Roosevelt. It was not for lack of suitors that at 25 years of age she found herself unmarried. It was due, rather, to the fact that she was very much her father's daughter. She adored him, and he was reluctant to give her up. She would never go against his judgment; to her, he was all-wise.

Perhaps it was this father figure she saw in the widower, James Roosevelt. He was twice her age, and had a son barely six months younger than she. Wellbred, poised, and urbane, he was a gentleman; and he paid her a good deal of attention. Despite James's background and personal attributes, Sara Delano would later in life insist that Franklin was "a Delano, not a Roosevelt at all." She would irritate her daughter-in-law by telling her of Franklin's lineage, his pure blood. In fact, some of Sara's relatives claimed to trace their family all the way back to "the Actii," a Roman Patrician family of 600 B.C.

During the summer of 1880, Sara Delano and James Roosevelt were married. Throughout October and the first week of November, the newly married couple remained on the Hudson estate. After the election in November, the couple sailed for Europe on the White Star ship, *Germanic*. For ten months they did nothing but enjoy themselves. They traveled in the best of style and met the most elegant people. It was during this trip that Sara realized that she was pregnant, whereupon the Roosevelts returned to the United States.

The pregnancy was an easy one, but not so the birth. It almost caused Sara's death. On January 30, 1882, James Roosevelt wrote in his wife's diary: "At a quarter to nine my Sallie had a splendid large baby boy. He weighs 10 lbs., without clothes." The boy was named after Sara's Uncle, Frank—the Franklin Delano who had married Laura Astor.

Franklin's early years were exciting ones. His parents travelled much, and wherever they went young Franklin went with them. They were once invited to visit with President Cleveland, who at the time seemed tired and disappointed. He had vetoed every bill that smacked of paternalism, and had thereby made many enemies. When the Roosevelts were about to leave the White House, President Cleveland turned to Franklin—then age 5—and said, "My little man, I am making a strange wish for you. It is that you never be President of the United States."

Each year Franklin would visit the family seat of the Warren Delanos at Fairhaven; would summer at Campobello; would go to Algonac for days at a time; and would spend several months in New York City. He accompanied his father on railroad inspection trips. He went with him to Wisconsin, to Chicago, and to many other cities. But, for Franklin, home was always Hyde Park, in upstate New York.

Franklin's parents were overprotective, and, although they claimed not to be imposing their way of life on him, they guarded and guided his every step. Determined to make him a "gentleman," they taught him the importance of being polite, courteous, respectful, charming; and tried to develop within him fine habits and tastes.

Franklin learned to ride horseback at an early age, and at seven was presented with a Welsh pony. He was also held responsible for the care of his dog.

He developed an early passion for boats and open water. When he was nine, he happily announced in a letter to an aunt that "Papa is going to buy a cutter that will go by naptha and we are going to sail it to Campobello and here." Six months later he was photographed, short-pants sailor suit and all, on the boat his father had purchased—the *Half-Moon*.

Before the age of 10, Franklin had started a stamp collection and pasted his stamps with the utmost care. At the same time, he began collecting birds' eggs, and then decided to collect birds themselves. He developed a competency as an ornithologist by the time he was 14, and became quite an authority on the subject.

His years at Groton, a very exclusive private school, opened a new world for him. For the first time in his life he was on his own, away from both his parents. From time to time, he jotted down a few words to his parents: "I am getting on very well."

Though he was not the greatest student, he did win the Latin Prize when he was graduated. Many years later, Endicott Peabody commented: "There has been a good deal written about Franklin Roosevelt when he was a boy at Groton, more than I should have thought justified by the impression that he left at the school. He was a quiet, satisfactory boy of more than ordinary intelligence, taking a good position in his Form but not brilliant. Athletically, he was rather too slight for success. We all liked him."

If his years at Groton opened the world for him, his years at Harvard matured him, and he became interested in many activities, not all of them scholastic.

Although he received his B.A. degree in June 1903, he decided to spend an additional year at Harvard. He was in no rush to enter business, or any profession for that matter.

Franklin Roosevelt attended the Harvard Commencement activities, but he was more interested in Groton's Prize Day. He wanted to be there because Theodore Roosevelt was to be the guest speaker.

It was at this point in Franklin's life that Eleanor appeared on the scene. Christmas time with the Roosevelts was a happy time when cousins and other relatives assembled. In fact, Eleanor met her handsome cousin Franklin at such a Christmas party. Normally, she was not permitted to mingle with young men her own age. Her grandmother was very prudish in her attitudes about coed meetings. However, this holiday was the one time during the year when an exception was made.

But Eleanor felt like an outsider, because everyone seemed to know everyone else. They had met many times before and had a great deal in common. Conversation came easy to them. Dressed the way she was, she knew she was not going to attract any real attention. Her grandmother had insisted that she wear a little-girl's skirt that barely reached her knees. This, of course, exaggerated her height. At almost 18, she looked and felt out of place.

In addition, other factors bothered her. She was not good-looking, was a poor dancer, and was awkward. She watched with some envy as the girls danced and flirted with her handsome cousin, Franklin. When he walked toward her and asked her to dance, she could hardly believe her ears. She was utterly overwhelmed and grateful.

The two cousins met a second time on a New York Central train. He was walking through the cars when he spied her.

At the time, she was 18, and was returning from school in Europe.

A few months later, Eleanor was introduced to New York society at an Assembly Ball. This was an affair attended by many New York city and state politicians. But, once again, Eleanor suffered the agonies of not being popular. Here, too, she felt as if she didn't belong and left the ball as quickly as possible. The humiliation was more than she could bear.

In time, and with the help of her Uncle Stanley and Aunt Tissie, a series of social events was planned for her: theaters, luncheons, teas, dinners, dances and suppers. At one of these functions, she again met her fifth cousin, Franklin, and, from then on, they saw each other off and on through the autumn of 1903. They became good friends.

As their friendship ripened, it grew into love, something no one would have dreamed could happen. Friends were surprised, relatives were astonished, and Sara Delano Roosevelt, Franklin's mother, was shocked. Actually, she was hurt and outraged; especially when at age 21 Franklin had still not earned a dollar of his own, nor had he even decided on a career. When he firmly announced that he was going to be married to "that unattractive girl Eleanor," it was more than his mother could bear.

Eleanor did have a good family background. She was a niece of the President of the United States. She was sweet, eager to please, grateful for every act of kindness. But as far as Sara was concerned, she was not for her Franklin. How could he fall in love with a girl so unattractive! True, she had a good figure, but her protruding teeth, receding chin, and clinging vine personality were not at all appealing.

Nor was she compatible with Franklin in other areas. He was actively interested in sports. She, on the other hand, was a poor sailor, couldn't swim, and didn't play tennis or golf. What did her Franklin see in this plain, self-conscious girl who at age 19 looked staid, and acted like a woman 30 years old?

After a visit with her future mother-in-law, Eleanor wrote to her cousin Sallie in Hyde Park:

Dear Cousin Sallie,

I must thank you for being so good to me yesterday. I know just how you feel and how hard it must be, but I do so want you to learn to love me a little. You must know that I will always try to do what you wish, for I have grown to love you very dearly during the last summer. It is impossible for me to tell you how I feel toward Franklin. I can only say that my one great wish is always to prove worthy of him.

Two days later, writing from Cambridge, Franklin wrote to his mother:

Dearest Mama,

I know what pain I must have caused you, and you know I wouldn't do it if I really could have helped it—*mais tu sais, me voilà!* That's all that could be said—I know my mind, have known it for a long time, and know that I could never think otherwise: Result: I am the happiest man just now in the world; likewise the luckiest. . . And for you, dear Mummy, you know that nothing can ever change what we have always been, and will always be, to each other—only now you have two children to love and to love you—and Eleanor, as you know, will always be a daughter in every way.

Sara Delano Roosevelt now began to use practical logic on her son. She was certain he was not yet ready for marriage. She decided to use the tactic of why not wait for some better (but indefinite) time in the future. You're both too young to know what you really want, she told him, let alone to accept the grave responsibilities of marriage. She pointed out to Franklin that his father had married at the age of 33, when he had already established a name for himself.

She then dangled the promise of an extended Caribbean cruise before Franklin, hoping that he would become so concerned with new places and new people that he would change his mind about Eleanor.

Eleanor understood the motive behind the cruise offer, and resented it—especially when Franklin accepted it. She now had no choice but to wait. As she waited for the return of her cousin, her anxiety bordered on despair.

Thoughts and fears of her childhood began to surge through her mind. She recalled how she had been shunted aside—how her brothers Elliott and Hall were always with mother, while she was left alone to suffer a sense of alienation. John, the baby, would sit on his mother's lap and be cuddled and caressed. Elliott, obviously loving and being loved by his mother, stood nearby. Only she felt excluded from this inner circle of love and affection.

Although still a young child, Eleanor knew that her mother didn't love her nearly as much as she loved her two brothers. She realized that her mother found her unattractive both in appearance and in personality. And then, her mother nicknaming her "Granny" had a devastating effect. She had heard her mother explain, "She is such a funny child, so old-fashioned, that we always call her 'Granny'." At such times, Eleanor hoped that the earth would open up and swallow her. Why live when this is what your own mother thinks of you!

Perhaps the hurt was even greater when Eleanor, who slept in her mother's room, observed how she dressed to go out. Her mother was admired in the city for her beauty and charm. Eleanor once wrote: "She looked so beautiful, I was grateful to be allowed to touch her dress or jewels or anything that was part of the vision which I admired inordinately." The more she longed for her mother's approval and affection, the more she felt, "I was disgracing my mother."

Once, while the family was touring Italy (the summer Josh was born), Eleanor was placed in a French convent. She was terribly lonely and unhappy there, and felt once again that she had been abandoned. She realized how unattractive she was, how different she was from other girls.

It so happened that one day a girl swallowed a penny, and so became the center of much attention and activity. This made an impression on Eleanor who later went to the sisters and claimed to have swallowed a penny. The sisters knew she had not swallowed a coin, and accused her of lying. They browbeat her, not understanding the need of this plain girl for attention. Finally, her mother was sent for, and Eleanor left the convent in disgrace, after being compelled to admit that she had lied.

The only time she ever received any real attention from her mother was when a sick headache sent her mother to bed. Since these headaches were frequent and quite severe, Eleanor found herself sitting on her mother's bed massaging her throbbing temples and sore neck for hours on end. Eleanor never felt happier: she loved her mother and she was alleviating her pain! How needed and useful she was!

It was different with her father. He loved Eleanor, and this fact was the one bright spot in an otherwise dismal childhood. He called her "Little Nell,"—a nickname of endearment; he never made fun of her. With him, she was always "perfectly happy." It was her father who came to her rescue when she was turned out of the convent, and he did not treat her as though she had disgraced the family.

Eleanor appreciated his kindness and his warmth. Once, when he first went away to Abingdon, Virginia and she could not understand his leaving her, she was reassured by a letter from him which read:

My darling little Nell,

Because father is not with you is not because he doesn't love you. For I love you tenderly and dearly—and maybe soon I'll come back well and strong, and we will have good times together, like we used to have.

Unfortunately, things got even worse. In early December 1892, Anna Hall Roosevelt was stricken with diphtheria. Eleanor was sent to stay with her cousin Susie. And it was there on December 7, that Eleanor learned that her mother had died.

There was one bright spot on the horizon at this time, and it lay in the knowledge that her father would soon come for her and make a home for her. He came, was kind, loving and charming, but was totally unable to make a home for his children.

His drinking and his poor physical condition made it impossible for him to raise his children. Eleanor was sent to live with Grandmother Hall who lived in a brownstone house on West Thirty-seventh Street.

Eleanor never forgot their parting. She and her father stood in the gloomy library of that house. Her father was dressed in black, and was obviously distressed. He took her into his arms and told her about his bereavement, and how now he had only his children; he wanted his children to remain close to him. To Eleanor this statement was a hope, a promise for the future.

Life with grandmother was not without its difficulties. She was afraid of everyone, especially the French maid who cared for her and who would scold Eleanor and pull her hair when anything was done to displease her. The strictly disciplined life in her grandmother's house left its scars on Eleanor.

From time to time, her father came unannounced for short visits to his mother-in-law's house—visits that Eleanor longed for. She had hopes of leaving with him, but it was obvious that her father was in no condition to become a responsible parent.

On August 14, 1894, shortly before her tenth birthday, Aunt Maude and Aunt Pussie told Eleanor that her father had died. Suddenly, her world collapsed; the dream she harbored of living together with her father was completely shattered. Here she was, without a mother or father—and only 10 years old!

In bed that night, she could not sleep. Succumbing to fits of weeping, she could not and would not accept the finality of his death. Her grandmother did not permit Eleanor, nor her brother, to attend the funeral, and Eleanor never really accepted her father's death. For a very long time, he lived very close to her in her thoughts.

When Eleanor was 15, she was enrolled in a school in England. It was here that Eleanor started to emerge as a person in her own right. Here she felt removed from the past, and, for the first time in her life, was free of the fears that had been haunting her. She was accepted by the girls, and was even popular.

Mlle. Marie Souvestre, the remarkable Frenchwoman who headed the school was a special joy to Eleanor. It was this woman who cured Eleanor of her habit of lying. Here she learned how to dress, how to speak, how to conduct herself. Over three school terms, Eleanor grew emotionally and intellectually.

Unfortunately, her mother's family would not leave her alone, they continued to chip away at the small amount of self-confidence Eleanor had developed.

During a visit with her Aunt Pussie at Northeast Harbor on Mount Desert Island in Maine, Eleanor was almost destroyed. Pussie did her best to kill the little bit of self-esteem Eleanor had developed while studying in Europe. She told Eleanor flatly that she must never expect to have a real *beau* because, she, Eleanor, was the ugly duckling of the family. To make matters worse, she told the girl about Elliott Roosevelt's last years, spitting out all the morbid details that had been kept from her.

All of the past came back to her when she met Franklin. And when he indicated that he loved her, she worried about the events that had happened years ago, and felt the horror of its implications. Somehow she felt that Franklin would find her real self, the girl she once was. And so, because she did not want to be disappointed with a relationship that she thought might end, she kept her inner feelings buried.

Eleanor was concerned about what might happen to Franklin on the cruise. Were his feelings for her deep enough, strong enough to survive the separation? Would his mother succeed in changing his mind? The months now, without him, frightened her. However, she was determined to make them meaningful. She visited the White House and spent time with her uncle, the President. She began to blossom, gained poise and self-confidence, and was even ready to accept a broken engagement from Franklin.

When Franklin returned, he continued to woo Eleanor relentlessly. In late November, Franklin Delano Roosevelt formally announced his engagement to Anna Eleanor Roosevelt. At the time, Franklin was attending Columbia University Law School and was living with his mother at 200 Madison Avenue in New York City.

On March 4, 1905, Eleanor and Franklin were invited to be present at the inauguration of Theodore Roosevelt as President of the United States. They were very much in the center of activities on this occasion. Thirteen days later, on St. Patrick's Day—also the birthday of Eleanor's mother—they were married.

Eleanor, as a bride, was radiant. She was graceful, tall, and slender. Her dress of stiff white satin, with shirred tulle at the neck, and a long bridal veil of rose-point Brussels lace, accentuated her height. Around her neck was a dog collar of pearls given her by her mother-in-law; and in her arms she held a huge bouquet of lilies of the valley.

However, the center of attraction was neither Eleanor nor Franklin. The tremendous crowds that gathered at the corners of Fifth and Madison Avenues, held back by about 75 policemen, were not there because of the young couple. Even as the bride descended the stairs, she was not the center of attraction. All eyes were on a bespectacled man with a mustache who was almost a head shorter than she. She leaned upon his arm. And when the minister asked, "Who giveth this woman to be married to this man?" a loud voice responded, "I do!" It was Eleanor's uncle, Theodore Roosevelt, the President of the United States.

Although the marriage had all the elements for success, involving as it did two very fine families, it was destined to fail. And the reasons became obvious before long.

Franklin Delano Roosevelt's reputation as one who had an "eye for the ladies" began when he was a young, good-looking, wealthy, Assistant Secretary of the Navy during the Wilson administration. He was the most handsome man to appear on the Washington scene. He had great charm, and was attracted to good-looking women. It was not difficult for him; he had a flair for establishing social relationships easily. He liked to hear and to tell a good story, and, when an anecdote pleased him, he would toss his head back and roar with delight.

Eleanor was unable to share with him the joy of such social contact. She was always very serious. This lack of compatibility helped dull their romance.

Elliott Roosevelt, in his book, *An Untold Story: The Roosevelts Of Hyde Park*, wrote that after the birth of John, the youngest son, in 1916, his parents never lived together as man and wife because she did not want to bear any more children.

Anna Roosevelt Halstead, Elliott's sister, disassociated herself completely from his version, although she did agree that there was dissension between her parents. She recalled: "If father became friendly with a princess or a secretary, he'd reach out and pat her fanny and laugh like hell, and was probably telling her a funny story at the same time, whereas to mother that was terrible. . . He loved to outrage Granny, to tease her. He could never do that with mother. She was much too serious. Mother was inhibiting to him. She would never go along. That's why he turned elsewhere."

The facts indicate that he did look elsewhere.

There was a time when Washington gossip focused its attention on his relationship with Miss Marguerite(Missy) LeHand. She was in her thirties when FDR became President, but she had been his private secretary since the early 1920s. She was tall, slim, had silver hair, and grey eyes—and had a great sense of humor that matched the President's. They were together a great deal. She would travel with him most of the time. She supervised his executive staff, lived in the White House, and would spend many an evening with Roosevelt. In the absence of Mrs. Roosevelt, Missy frequently entertained friends whom she and the President both found interesting.

From 1924 to 1926, Roosevelt took long cruises, each one lasting two months. Missy, except for a few emergency absences, was always aboard. Eleanor made one very short visit in the last of those three winters. Eleanor accepted this arrangement, although it did not sit well with her mother-in-law. Franklin needed Missy to handle the mail, was the excuse Eleanor offered.

When Roosevelt, already stricken with polio, decided that swimming in the natural spring waters at Warm Springs would hasten his recovery, Missy accompanied him. On April 1, 1925, such a trip lasted for 15 weeks, with Eleanor absent and Missy on hand. She had a room in his cottage, and spent considerable time with Roosevelt.

One writer calculated that, during the years 1925 through 1928, FDR was away from home a total of 208 weeks. During this absence, Eleanor was with him for four weeks; Sara Delano (Mama) for two; and Missy was with him day and night for a total of 116 weeks.

Doris Fleeson, writing in the *Saturday Evening Post*, observed, "No invitation is accepted by Missy if it means leaving the President alone. . . Missy is attuned to his moods, knows how to keep him company both with conversation and with silence."

Grace Tully, a member of Roosevelt's staff, wrote: "She'd sit with him in the evening when he was reading or playing with his stamps. Sometimes she'd sit with him while he was doing mail. He liked somebody around in case he wanted to say something. He didn't want to talk to the air. He liked to think out loud, and if he thought out loud he wanted somebody to listen."

During a visit with the President, Fulton Oursler observed

that Missy was present, not Eleanor. And when the President was asked the whereabouts of Eleanor, he replied that he did not know. During the supper that followed, "not once was the name of Eleanor Roosevelt mentioned."

More and more did Roosevelt begin to rely on Missy, sometimes to the embarrassment of his supporters. Hundreds of people kept their contacts with the President almost solely through Missy.

Eleanor Roosevelt, in her own recollections (*This I Remember*), wrote about Miss LeHand:

> Missy was young and pretty, and loved a good time; and occasionally her social contacts got mixed up with her work and made it hard for others. Some of the people who worked closely in the administration with my husband were brought in through Missy LeHand's efforts. I think none of them ever meant a great deal to Franklin. I also think they exploited Missy's friendship, believing her more interested in them personally, than in what they could contribute to Franklin's work.

Another time she wrote:

> As Miss LeHand lived at the White House she very often, when I was not there, invited people she thought my husband would enjoy, or whom she personally wanted, but he never gave this type of social gathering a thought.

In June 1941, there was a party given for the White House staff. Toward the end of the dinner, Missy looked sick. When Grace Tully advised her to go to her room, Missy refused. She would not leave before the boss left at 9:30. A few minutes later, Missy fell unconscious. Dr. McIntire recognized the signs of a stroke. Her left arm and leg were paralyzed. Her speech was gone. After some hospitalization, she left for Warm Springs for rest and medical attention.

When Roosevelt visited her late in November, he could hardly keep his composure. Here was Missy unable to say a word. Gone was her wit, her humor, her warmth. Roosevelt, who hated illness, could not face what he saw. His visit was strained.

When she returned to the White House, she was resettled in her same room. FDR visited her regularly, but the visits were painful. Evidently, the White House was not a good place for her, and so she was sent to Somerville—to the house on Orchard Street from which, two decades earlier, she had set out for New York in search of excitement and a career.

For a while she seemed to be improving. She began to walk with a cane. In November of 1942, on the morning of a congressional election, she sent a wire to Roosevelt at the White House which read:

"Am Fighting For You, Love Missy."

On the evening of July 30, 1944, Missy went to the movies. There she saw a newsreel of Franklin Roosevelt, and was shocked at the way he looked, and at the way his voice sounded. Back home, she looked at some old pictures, and went to bed. Her arm, that had been useless for so long, began to move. She thought that feeling was returning to it. She called in her sister who had been staying with her. As her sister approached the bed, Missy slumped over. She was dead.

Roosevelt was aboard ship at that moment, having departed from Honolulu where he had conferred with General MacArthur and Admiral Nimitz. A radio message from the White House was handed to him:

July 31, 1944

MEMORANDUM FOR THE PRESIDENT: RE-
GRET TO INFORM YOU THAT MISS LEHAND
DIED IN THE NAVAL HOSPITAL AT CHEL-
SEA, MASSACHUSETTES, AT 9:05 A.M. TO-
DAY. ADMIRAL SHELDON, OF THE BUREAU
OF MEDICINE AND SURGERY, STATES THAT
THE CAUSE OF DEATH WAS CEREBRAL EM-
BOLISM. MISS LEHAND WAS TAKEN TO
THE HOSPITAL AT 2:00 O'CLOCK IN THE
MORNING. ADMIRAL SHELDON SAID THAT
SHE HAD ATTENDED THE THEATER LAST
EVENING AND THAT THE CHANGE FOR
THE WORSE WAS UNEXPECTED. HAVE NO-
TIFIED MRS. ROOSEVELT AND MISS TULLY.
AWAIT INSTRUCTIONS. WILL ISSUE STATE-
MENT IN THE PRESIDENT'S NAME AND
WILL SEND TEXT TO YOU FOR YOUR INFOR-
MATION.

Upon her death, rumor about FDR's relationships with other women began to surface. One such was the Crown Princess Martha of Norway who spent most of the time during World War II in the United States separated from her husband. Evidently, Roosevelt went out of his way to play host to this lithe, lovely young lady. She (and when her husband was in America, he as well) were frequent guests at the White House.

Gossip had it that when her husband was not in America— which was most of the time—the Crown Princess would spend entire weeks at the White House. When the First Lady was absent, and that was often, the Princess would lunch with the President. Occasionally, he would visit her at Pook's Hill, where she lived. Again and again it was reported that this beautiful matron had flirted with the President.

Once again, Eleanor took an emotional beating. This time she was referred to as "Princess Martha's Lady-In-Waiting," hardly an appellation a wife would appreciate.

All of this must have amused FDR because, even before Martha left for home in October of 1944, he was spending much time with Mrs. Rutherford, the former Lucy Mercer. It was with Lucy that FDR spent the remainder of his life. She was at the White House when Eleanor was not. She was everywhere he wanted her to be. And through the last days of his fatal illness at Warm Springs, Georgia, Mrs. Rutherford was at his side. She left him only a few hours before his death so that Eleanor alone would be at the side of her husband when he died.

When Eleanor was the wife of the Assistant Secretary of the Navy, she found herself unable to take care of all the paper work with which she was burdened, and decided to engage a social secretary. The girl was Lucy Page Mercer. She was very poor and the product of a broken home. Her mother, Minnie Mercer, was a remarkably handsome woman and was still socially prominent, being listed in the highly exclusive Washington Social Register. The fortune she had inherited from her father had long disappeared, having been spent in reckless fashion.

Minnie had been married twice. She divorced her first husband on the grounds of adultery when she was only 23. She then married Carroll Mercer in London on July 30, 1888. He was a lieutenant in the U. S. Marines, and at least once was suspended for being drunk while on duty.

In 1889, he resigned his commission, and came to live on Minnie's money in her luxuriously furnished house in Washington. It was there that Lucy was born, the second and last child of the Mercers.

Lucy's childhood years were anything but happy. They were bad financial years for her parents. Her mother and father quarreled often and bitterly. They were separated for a while when Carroll obtained a commission as captain in the U. S. Army in June 1889. As soon as he rejoined his family, the quarreling resumed and, once again, they separated. This separation was to be final, although the Mercers never officially divorced because Carroll was a practicing Catholic.

However, unlike Eleanor who felt unloved as a child and ugly as well, Lucy knew that she was loved and was regarded as a beautiful child. When she became a teenager, she was virtually

radiant and beautiful. She was well-poised and dignified, graceful in movement and reserved in manner. Still, she was a warm,
generous lady, with a capacity for great passion and compassion.

In 1914, Lucy did not have a full-time position, and so, when
she was offered the post of social secretary to Mrs. Franklin Roosevelt, she accepted. At the outset, Lucy was practically a servant
to the Roosevelts, but this did not last long. As her efficiency and
tact became evident, she was asked to handle the hundreds of
social calls, afternoon luncheons, dinners, balls, and theater parties. She was almost considered a member of the family. Soon,
Franklin Roosevelt began arranging bachelor escorts for Lucy so
that she might join in his recreational outings.

In *The Roosevelts of Hyde Park*, Elliot Roosevelt discusses this
period:

> Father would come downstairs at the same
> brisk pace that took him everywhere. He was
> considered a stylish dresser, from his high col-
> lars to his Peel shoes, bought in London. His
> English cut, dark business suits lasted him for
> years, but they kept their impeccable fit. He
> seemed permanently to be overflowing with en-
> ergy, but never more so than in the mornings.
> And then off to work. At this moment, another
> caller was lifting the hem of her long skirt to
> climb the front steps. She wore a lace jabot at
> the neck of her blouse, encircled by a black vel-
> vet ribbon. She was fair, slender, fullbreasted
> and smiling. Lucy Mercer had lived in this
> same row of houses, at Number 1761, as a child
> before her family's fortune was dissipated.
> Now she returned on most mornings of the
> week to work for mother as a very social secre-
> tary and guide on the finer points of Wash-
> ington's social protocol, which she knew like
> the back of her slim hands.

Blue-eyed Lucy was tall, slender, and erect. FDR called her
"the lovely Lucy." Her voice was warm, rich and friendly; her
smile was most attractive. She had gaiety and wit, and possessed
a great deal of feminine charm which attracted and pleased men
in social situations. Whatever it was, she had something that
especially pleased Franklin Roosevelt, who was greatly drawn to
her.

Lucy had the same brand of charm as Roosevelt—everybody
who met her spoke of that—and there was a glint of fire in her
warm eyes. Lucy was impressed by her employer's husband, the

very prominent and greatly admired figure on the Washington scene. He was so kind, warm, and friendly.

Her feeling was not uncommon to those who met Roosevelt. Men and women alike were impressed by his sheer physical magnetism. The first impression he gave was abounding energy and virility. He would leap over a rail rather than open a gate, run rather than walk . . . Old ladies maneuvered to have him take them out to dinner. Young women sensed the innate sexuality of the self-confident assistant secretary who liked to work at his desk in shirt sleeves.

At the start, Lucy felt that he was an unlikely mate for the plain, dutiful and conscientious Eleanor who appeared wholly dedicated to childbearing and household management. He was so handsome a man, so fun-loving; his wife was so much the opposite.

Eleanor's awareness of her husband's new romantic interest made her nervous, more jealous, and more resentful of younger women. Because the sexual side of her nature had never been aroused, she could not have been able to analyze the stark biological reasons for her husband's wandering attention, and for the tension that was growing between them.

Said Elliott, "Mother, jealous in spite of herself when other women cast admiring looks at Father, and he returned them, seemingly had begun to have qualms about leaving him as a summer bachelor when she made her annual departure."

In the year 1917, Eleanor realized that Franklin had lost interest in her. This was a period of great unrest in their lives. Her husband had become emotionally involved with another woman, an involvement that would weave its way through the rest of Franklin Delano Roosevelt's private life.

Lucy Mercer recognized and understood Franklin's need for feminine companionship; his need for a woman with whom he could relax, forget, and have fun. They found pleasure in one another, and soon their delight turned into an emotional attachment so deep that it completely absorbed them both. But the affair was disconcerting and dangerous for both as well. If discovered, their furtive meetings could prove embarrassing for him; and she was toying with the love of a married man. She was not rich, and had no husband—not even a prospect.

Eleanor sensed a change in her husband, even though he did his best to hide his feelings. She sensed that Franklin was eager for her to leave for Campobello. When she left, he wrote her:

I had a vile day after you left, stayed at
home, coughed, dozed, tried to read, and failed
even to play Miss Millikin (Solitaire) . . . I really
can't stand that house all alone without you,

and you were a goosy girl to think or even pretend to think that I do not want you here all the
summer, because you know I do! But honestly
you ought to have six weeks straight at Camp,
just as I ought to, only you can and I can't. I
know what a whole summer here does to people's nerves, and at the end of the summer I
will be like a bear with a sore head until I get a
change or some cold weather—in fact as you
know I am unreasonable and touchy now—but I
shall try to improve.

During Eleanor's absence, Franklin and Lucy were seen together quite often. Gossip began to reach Eleanor's ears. Her
worst fears were confirmed in the autumn of 1918, shortly after
her husband had returned from a European mission. He was
quite ill and upset.

While on his European trip, he wrote to Lucy daily and
repeatedly told her that, in time, everything would work out for
them. Alone, Lucy took refuge in religion, trying to gain emotional strength. Her letters to him spoke about her worries, her
religion, and her doubts about marrying a divorced man with
children.

Lucy was a devout Catholic, but she did love Franklin,
loved him so much that she would have married him had things
worked out as both hoped. In fact, the longer the relationship
continued, the more convinced was Lucy that Franklin was not
going to divorce his wife. At the same time, Lucy, too, was
entertaining second thoughts. She did not want to hurt Eleanor,
and feared that some day she would be held responsible for
breaking up the Roosevelt home.

To carry on a clandestine affair was completely alien to Franklin's nature. From his boyhood, his mother drummed into him
the concept of *noblesse oblige*, which was defined as, "People of
social position like ourselves should behave *nobly* toward
others." Roosevelt did not flaunt his growing fascination with
the charming girl, but he made no secret of it either.

Roosevelt was slowly becoming less discreet about his love
for Lucy. They were seen driving together by more people than
just his cousin, Alice Longworth, who invited them to her house
for dinner, happy to plot against Eleanor. Friends were gossiping
because they realized that something much more serious than a
bachelor's summer flirtation had developed.

When Eleanor returned from Campobello to Washington in
the fall of 1918, Franklin had already told Lucy that he wanted to
obtain a divorce and marry her. She kept postponing a final
decision, because she did not want to bear the responsibility for

breaking up a home. Franklin, however, kept assuring her that he and Eleanor had no romantic involvement, and that their marriage was merely a business arrangement.

Eleanor was jealous of Lucy, as she was of any female who was close to her husband. Nevertheless, when Lucy was relieved of her Navy job, Eleanor engaged her again as a social secretary.

While Franklin was sick with pneumonia following his European mission, Eleanor came across letters written by Lucy to Franklin. Eleanor had suspected for some time that her husband and Lucy were in love, but the letters, at last, gave her the ammunition she needed to finally confront them.

Elliott Roosevelt describes the confrontation between his father and mother in these words:

> It was September 20, when he (Father) lay in bed with pneumonia in Granny's bedroom. Mother, unpacking for him, found Lucy's letters. She had no compunction about reading them. They were the concrete evidence she had lacked and long waited for. She immediately called on Granny as the ally who would back her to the hilt. Mother would have preferred a divorce. That was her first thought, and her first tactic was to offer it. She had grounds in the State of New York, which recognized only adultery. The letters were her proof. But Granny held ironclad views about *noblesse oblige* and broken homes. If divorce were the answer, she would cut off father's money as punishment for his offense. He could never support two establishments. And to be divorced for adultery would mean political suicide for a man who was already being talked about by a handful of people as a future President.

It was at this time that Eleanor summoned Franklin and Lucy to a meeting.

The meeting has been described by a friend of Lucy in this way:

> Shaken and in tears, Lucy came to my apartment straight from the meeting. She said Eleanor had told her and Franklin that she had found out they were in love and warned them of the serious consequences on his children and his career if the affair continued. She did not offer to give him a divorce; it wasn't even mentioned.

Drew Pearson, in one of his columns, wrote that Eleanor had said to her husband: If you want to be President, Franklin, you'll have to take me with you."

Anyway after Eleanor finished talking, Lucy did not wait for Franklin to speak up. She simply said she had already resolved to end the romance because of her religion. She then solemnly promised she would never be alone with Franklin again. Eleanor then said that she could continue as her social secretary and that ended the meeting.

Eleanor's agony at this time is understandable. During her lifetime, she needed to love and to be loved, and it had always been denied her. Knowing that she was far from beautiful, being painfully shy, actually feeling that she was being pitied or laughed at, and belittled by her domineering mother-in-law, her life was filled with an overdose of misery. She was the castaway wife who wanted to believe her husband's "I will never see her again," only to find reasons to doubt his protestations and avowals.

Eleanor set a price for her compliance when she laid down the rules in private with her husband. This, she told him, meant that their marital relations could never be resumed. She was willing to have him as a partner in private life, but not ever again as a husband.

For many years Lucy kept her promise. Though Roosevelt communicated with her after he became President and tried to arrange a meeting during her several visits to Washington to see her mother, she refused to meet him. There is little doubt that Roosevelt kept close track of Lucy Mercer's movements during the first two years after the agreement to terminate their relationship. She did a bit of traveling, and visited relatives in North Carolina for extended periods. In 1919, she actually lived in an apartment in Toronto.

On February 13, 1920, there appeared in the *Washington Post* a social item which said: "Mrs. Carroll Mercer announces the marriage of her daughter, Lucy Page, to Mr. Winthrop Rutherford of New York." Mr. Rutherford was 56, and Lucy was young enough to be his daughter.

Roosevelt read this social item, but at the time was so involved with political affairs that he had little time to brood. In a way, Lucy Mercer's wedding restored some order to his private life. It absolved him of possible guilt feelings. Better still, it removed him from future temptation.

More than 20 years later, in 1944, Roosevelt was again spending time with Mrs. Lucy Rutherford. Once, during a campaign, FDR's train stopped in New Jersey so that he could visit with her. She was now a 53-year-old widow whose husband had died only a few months earlier. She was still as beautiful as ever, and even more charming than when Roosevelt, as a young man, had first fallen in love with her.

For the remainder of his life, Franklin spent as much time

with Lucy as possible. They lunched or dined together at the White House when Mrs. Roosevelt was not present, although always in the company of others. They saw each other outside Washington as well. These meetings were kept from the press, and surely from Eleanor.

Theirs was a genuine true and great love. Their relationship gave him a fulfillment he had not experienced in marriage, and filled his final years with warmth and understanding. Their romance was never a complete sexual relationship. Had it been, it would have terminated many years earlier.

Not long after Roosevelt's death, Eleanor confided to her son Elliott: "He was a very lonesome man. I wish I had been able to be closer to him, to comfort him sometimes, but I suppose that could not be."

*   *   *

For all of sad words of tongue or pen,
The saddest are these: "It might have been."

These words of Whittier were used by Elliott as the closing lines of his book about his famous parents—Franklin and Eleanor.

9
George Bernard Shaw: The Pseudo-Lover

In the course of his long and successful career, George Bernard Shaw dominated the English theater, campaigned for social reform, produced newspaper analyses of unsurpassed quality, stimulated original thought in many people, and was hailed as one of the most clever humorists of his era.

He was considered a crank by some, a sage by others, a playwright and protagonist by many. He claimed to be a pioneer in science (although he never stepped into a laboratory), a musician, a man of letters, a businessman, a critic, a columnist, and a calm, detached, unemotional lover.

Summarizing his own personality, Shaw wrote: "To one biographer I am a Saint and an Idealist; to another a Don Juan with a woman in every theater .·.. My life has been a hell, but because I have kept the lid on, nobody peeped into it . . . My trifling, and lying, and ingrained treachery and levity with women . . ."

He supplied the thought for his own obituary. He suggested: "Tell them that I have provided for the greatest players a modern repertory comparable only to that left by Shakespeare." Max Beerbohm, the esteemed writer, recognized him as an individual who could be described as "immortal."

George Bernard Shaw was born at 33 Synge Street, Dublin, on July 26, 1856. His parents, who shared little in common with one another and who finally separated, endowed him with tremendous talents and qualities of character. From his father he derived his humor, and from his mother his vivid, colorful imagination.

George Bernard's father, George Carr Shaw, came from a family that had first set foot in Ireland towards the close of the 17th century. The family had produced bankers, clergymen, stockbrokers, civil servants and even baronets. In fact, the Shaws felt they were a race apart from the rest of humanity.

As a youngster, George Carr Shaw was not too fortunate. He was raised by a widowed mother together with his 13 brothers and sisters. She lived in poverty and kept every member of the household on a skimpy diet. George, however, did not permit poverty to get the better of him. Possessed of a good sense of humor and a kind heart, he met the day's troubles with a joke and a jest. His humor was aimed at events that befell him that might have caused other people to weep. He was a thoroughly amiable fellow with an agreeable appearance in spite of a squint.

George went into the corn business only to go bankrupt. Never, though, did he permit his sense of humor to leave him. When George Carr Shaw was past 40, he fell in love with Elizabeth Gurly and asked her to marry him. She was half his age.

Because she wanted to escape from a humpbacked, tyrannical aunt who scolded and bullied her, Elizabeth accepted his proposal. By doing this, she sacrificed her home and her very real prospects of comfort and luxury. It is doubtful that she ever loved him. Her aunt disapproved of the marriage and, consequently, cut her disobedient niece out of her will.

It wasn't long before Elizabeth had an unpleasant surprise. She discovered that her husband was a chronic drunkard, who, without intending to do harm, relieved himself of all responsibility, and placed it all on his wife's shoulders.

Elizabeth was an impassive woman, not given to emotion. She was quiet, resolute, and never lost her temper. Above all, she was a talented musician, with one absorbing interest: she was passionately devoted to singing and studied under George Vandeleur Lee, a Dublin teacher. Soon, she organized concerts, and spent much of her time working with Lee. Eventually, George Lee moved in with the Shaws. The money he paid for his room and board plus the government pension was all that kept the family fed, housed, and clothed.

The musical activity within the family was the most significant part of George Bernard Shaw's home influence. Operas, concerts and oratories were constantly being rehearsed at home. Before he was 15 years old, he knew many of the works of Handel, Beethoven, Verdi and Gounod by heart. George Bernard Shaw was taken to operas and plays very often. Though he loved the stage, Shaw, during his youth, did not dream of being a writer, let alone a playwright, despite the fact that story-telling came very naturally to him.

George Bernard hated school. He said: "I learned nothing of what it professed to teach . . . My school was conducted on the assumption that knowledge of Latin is still the be-all and end-all of education . . . The method of teaching was barbarous: I was ordered to learn the declensions and conjugations and instalments of the vocabulary by rote on pain of being caned or 'kept in' after school hours if I failed to reel off my paradigms without prompting . . . I escaped from classical school just as Homer was threatening, but not before I was confronted with algebra without a word of the explanation that would have made it interesting to me."

At 15, Shaw started to work for an estate agent called Charles Townshend. He was an excellent employee—accurate, efficient, and industrious; and was liked by his fellow employees with whom he discussed art, music and literature. George Bernard was not adverse to giving impromptu renderings of an aria from *Il Trovatore* when the spirit moved him.

At home, the situation between his parents didn't improve. In fact, his mother, together with his two sisters, had deliberately deserted George Carr, husband and father. She put the Irish Sea between him and her, taking Agnes and Lucy with her to London. Now George was left alone with his father.

George Bernard never explained why he did not go with his mother and sisters when they left for London. He was no "mother's boy," although an only son. There is no evidence that his mother ever wanted his company, nor that he longed for hers; rather, the contrary may be pretty safely presumed.

For five years, Shaw lived with his father during which time he taught himself to play the piano. But his true love was writing. It wasn't long before Shaw moved to London and joined his mother, determined to become a novelist. Every day he set himself to write five pages—no more, no less.

When he left Dublin in his twentieth year, he had neither found himself, nor a career which he loved. He was very aware of his inability to find a suitable direction for his life. Without any show of emotion, George left his father who was a lonely, sad, little man.

When he arrived at his mother's house in England, he was received with little, if any enthusiasm. His mother was a disappointed, disillusioned woman who felt bitter about her husband and who had just buried her younger daughter. To her, the George Bernard who had arrived at her doorstep could have been a stranger. They had not seen one another for five years, nor had they corresponded, and the boy had become a gawky youth, on the threshold of manhood. In any event, she was too preoccupied with making a living to worry about the fresh demands his presence in the home would make. There was hardly enough money on hand to sustain them despite the fact that she was receiving a legacy of 4,000 pounds—a substantial sum in those days—and was earning some additional money as a music teacher. Shaw later commented, "My mother and I lived together but there was hardly a word between us."

George Bernard Shaw seldom had anything good to say about his mother and father. "Technically speaking, I should say she was the worst mother conceivable," he once wrote. He said that he himself had been "begotten after a brawl when his father was fuddled with drink." Later in life, he confided to the famous actress, Ellen Terry, this cry of anguish: "Oh, a devil of a childhood, Ellen, rich only in dreams, frightful and loveless in realities."

Between his twenty-first and thirtieth year, he earned almost nothing. A few jobs did come his way. He ghosted a few articles, and worked in the offices of the Edison Telephone Company. Many of the articles he wrote were returned—as were his novels. He was miserably depressed and would go about sulking, dressed in a familiar rusty-black suit, frayed at the collar and cuffs.

When not writing at home or visiting the National Gallery, he spent most of his time in the British Museum Library, which cost nothing and offered so much. He managed to obtain a job as a telephone engineer at a salary of 48 pounds a year plus commission. In six months, he was promoted, with a raise in pay. In twelve months, he quit and returned to writing novels.

His first novel, *Immaturity*, was returned by publisher after publisher. The great novelist, George Meredith, refused it with one word: "No."

Now followed a succession of novels: *The Irrational Knot*, *Love Among the Artists*, *Cashel Byron's Profession* and *An Unsocial Socialist*. Not one of them was remotely successful and Shaw gave up the writing of novels for good. In nine years he had earned only 6 pounds as a writer, and most of that from a patent-medicine advertisement.

During the writing of Cashel Byron, he got himself converted to socialism by attending a meeting at the Memorial Hall, which was addressed by Henry George, the American single-taxer.

Women were not of primary importance in the real life of Shaw, although they were of primary importance in his writing. From boyhood on, he dreamed of beautiful women, although he frequently prevented himself from realizing in the flesh what was in his mind. He longed to live the physical experience, but did not get very far.

In a conversation with Stephen Winsten, he said: "Women have been a ghastly nuisance in my life. Do you think impotent people, as we are called, are sexless? We fall for women more passionately than the so-called normal creatures. Nature can be very cruel . . . I was inadequately equipped for love."

In a letter to Frank Harris, when Shaw was 74, he wrote: "If you have any doubts as to my normal virility dismiss them from your mind. I was not impotent; I was not sterile; I was not homosexual; and I was extremely though not promiscuously, susceptible ... I never associated sexual intercourse with delinquency. I associated it always with delight."

To Cecil Chesterton, who had asked whether he was a puritan in practice, he replied that the sexual act was to him monstrous and indecent, and that he could not understand how any self-respecting man and woman could face each other in the daylight after spending the night together.

Shaw doubted whether it was right for children to know who their parents were. The most satisfactory method, Shaw thought, would be for a crowd of healthy men and women to meet in the dark, to couple, and then to separate without having seen one another's faces.

At 28 years of age, he thought he had fallen in love with Alice Lockett. She was a music pupil of his mother's. She was also a nurse. Shaw wrote poetry and love letters to her. All in all, his correspondence with Alice seems to have lasted about two years—from September, 1883, to October 1885. In due course, she married R. Salisbury Sharpe and gave birth to a number of children.

No sooner did Alice walk out of his life that Mrs. Jenny Patterson, an experienced woman, walked in. G. B. S. was now 29 years old, and strange to relate, had never known any woman. His chastity, however, was not in the least dictated by moral scruples. He attributed it to a fastidiousness which could not endure the streets; and to the shabbiness of his attire.

Shaw, in 1885, was now on the Executive Board of the Fabian Society. Like his mother, he had found a creed and cause for which to live.

The moment he could afford to dress presentably, one of his mother's singing pupils, a wealthy widow named Mrs. Jenny Patterson, invited him to tea and virtually raped him. "I permitted her," he explained, "being intensely curious on the subject. Never having regarded myself as an attractive man, I was surprised; but I kept up appearances successfully. Since that time whenever I have been left alone in a room with a susceptible female, she has invariably thrown her arms around me and declared she adored me."

Shaw believed that "sexual experience was a necessary completion of human growth," and he preferred to gain his knowledge from one who knew how to impart it, and allowed himself to be seduced. He recorded the occurrence with Mrs. Patterson in a story that he wrote two years after he had met her. In the story, it is Don Giovanni who is relating the seduction:

> At last a widow at whose house I sometimes
> visited, and of whose sentiments toward me I
> had not the least suspicion, grew desperate at

my stupidity, and one evening threw herself into my arms. The surprise, the flattery, and my inexperience, overwhelmed me. I was incapable of the brutality of repulsing her; and indeed for nearly a month I enjoyed without scruple the pleasure she gave me, and sought her company whenever I could find nothing better to do. It was my first consummated love affair; and though for nearly two years the lady had no reason to complain of my fidelity, I found the romantic side of our intercourse, which seemed never to pall on her, tedious, unreasonable, and even forced and insincere except at rare moments, when the power of love made her beautiful, body and soul. Unfortunately, I had no sooner lost my illusions, my timidity, and my boyish curiosity about women, that I began to attract them irrestibly. My amusement at this soon changed to dismay. I became the subject of fierce jealousies; in spite of my utmost tact there was not a married friend of mine with whom I did not find myself sooner or later within an ace of a groundless duel.

Later, he wrote to Frank Harris: "Sexual experience seemed a natural appetite and its satisfaction a completion of human experience necessary for fully qualified authorship." At another time, he wrote: "I liked sexual intercourse because of its amazing power of producing a celestial flood of emotion and exaltion of existence."

Jenny Patterson was not only "sexually insatiable" but insanely jealous; and as Shaw continued to flirt with other women she provided him with enough material to make his fortune as a writer of emotional scenes. She became the Julia in his novel, *The Philanderer*. She dogged his footsteps, invaded his home, exploded into hysteria, and generally made his life miserable. There were violent scenes and she had reason to be jealous, for she had discovered, and read, one of Annie Besant's letters to him. She also spied on them walking together in the London streets. In May, 1890, he visited her, but "found her so fractious that I presently shook the dust off my feet and went away." The same month he recorded: "It looks like breaking off."

Annie Besant was the finest platform orator of her generation. When they first met, Annie took a strong dislike to Shaw, mostly on account of his lightheadedness. However, his charm seemed to have a devastating effect on her. Soon, she was inviting him to spend an evening at her house where they would play piano duets. In fact, she so wanted to please him that she practiced alone like a school girl, and always played the right notes coldly and accurately at a moderate speed. He played the wrong ones with enthusiasm. Often, he could be seen walking home with her, carrying the handbag of hers he always complained about.

Nothing happened between duets. She waited for him in the evenings, but her waiting was in vain. However, Annie was not a woman to be neglected or trifled with. Shaw insisted that their relationship be put on a serious level. Since her husband was alive and she could not marry, she drew up a contract setting forth the terms on which they were to live together as man and wife, and presented it to him for his signature. He read it and exclaimed, "Good God! This is worse than all the vows of all the churches on earth. I had rather be *legally* married to you ten times over."

She insisted on his signing the contract, and, when he refused, she demanded her letters back. He collected what he could of them, and returned them to her. She produced a casket in which she kept all his letters, and, convulsed with tears, handed them back to him. "What! You won't even keep my letters!" The correspondence went into the fire.

She insisted on his signing the contract, and, when he refused, she demanded her letters back. He collected what he could of them, and returned them to her. She produced a casket in which she kept all his letters, and, convulsed with tears, handed them back to him. "What! You won't even keep my letters!" The correspondence went into the fire.

His association with Annie Besant ceased suddenly. It may very well be that when Shaw transferred his affection from her, Annie discovered his true character.

George Bernard Shaw believed himself to be especially attractive to women, and there is a good amount of evidence to show that his assumption was correct. Yet it is difficult to see why young George Bernard should have been found attractive by women. Shaw, as a non-earner, was a poor marital risk. His face was dead white with sparse patches of orange whiskers sprouting on cheek and chin. In fact, H. H. Champion, a once fellow socialist, described Shaw's face as "an unskillfully poached egg."

Wilfred Blunt, the poet, described him in his book, *My Diaries*, as:

> A grotesque figure. An ugly fellow. His face a pasty-white with a red nose and rusty red beard and little slately blue eyes. . . .: Shaw's appearance matters little when he begins to talk

—if he can ever be said to begin—for he talks
always . . .

Another woman who openly surrendered to George Bernard's charm was Edith Nesbit. She was a poetess married to Hubert Bland, a man who eagerly sought the affection of many women. There were moments when Mrs. Bland might have exchanged her impulsive husband for the villa, the carriage, and several thousand pounds a year, because his enormous physical strength and virility not only taxed her severely, but involved the responsibility of caring for two other of his "unofficial wives" whom she had to see through maternal difficulties.

Bland was a journalist, writing articles expressing the Tory democratic viewpoint. He was of the school of Randolph Churchill. He was a very aristocratic-looking man with a monocle; he liked both boxing and women.

When he had married Edith, then 17, he already had a mistress and an illegitimate child. Later, he impregnated one of Edith's friends. There was a time when Edith was saddled with his mistress and her bastards.

However, Bland was useful to Shaw. He put into serial form, *An Unsocial Socialist,* Shaw's novel which had failed to get publication. Perhaps this was one of Shaw's reasons for not speaking out about Bland's excessive philandering.

Edith had no scruples about falling in love with Shaw, whom she described as simple, but "one of the most fascinating men I ever met." His handsome figure, rich voice, and Irish accent made an impression on her; and she expressed her emotions fully in her poems. Although she knew of his faults, and considered him untrustworthy because he had a habit of embroidering the truth, especially in his flattery of women, her passion for him was evidenced in her poems. In one poem, she spoke of Shaw's "maddening white face."

There came into existence at this time the Fabian Society, of which Shaw, Bland and Edith Nesbit were members. The Fabian Society was started by Thomas Davidson, as The Fellowship of The New Life. Its purpose was to reconstruct society in accordance "with the highest moral possibilities." Some of the original members included Havelock Ellis, the future British Prime Minister, James Ramsay MacDonald, and Herbert Bland.

The time came when some of the down-to-earth members wanted something more realistic than the highly idealistic "Fellowship," and thus the Fabian Society was formed.

On May 16, 1884, George Bernard Shaw, who (like the society itself) lived in Osnaburg Street, attended a meeting. He was convinced that this group was what he was seeking: a forum for ideas and self-expression on socialistic lines. In truth, the Fabians were the Jesuits of English politics. They worked chiefly in secrecy, knowing that socialism was feared and hated in Britain. For years, the press reported nothing about the Fabians whatsoever.

George Bernard Shaw was a true philanderer during those early Fabian days. He courted six or seven women at once, and it was often difficult to keep them from colliding with one another. They were either his mother's music pupils, like Alice Lockett and Jenny Patterson, or they were in the socialist circle, like his Annie Besant, Geraldine Spooner, May Morris, Eleanor Marx and Edith Nesbit. The time came when coterie actresses like Florence Farr and Janet Achurch were added to his life.

Edith Nesbit cared little about politics, but her tastes and talents were literary. To draw attention to herself at Fabian meetings, she developed a technique of fainting and creating scenes. When Shaw aroused her interest, she asked him to sit next to her at committee meetings. He consented only when she promised not to cause any further scenes.

Edith, a clever woman herself, found Shaw's cleverness irresistible. His reservoir of Irish humor and wit never ran dry. Her desire for Shaw made her keep her eyes open for any possible rival, and there were plenty around.

However, Shaw began to fear Edith's jealous husband, who was so adept at boxing. He was afraid that the ferocious Bland would explode, and so began to think about extricating himself from the perilous situation. Although restraining himself was easy, controlling Edith was difficult. She was not about to "release" him too quickly.

Shaw's method of discouraging Edith showed tact, skill, and wisdom—not to mention uniqueness. He set himself about boring the lady to tears by long discussions on the dullest of economic topics. He dropped words about her to people he was certain would repeat them to her. After awhile, his method worked and Shaw freed himself from a situation he no longer enjoyed.

There were those who claimed that Shaw philandered in order to provide himself with material for his plays. Shaw himself admitted this, saying, "My pockets are always full of the small change of love-making; but it is magic money, not real money . . . I am fond of women (or one in a thousand, say); but I am in earnest about quite other things. To most women one man and one lifetime make a world. I require whole populations and historical epochs to engage my interests seriously and make the writing machine, for that is what G. B. S. is: work at full speed and pressure. Love is only diversion and recreation to me."

On May 1, 1891, Shaw wrote to Florence Farr about Jenny Patterson. Florence was a leading lady in one of his early plays, and he was sexually intimate with her. Florence was a young, independent, professional woman who moved freely in artistic London circles. She was clever, good-natured and very pretty, and all her male friends fell in love with her. This was such a common occurrence that she would often show impatience with her lovers. Once, when a stammering suitor seemed to indicate that he was in the mood for love, she grabbed him firmly by the wrists, drew him into her arms with a smart pull, saying, "Let's get it over with."

Shaw found Florence a pleasant change, for she felt about sex exactly as every man likes the woman he is not in love with to feel about it. She was incapable of jealousy, and never gave him the least bit of trouble. He once pointed out that Florence Farr attached no more importance to what you call "love affairs" than Casanova; and she was too good-natured to refuse anything to anyone she really liked. I think she was rather proud of her Leporello list which, in 1894, contained 14 names.

Actually, Shaw's intimacy with Florence Farr had as little effect on him as on her. "In permanence and seriousness," he confessed, "my consummated love affairs count for nothing beside the ones that were either unconsummated or ended by discarding that relation." Shaw found sex hopeless as a basis for permanent relations, and never dreamed of marriage in connection with it.

"I liked sexual intercourse," he once said, "because of its amazing power of producing a celestial flood of emotion and exaltation of existence which, however momentary, gave me a sample of what one day may be the normal state of being for mankind in intellectual ecstasy. I always gave the wildest expression to this in a torrent of words, partly because I felt it due to the woman to know what I felt in her arms, and partly because I wanted her to share it. But except, perhaps, on one occasion I never felt quite convinced that I had carried the lady more than half as far as she had carried me."

"People were so enslaved by sex," he once argued, "that a celibate appeared to them a sort of monster: they forget that not only whole priesthoods, official and unofficial, from Paul to Carlyle and Ruskin, have defied the tyranny of sex, but immense numbers of ordinary citizens of both sexes have, either voluntarily or under pressure of circumstances easily surmountable, saved their energies for less primitive activities."

George Bernard Shaw's public activities were never neglected for the sake of women, because no woman could absorb his interests and energies sufficiently. "It is only when I am being used that I can feel my own existence, enjoy my own life. All my love affairs end tragically, because the woman can't use me. They lie low and let me imagine things about them; but in the end of a frightful unhappiness, an unspeakable weariness comes; and the Wandering Jew must go on in search of someone who can use him to the utmost of his capacity. Everything real in life is based on *need*."

He did persuade Florence Farr to divorce her husband, and Jenny Patterson was a widow. But the idea of marrying Shaw, which they were both quite free to do, seems never to have taken root. Shaw's sexual development came late but, once having taken the plunge with Jenny Patterson, his interest in women as a sex became vivid and intense.

There was a time when, in connection with Florence, Shaw did suffer the pangs of despised love. For a time, he loved Florence far more than she could bring herself to love him.

One love letter makes that clear. Evidently, she had forgotten to keep an appointment with him, and he wrote to reproach her: "When my need was at its holiest, I found darkness, emptiness, void. How could you do this thing? This was to have been the happiness of all my great happiness, the deepest and most restful of all my tranquilities, the very best of all my loves, and I was robbed of it."

Inevitably, the end came.

She left Shaw and picked up with the poet and mystic, W. B. Yeats. In spite of her desertion of Shaw, there was neither quarrel nor recrimination between the former lovers. Shaw had lost both his mistress and his leading lady. But it did not matter to him; there were others in the offing. Of the ending, Shaw says: "We detached ourselves naturally and painlessly; and presently I got married."

During the nineties, Shaw met a genuine, aggressive journalist named Frank Harris. Harris steered him toward a job with the *Saturday Review*. In his critical articles, Shaw made fun of cherished idols, laughed at Henry Irving, made jokes about Sarah Bernhardt, even dared to criticize the Immortal Bard, William Shakespeare himself.

Shaw wrote five plays, but only two were performed. One lasted two nights, and the other for 11 weeks, during which it lost 2,000 pounds. The first of Shaw's plays that made any impression on the public was *Arms and the Man*, written in 1894.

It was about this time that Shaw began to correspond with Ellen Terry, the famous actress, who later became his confidante. She had wit and character. She was admittedly the greatest actress of her generation, the darling of English theatergoers. Her face, figure and movements were beautiful. She was sweet-natured, kind and good.

Shaw was attracted to her, and watched out for her. He continually wrote to her, a correspondence that lasted for 26 years. Commenting on his love affair with Ellen Terry, he said, "The ideal love affair is one conducted by post. My correspondence with Ellen Terry was a wholly satisfactory love affair. I could have met her at any time; but I did not wish to complicate such a delightful intercourse. She got tired of five husbands; but she never got tired of me."

In the late summer of 1896, there was a Fabian house-party at Stratford St. Andrew Rectory, about three miles on the Ipswich side of Saxmundham in Suffolk. It was here that Shaw fell in love with Charlotte Payne-Townshend.

Charlotte was Irish on her father's side. She had inherited wealth as Shaw inherited poverty. Her father, Horace Payne-Townshend, was an Irish barrister and landowner. Her mother was an English lady from Worcestershire who disliked Ireland. Charlotte had successfully eluded a number of money-mad suitors. She was trying to fulfill a promise she had made to herself as a child: "that she would marry a *genius*." At the age of 34, in 1891, she was considered to be very much on the road to becoming "an old maid."

Charlotte, though wealthy, was a member of the Fabian Society. She was described by Beatrice Webb, a Fabian leader, with these words: "She is romantic but thinks herself cynical. She is a socialist and a radical not because she understands the collectivist standpoint but because she is by nature a rebel . . . She is fond of men and impatient of most women; bitterly resents her enforced celibacy, but thinks she could not tolerate the matter-of-fact side of marriage. Sweet-tempered, sympathetic and genuinely anxious to increase the world's enjoyment and diminish the world's pain."

Once Shaw met her, they were constant companions. Their friendship strengthened and deepened.

On August 28, Shaw broke the news to Ellen Terry, whom he had never met in person: "We have been joined by an Irish millionairess who has had cleverness and character enough to decline the station of life—'a great catch for somebody'—to which it pleased God to call her, and whom we have incorporated into our Fabian family with great success. I am going to refresh my heart by falling in love with her. I love falling in love —but, mind, only with her, not with the million; so somebody else must marry her if she can stand him after me."

Three weeks later, he wrote again to Ellen Terry: "Shall I marry my Irish millionairess? She . . . believes in freedom, and not in marriage; but I think I could prevail on her; and then I should have ever so many hundreds a month for nothing. Would you ever in your secret soul forgive me, even though I am really fond of her and she of me? No, you wouldn't."

The next day he again wrote to Ellen Terry: "She doesn't really love me. The truth is, she is a clever woman. She knows the value of her unencumbered independence, having suffered a good deal from family bonds and conventionality, before the death of her mother and the marriage of her sister left her free. The idea of tying herself up again by a marriage before she knows anything—before she has exploited her freedom and money-power to the utmost—seems to her intellect to be unbearably foolish."

Shaw was being cautious. The lady's wealth bothered him. The thought of marrying her without a prospect of financial success was intolerable to him. Ellen Terry, with her open-hearted generosity wrote back: "How very silly you clever people are. Fancy not knowing! Fancy not being sure!!"

The autumn of 1897 found Shaw and Miss Charlotte Payne-Townshend staying with the Webbs at The Argoed, Penallt, Monmouth. By the beginning of 1897, Charlotte had become his secretary. He dictated articles to her and she nursed him when he was tired. He wrote: "I lay like a log whilst the faithful secretary petted me and rubbed the bicycle gash in my cheek with vaseline, in the hope that diligent massage may rub it out and restore my ancient beauty."

He began to spend more and more time in her flat at 10 Adelphi Terrace, above the London School of Economics. At long last there were no more doubts as to their mutual affection and suitability. Also, by 1898, the financial success of Shaw's *The Devil's Disciple* had made him much less unequal to her. When Charlotte saw how Shaw was living under the roof of his mother who cared little about life's comforts, she was horrified. She invited him to stay at her house in the country. But he refused to do so unless they were united as man and wife.

In 1898—by now both in their forties—they married in Charlotte's flat in Adelphi Terrace over the London School of Economics. The actual marriage ceremony could have been made into a slapstick scene in a movie. Shaw looked so comical in his old clothes as he walked on crutches; and Graham Wallas, one of his witnesses, looked so meticulous and distinguished that the registrar took him to be the bridegroom, and assumed Shaw to be the inevitable beggar who found his way to all weddings.

What was the nature of their marriage? Charlotte hated sex and the procreation of children, and G.B.S. had experienced sex in plenty with Jenny Patterson and Florence Farr. This was a sexless marriage. "She married me because she thought I was a genius," Shaw stated. Who can doubt that he married her for "the hundreds a month he could derive." Shaw bragged that "marriage has not made an iota of difference to my working. I write what I like and I do what I like."

Like nearly all unions, the Shaw marriage had its ups and downs, but the marriage itself was a happy one. Both were comfortable with each other. Charlotte, an intelligent, curious woman, brought a great deal of excitement to her husband. She fit into George's life like the last piece of a jigsaw puzzle.

Their lives were quiet; puritanical rather than flamboyant. And Shaw once wrote to Ellen: "I wonder what you would think of our life, our eternal shop; our mornings of dogged writing, all in separate rooms, our ravenous plain meals; our bicycling; the Webbs' incorrigible spooning over their industrial and political science . . . You'd die of it all in three hours, I'm afraid."

Charlotte was not a warm woman. Had she been, Shaw's own personality might have developed and he might have been less callous to the feelings of others. Charlotte was not fond of children. Indeed, she was firmly resolved against bearing any, and it was rumored that this was the reason for the breakup of her earlier love affair with Axel Munthe, the Swedish writer. But Shaw was content with what he had, although he was well aware that it was not fully what he would have liked. He once observed: "What can childless people with independent incomes, marrying at forty as I did, tell you about marriage? I know nothing about it except as a looker-on."

"What do you call married life?" he once questioned. "Real married life is the life of the youth and maiden who pluck a flower and bring down an avalanche upon their heads. Thirty years of the work of Atlas and then rest as pater and mater families."

Later, he wrote: "The years make no earthly difference. I still fall for women but they regard it as one of my jokes and tolerate me. Charlotte took it very nicely and bravely; she wept and poured out her soul to one or two young men. I did not interfere. It will all come out when I am dead."

Shaw now settled down into a rather normal home life, and began his ventures in the theater. His efforts met with little success. Then at 42, he decided he would publish his plays in book form. It was not until he reached the age of 48 that his plays were looked upon favorably, and were in demand.

Shaw's role in the production of his plays was not passive. He selected the cast of each one, trained the actors, worked out staging and was very much present at rehearsals. His plays became more and more sucessful, and Shaw soon found that he was a celebrity—although to many he was still considered a crank and a nuisance. Press photographers followed the Shaws everywhere, and shot pictures of them bathing and even basking in the sun.

Despite the many photographs taken, Charlotte insisted that her husband's portrait be done by the great French artist, Rodin. After the sittings, Rodin was asked how Shaw spoke French. "Mr. Shaw does not speak French well," he replied, "but he expressed himself with such violence that he imposes himself."

Charlotte also insisted that they do more traveling. He accommodated her mostly under protest. In the Sistine Chapel in Rome, he accidentally met Anatole France who had become a legend in his own lifetime. When France asked him who he was, Shaw merely replied, "Like yourself, a man of genius."

Ever since the Jenny Patterson episode, Shaw became accustomed to women admirers. Now, in his late middle age, and for the first time in his life, he himself became entirely hynotized by a woman who was herself the idol of most men.

Shaw described what happened to him in a letter to Ellen Terry: "I went calmly to her house to discuss business with her, as hard as nails, and, as I am a living man, fell head over ears in love with her in 30 seconds. And it lasted more than 30 hours. I made no struggle. I went head over ears and dreamed and dreamed and walked on air for all that afternoon and the next day as if my next birthday were my twentieth."

The woman was Mrs. Patrick (Stella) Campbell, and she so affected Shaw that he became a man parched by thirst for a woman's love and affection. Stella Campbell was a highly intelligent woman, a woman of great perception. Back in the early nineties, she had captivated him by her piano playing in *The Second Mrs. Tanqueray*, and when she became Forbes-Robertson's leading lady, he began to rave about her physical dexterity, declaring, to her great indignation, not that she was a great actress, but that she could thread a needle with her toes.

When he saw her act as Ophelia, it gave him the idea for *Pygmalion*, which he wrote 15 years later. His thoughts kept returning to "that rapscallionly flower girl."

The years passed, and for a while Shaw succumbed to love with emotion. He was present when Stella had a splinter removed from under her thumbnail and the pain he saw her suffer made him aware of all that had become artificial and remote in his attitude towards other people. He wrote:

My Dearest love,
I think all that was good for my soul, because it tore everything that was selfish and imaginary right out of me, and made you a real fellow-creature in real pain. (O Lord! my fibres all

twist and my heart and bowels torment me when I think of it); and the more real you become the more I discover that I have a real real kindness for you, and than I am not a mere connoisseur in beauty, or a sensualist, or a philanderer, but a—but a—a—a—a—I don't know what, but something that had deep roots in it that you pluck at. Only, why should you have to be hurt to cure me of selfishness and little fits of acting?'

For months, he plied her with letters filled with the most ardent emotion, while, at the same time, accompanying his wife and sister-in-law around Eurpoe, or rehearsing plays in London. Her name was so constantly on his lips that Sidney Webb declared that it was a clear case of sexual senility.

Shaw went to a Fabian summer school at Sedbergh to take his mind off her—and spent most of his time walking over the fields talking about her to Rebecca West, a brilliant young journalist. He worried about her health, her finances, her career. He revelled in dreams, but all the while knew that they were dreams and were not part of real life.

There was no doubt, Charlotte was a *real* woman; and Charlotte was bitterly jealous of what she learned or suspected of the affair. "I am all torn to bits," she said. "You don't know what it is to me to be forced to act artificially when everything has been freshly stirred in me . . . But the worst of it is that all our conversation was overhead, and the effect was dreadful . . ."

Reality returned, and the Shavian personality again began to reassert itself. Even at the height of the fury, Shaw had always been considerate of Charlotte's feelings. Once, at the house in Kensington Square, Stella teasingly attempted to hold him back by force and a servant came into the room just as they fell on the floor in a scuffle.

Realizing the anguish he was causing his wife, and though he deplored it, he kept persuing Stella. He behaved like a lovesick youth. He could think of nothing but "a thousand scenes in which she was the heroine and I the hero."

He pursued her when she had left London for Sandwich to get away from him. There was no doubt that he intended to seduce her. She fled, leaving him this brief note:

Please will you go back to London today—or go wherever you like but don't stay here—if you won't go I must—I am very very tired and I ought not to go on another journey. Please don't make me despise you.

Stella

Shaw was humiliated and gave up all hope of possessing her. On paper, he raged at her:

> Infamous, vile, heartless, frivolous, wicked woman! Liar-lying lips, lying eyes, lying hands, promise-breaker, cheat, confidence-trickster.

She retorted in kind. It wasn't long before she married George Cornwallis-West, the Duchess of Westminster's brother, a handsome, picturesque, romantic, extravagant, fashionable, spendthrift playboy. The marriage did not last long.

Shaw had lost his heart but not his head and soon the entire affair was dim in his memory. He wrote about love this way: "I have been in love, like Beethoven; and have written idiotic love letters, many of which, I regret to say, have *not* been returned; so that instead of turning up among my papers after my death, they will probably be read by inconsiderable admirers during my lifetime, to my utter utter confusion. My one comfort is, after whatever they may contain—and no more man is more oblivious of their contents than I am—they cannot be more fatuous than Beethoven's."

The affair with Mrs. Campbell was ended. Her fortune had dwindled. She was getting old, but still had great beauty and talent. She found it more and more difficult to obtain parts in plays. What little money she earned she mortgaged in advance, for she was always in debt.

Many years later, after Ellen Terry had enormous success with her published book of Shaw's letters, Mrs. Campbell decided that she, too, would do the same. In fact, she wanted to eclipse the success of Ellen Terry. However, Shaw was adamant in his refusal to allow this. It would be time enough, he pointed out, when the copyright would expire long after his death. Then, he felt, Mrs. Shaw could no longer be annoyed by misunderstandings.

However, Mrs. Campbell wrote her own memoirs, and promised the publisher such an incomparable collection of love letters —from a well-known duke, from a famous painter with illustrations, from James Barrie, from Shaw, and from a host of others whom she had enchanted—that he advanced 2,000 pounds on it. But she had not reckoned with the attitudes of the executors of the estates of the letter-writers who absolutely refused to authorize publication of these documents, and Mrs. Campbell was left in debt to the publisher with nobody to extricate her but Shaw and Barrie. They decided to allow her to use a few edited samples and thus save the situation for her.

She refused to permit Shaw to see the book in manuscript form lest it be said that he helped her write it; not did she send him a copy after publication. Long after the book was forgotten, he came across a copy in New Zealand, and read it there for the first time. "Without the lady herself," he said, "it was nothing."

By now, the fever which had once burned in Shaw had been completely extinguished; he could not even remember what it had felt like, and he reread his letters with embarrassment. He now was viewing the activities of the rest of the planet from a loftier perch. In his mind, the whole affair had been a sordid escape from the problems of life, and his wish was that the letters of earlier years be buried and forgotten. He put it this way: "Do you ever read breach-of-promise cases? Or divorce cases? Do you ever shudder at the way in which the letters are served up cold to the ridicule or the pruriency or the simple, scandalous curiosity of (the public)?"

Stella Campbell married a second time, but this too ended in divorce. It was said that "to love Stella was inevitable, to live with her impossible." She finally moved to Pau in the Pyrenees, where she died. The last words on her lips were about "Joey," her favorite name for Shaw. Her old, devoted worshipers were free at last to remember only that side of her which was noble, generous, and proud. And so ended Shaw's post-marital love affair.

Charlotte Shaw knew this facet of her husband's character well enough. She regarded it with contempt. She despised this side of him in her heart. She regarded it unimportant but that knowledge did not prevent her jealousy.

Shaw now went on to win world-wide acclaim. In 1925, he was awarded the Nobel Prize. He donated the prize money to the Anglo-Swedish Literary Alliance for the promotion of intercourse and understanding in literature and art between Sweden and the British Isles. He refused knighthood or peerage when offered to him by Ramsey MacDonald. Three of his plays had been filmed with tremendous success.

In 1943, his wife Charlotte died after a long and painful illness. Shaw had now become ill, suffering from anemia. The cure, which called for liver injections, caused him, a conscientious vegetarian, much concern. As he grew older, Shaw began to see more and more people whom he loved as friends and associates being reclaimed by Mother Earth.

"I don't want to see anybody, and I don't want anybody to see me," he said to those who wanted to interview him. "You don't know what it is to be as old as I am. Do you suppose I want the great G. B. S. to be remembered as a doddering old skeleton?"

He spent his 94th birthday at the Arts Theater, where his play, *Heartbreak House,* was being performed. On September

10th of the same year, he was trying to lop a branch from a tree in his garden. It broke off too suddenly, and he lost his balance. He fell and fractured his thigh. He underwent surgery and made good progress. After the operation, he was alert enough to tell the surgeon: "It will do you no good if I get over this. A doctor's reputation is made by·the number of eminent men who die under his care."

The *Radio Review* of Dublin telegraphed to ask if he would like any particular tune to be played. He replied: "Play the tune the old cow died of." A few days later, his prostate gland failed to function, and a minor operation was performed.

One of his friends called at the hospital to inquire as to his health. Shaw was provoked: "Everyone asks me this. It's so silly, when all I want is to die; but this damned vitality of mine won't let me."

"Are you looking forward to dying?"

"Oh, so much, so much," he said. "If only I could die! This is all such a waste of time, a waste of food, a waste of attention. But they won't let me alone." Then, raising his voice, he shouted: "I'm in HELL here. They wash me all the time, and they massage me. When I'm asleep they waken me; when I'm awake they ask me why I'm not asleep! Routine, routine, I'm sick of it. Each time they pounce on me they tell me it will be just the same as last time, and then I find they've added a new torture!"

"Never mind. You are going home on Wednesday. Your room is all ready and looks comfortable. Then you'll feel happier."

"Happier? No. But at least I shall be able to die in peace . . ."

He was taken home on October 14th, and spent the final month of his life in comfort, displaying little interest in anything.

Just before lapsing into unconsciousness on Tuesday, October 31st, he spoke his last words, with all the conviction of one who intended to carry out his promise: "I am going to die!"

One minute before five o'clock, on the morning of November 2, 1950, George Bernard Shaw fell asleep for ever.

10
Frederic Chopin and George Sand

They were destined to meet. He needed a strong supporting hand; she, another lover. "Destiny," as defined by William Jennings Bryan, "is not a matter of chance, it is a matter of choice; it is not a thing to be waited for, it is a thing to be achieved."

Frederic Chopin, the frail pianist and composer, and George Sand, the internationally famed writer, lived together, on and off, for 10 years, sharing moments of success and happiness, and, with great understanding, dividing their sorrows. They lived in the same house, ate at the same table; yet today, many doubt that they ever shared the same bed.

Frederic Chopin achieved universal acclaim as one of the world's greatest composers of music in the course of a lifetime that was brief and tragic. Though his life was short (he lived to be only 39), his music still lives on, and continues to stir those who hear it. To echo the words of Victor Hugo, "Music expresses that which cannot be said and on which it is impossible to be silent."

Frederic's father, Nicolas Chopin, was a Frenchman who migrated to Poland just after graduating from high school. He was not very happy in France, and when he left, all he took with him was his violin and his flute.

When young Nicolas arrived in Warsaw, Poland was in the midst of a political crisis—one of many in its turbulent history. Russian troops had been sent into Warsaw, and Nicolas witnessed fighting in the streets. He was greatly moved by what he saw and experienced. Later, he became an ardent Polish patriot, and an officer in the army.

Making a living in a strange country was far from easy. He took job after job, but was unable to find himself. Finally, his knowledge of French made it possible for him to obtain a position as tutor to children of well-to-do families. It was while teaching one of his students that Nicolas met 20-year-old, blue-eyed, pretty Justina. She was a housekeeper for Countess Skarbek, a distant cousin.

They became friends and before long they found much joy in their mutual love. They were married on June 2, 1806. Nicolas was 35; Justina 24. Their first child, Ludvika, a girl, was born on

April 6, 1807 in Warsaw, and a second child, Frederic Francois, the future great pianist, was born on February 22, 1810 in the couple's small, three-room cottage.

Very early in his life, Frederic and his sister were exposed to the sound of music. Not only did Justina give private music lessons, but often she would sit at the piano and play, and Nicolas would accompany her on the flute or violin. This musical environment had its happy effect. Both children loved it. Ludvika could play the piano, and little Frederic begged her to teach him. Before very long, Ludvika became her brother's first piano teacher. Later, when she began to take piano lessons from Adalbert Zhivny, Frederic, then just six, begged to be allowed to sit in. He was granted his wish, and in time became Zhivny's student. Never did either teacher or student forget those early moments in their lives. They forged a friendship that lasted until the time of Zhivny's death.

Zhivny taught Frederic to appreciate Bach and Mozart. He was much more to Frederic than a music teacher; he was a friend. Soon, the music teacher was part of the Chopin household. He came for tea, to play cards, or just to talk. And he was always received with open arms and warm hospitality. It was to Zhivny that Frederic once confided his secret desire to compose his own music. And very early in his boyhood he began. Chopin's phenomenal memory made it possible for him to remember his own improvisations, and to play them again and again until Zhivny wrote down the entire score. Frederic could not do this himself, since he did not know how to write music. Zhivny was important to him, a fact that Chopin did not forget even when he was at the height of his fame. He owed a heavy debt to his teacher for the love, training, guidance, and inspiration he gave him.

Chopin was only eight years old when he gave a concert before Countess Zofia Samoiska. Although scarcely in the same categaory as Mozart or Handel, when fragile Chopin sat down at the pianoforte to play, dressed in knee-high pants and velvet jacket with a large white collar, little did that first audience realize that this little boy would one day be acknowledged as one of the musical greats. They looked at the young lad who had the temerity to sit before them, with some degree of suspicion. But when they heard the beautiful tones he was able to call forth from the piano, they were hypnotized. The child Chopin was already on his way to fame. Soon, everyone was eager to flatter him and to have young Frederic as one of their house guests.

Between Frederic's eighth and fifteenth birthdays, he could have appeared at any number of public performances, but his parents, Nicolas and Justina, would not exploit the musical genius of their son. They wanted him to lead a normal life, to play with friends, to have the benefits of growing up naturally. However, his inner creative urge would not be denied and Frederic was compelled to compose. His soul cried out and played tunes in his mind. In 1820, he dedicated a Military March to the Grand Duke. In 1821, he composed a polanaise in A-flat to honor Zhivny's birthday. He was only 11 years old at the time. Music had already become a way of life for the young composer.

Joseph Elsner was Chopin's second teacher. He was a more experienced teacher than Zhivny. It wasn't long before Elsner realized that his pupil was in every way a better musician than he. To his credit, he admitted this fact to Chopin.

In 1825, Chopin made his second public appearance. This was at the Conservatory. He was a great success, and received such excellent notices that the Tsar expressed a wish to hear Chopin play. He was now a celebrity, and received invitations to play in the homes of the rich, and in the palaces of royalty.

It was time for Chopin to project to a larger audience, and Vienna was the first foreign city in which he offered his skill as a composer and pianist. Here was a metropolitan audience intimately acquainted with all the great musical geniuses. After his appearance, he wrote to his parents:

> If I was well-received the first time, it was still better yesterday. The moment I appeared on the stage, there were bravos, three times repeated, and the audience was larger. Baron _____, I don't know his name, the manager of the theater, thanked me for the take, saying: "If such a crowd has come, it is truly not for the ballet, which everybody knows well." All the professional musicians are captivated by my Rondo . . .

Frederic wanted his parents to know of his success, for, with all the acclaim, Frederic was already a lonely person, lonely even in the midst of company. He needed and wanted whatever love and strength he could find. He needed the love of a woman, the feeling of well-being that comes from being loved and needed by another person.

On October 3, 1829, Chopin found it necessary to return to Vienna. Some thought he wanted to return because he was infatuated with Leopoldine Blahetka. In a letter to a friend, he said: "She is young, pretty, and a pianist, but I, perhaps unfortunately, have my own idea, which I have served faithfully, though silently, for half a year; of which I dream, to thoughts of which the adagio of my concerto (F minor opus 21) belongs, and which this morning inspired the little waltz (opus 70, no. 3) which I am sending you." Chopin's thoughts were of another woman who had impressed him greatly.

Chopin was infatuated with a young soprano, Konstantsya Gladkovska. She was young and unspoiled, and was musically talented. However, though he wrote about her to his parents and friends, marriage was never mentioned in any of his letters. His interest in her was more than physical, although he adored her looks, worshiped her when she sang, and considered himself to be completely in love. But his love was the love of the young and innocent, no more than puppy love; and Konstantsya was never aware of how the great Chopin felt about her. Frederic, held back by his timid nature, could not tell her.

Although a celebrity, Chopin was very often depressed. He was lonely, and his need for creating music was great and demanding. In the summer of 1831, he wrote of his state of mind in a notebook:

> I wish I were dead, yet I should like to see my parents. Her (Konstantsya Gladkovska's) image appears before me: I don't think I love her any longer, but I cannot get her out of my head. Everything I have seen abroad up to now seems to me old and hateful . . . The people here are not my people; they are kind, but kind by habit. I don't know what to do with myself. I wish I weren't alone.

What great yearning and need lay buried in the breast of this lonely man! Chopin later explained his feelings in these words: "Some of this sickly indecision arose from lonely eroticism, felt but unexpressed. Some of it was sexual—but more of it was Frederic-Francois Chopin's need for a guiding hand, if not that of Tytus, a friend he had now lost, then that of George Sand, whom he was to find within a few years."

In 1831, Chopin was in Paris. He had made new friends: Liszt, Rossini, Mendelssohn, Heine and others. It was also during this year that Chopin complained: "My health is poor." From that time on, he was never well again. He was already suffering from the early stages of tuberculosis. And he was deeply depressed, having learned that Konstantsya Gladovska had married Yosef Grabovski.

The next few years brought Chopin before the public on rare occasions. Several times it was reported that he had died, compelling him to issue statements denying rumors of his death.

During this trying period, he fell in love with 19-year-old Marya Vodzhinska. She was a bubbling young flirt, not particularly beautiful, but a firebrand who had attracted many men of stature, including Louis-Napoleon Bonaparte, the future emperor of France. The family of the young lady merely tolerated Chopin's attention. For Marya, he composed the A-flat major Waltz. Just before he left Dressen, Marya took one lovely flower from a bouquet of roses and presented it to him.

In July 1836, Chopin once again visited the Vodzhinski's villa. During the month of August, Chopin sat for Marya who sketched his portrait. On September 9th, Chopin asked her to marry him, and she accepted. He then asked Marya's mother for her consent. This she gave on condition that the engagement be kept secret until Marya could obtain her father's consent. Marya's father objected. He would not give his blessings to a marriage between his daughter and a frail, sickly musician. Frederic and Marya were separated, never to meet again. Chopin was devastated and referred to this episode as "Moja bieda"—my misery. After his death, when his belongings were collected, the rose the Marya had given him was found enclosed with a small packet of letters.

As 1836 drew to a close, Chopin met the woman who, for more than 10 years, was to be the most important person in his life. She was George Sand, a woman who was not against making the overture toward a man who appealed to her as Chopin did. As a result, a friendship and love developed.

Chopin had finally found the woman he needed, one who gave him the love of a mistress, a mother's care, and the helping hand of a friend. He was already 27, and physical love had been denied him for too long. Some students of Chopin, Edouard Ganche, in particular, claim that Chopin was impotent. George Sand herself claimed that their relationship was chaste because Chopin wanted it so.

George Sand was born Amandine-Aurore-Lucille Dupin, on July 1, 1804, into a family in which the amount of bastardy was so great that her family tree bears many uncertain lines.

George Sand, the name she chose as a pseudonym, developed quite a reputation as a writer, a novelist, and a lover. She loved Alfred de Musset. When he became ill, she nursed him under the care of a young doctor. She promptly fell in love with the doctor. Her love for him didn't last long. There was a lawyer named Michel de Bourges with whom she was involved; and there was also her son's tutor.

George Sand has been called a nymphomaniac, a female Don Juan, a lesbian, and a women in love with her own son. She was a cigar-smoking, trouser-wearing, intelligent woman who demanded from life more than it could give her. She was without fear, without shame—a fickle and often foolish mistress. She had been married to a man who gave her nothing in the way of stimulation, wisdom or inspiration. Nor had she received the tenderness she sought from her lovers. In Chopin, she met a man, who, while not as vigorous as she would have liked, gave her what she needed and could return. At the time of their meeting, she was 33; he was a young man of 27 or 28.

During the summer of 1838, both George Sand and Chopin had their own personal concerns: She, the health of her son; and, Chopin an almost constant depression. She suggested to Chopin that he accompany her to Majorca, and he agreed. He needed rest, and she needed the mild climate of that Balearic island.

Chopin enjoyed the beauty of this semitropical island. He went on short walking expeditions, believing that exercise and fresh air would help him regain his strength. Once, during such a walk, he was caught in a storm, and when he reached the villa, he was chilled and wet. He took seriously ill and George Sand summoned three local doctors. On December 3, Chopin commented on the doctors:

> One sniffed at which I spewed up, the second
> tapped the place from where I spat it, and the
> third poked around and listened while I spat it.
> The first said that I had already croaked, the
> second that I was dying, the third that I shall
> die. And today I am the same as always . . .

Once recovered, he went back to his piano, composing the music which has granted him immortality.

When spring came, the skies in Majorca turned blue again, and the warm air began to dry up the dampness. Yet, both Sand and Chopin were impatient to leave. He was weighed down by depression, and she was upset and distraught; they wanted desperately to be gone.

Up until now Chopin had attempted to keep his friendship with Sand secret. His first recorded mention of George Sand was in a letter to his friend Voitsyekh Gzhimala, dated March 27, 1839. In the letter, he refers to her as "my love." In another letter, he calls her "my angel." He wrote to another friend saying: "You would love her even more than you do if you knew her as I know her today."

By May, Chopin was strong enough to join Sand on a sea trip from Marseille to Genoa. Chopin had never been there, and he wanted to visit Italy. They were accompanied by Maurice, Sand's son. Sand was a passionate woman, and enjoyed having her lover with her on this unexpected vacation. But Chopin was not well, and the return trip was a trying one.

In October of 1839, Friederike Muller, a young girl, persuaded Chopin to accept her as a pupil. She wrote these words about her early lessons:

> Alas, he suffered greatly. Feeble, pale, cough-

ing much, he often took drops of opium on su-
gar and gumwater, rubbed his forehead with
eau de Cologne, and nevertheless he taught
with a patience, perseverance, and zeal that
was admirable.

No doubt, Chopin was getting weaker. It took tremendous
will to teach, to play and to compose. His coughing spells drained
him to the point that he could hardly function. Chopin and Sand
separated. He was ill and she was concerned with the various love
affairs of her son Maurice.

In November 1841, Chopin and George Sand were reunited,
living at their quarters on Rue Pigalle. They were still lovers
and her attitude toward him was as protective as ever. By this
time, she had become a woman of international fame, and was
much more sought after and discussed than Chopin. Her writings had crossed the ocean and her popularity as a provocative
writer had been established. Yet, the two spent a great deal of
time together, travelling from city to city as the will of Sand
demanded.

Chopin composed very little in 1845 and the fault has been
laid at the doorstep of George Sand. Her declining interest in
him, which dulled his ambition and sapped him of his determination, was not out of a lack of love for him, but rather because
there were now others close to her who seemed to demand much
of her time and attention.

George's son, then 22, had developed an increasing dislike
for Chopin. Maurice's adopted sister helped him undermine Chopin's position within the family. It was evident that weak Chopin
would not be a member of the Sand household for long.

The tension between Maurice and Chopin broke out in a
violent quarrel which took place in the middle of June 1846. In
this fracas, George Sand openly sided with her son. Maurice had
been widening his influence over his mother, and was establishing his position as head of the family. Chopin recognized the
fact that the regime was changing. "You no longer love me," he
said to George as he left the house, hoping that time would heal
the wounds and that he would return the following year.

Chopin went to Paris where he waited for Sand to join him,
but she was busy trying to straighten out the lives of her children. Neither Chopin nor Sand made a definite move to see one
another.

Chopin took seriously ill again.

On February 16, 1848, Chopin gave his final concert at the
Salle Pleyel in Paris. He was now very sick. He walked erect to
the piano, and carried through his performance solely by will.
The concert was well-received, and Paris held tight to their musi-

cal genius. Chopin was utterly spent.

Quite by accident, on March 4th of the same year, Chopin ran into Sand. Their conversation was brief; the past was not discussed. She returned to her home; he left for England. They never saw each other again.

One bright spot in the life of Chopin was his relationship with Countess Potocka. Many students of Chopin insist that she was the real love of his life. Chopin's own words speak for themselves. Once, in writing to the countess about his friendship with Sand, he said: "Only you and Sand have had my heart, and you more than anyone else, because you know and understand me as no one else does. I haven't opened my heart to her; she is a foreigner and would not understand me."

Chopin was a proud nationalist. He loved Poland, sacrificed his close ties with his family. If he were ever to marry, he could only marry a Pole.

It has been said and must be restated that Chopin was a deeply moral man. George Sand's reputation as a mistress of many must have affected him. Delphine Potocka was a beauty and an aristocrat as well; Sand was neither.

In a letter to Delphine Potocka, Chopin wrote: "The other women in my life were either youthful dreams buried long ago or winds of passion that blew only for a short while." In another letter, he said: "When a great love overwhelms me, when passion seizes me, and temptations tear at me like dogs, I forget about the world—as I once did with you—and I am ready to give up everything for a woman, to sacrifice my life and my work. With other women it wasn't so, with them I never lost my head."

Victor Seroff, in his book, *Frederic Chopin*, asks: "If George Sand was the only woman he ever loved, how did it happen that he did not dedicate a single composition to her? It was not so with Potocka."

Chopin's life now assumed a regularity about it. Winters were spent in Paris and summers at Nohant. He was as popular as ever, and was more and more sought after as a guest at parties.

In 1844, Frederic Chopin learned of his father's death. He had not seen his father for many years and this deeply troubled him. He was restless and depressed as he learned too of the death or departure of old friends. Zhivny had died; Julian Fontana had left for the United States. Chopin was beginning to feel more and more alone.

His sister Ludwika and her husband came to visit him, and the visit resulted in a seeming miracle—his health began to improve. He introduced them to his friends, took them to the theater and opera, spent hours listening to their stories. Friends told him that his sister was the best doctor he had ever had. Chopin felt he had been given a new lease on life. His peace of mind returned and, with it, better health.

Chopin was greatly affected by the Revolution of 1848, which broke out in several European countries. Polish patriots living in other countries hoped for a Polish revolt against Russian rule, and many left to join the fight against Russia. When Chopin became aware that his friends were leaving, he wrote: "Let us not expend our strength in vain, for strength is needed at the right moment. The moment is close, but it is not today. Perhaps in a month, perhaps in a year."

There were many demonstrations and much street fighting in Paris. Chopin decided to close his apartment and move to London. There, the musical season was in full swing, and he was welcomed by Miss Jane Stirling, a former pupil. She made certain that Chopin received invitations to the best gatherings that London society had to offer.

During this three-month stay in England, he played twice in public and three times at the homes of British nobility. However, he was not well. The climate aggravated his coughing spells, and made it impossible for him to gain satisfaction from his musical successes. The activity exhausted him.

He was restless and lonely, even when not alone. In July, the London musical season came to a close, and Chopin left for Scotland. There he spent time visiting some of the magnificent estates and castles. Soon, bored, he returned to London. His health began to worsen. He took to his bed with a chill, headache, and "all my bad symptoms." Yet, he managed one appearance at a concert for the benefit of Polish exiles. It was the last time he ever played in public.

A few days later, on the advice of his doctor, he returned to Paris. To his extreme delight, Potocka was there, and often she entertained him with song at his home. That winter he did little teaching, but managed to compose the two *Mazurkas*—his last composition.

In the spring, an epidemic of cholera broke out in Paris. Chopin was worried about his financial condition. "I haven't begun to play," he confided to friends. "I can't compose, and I don't know how I'll be living shortly."

Chopin was now very worried about his failing health. He wrote to his sister, begging her to come and visit him. Each day, he lay on a chaise lounge on the terrace of his apartment, waiting for his strength to return.

Ludwika arrived in July, and, with her help, Chopin moved to another apartment right in the heart of Paris. He knew his days were numbered. Although he was not a religious man, he asked for a priest to administer last rites.

When Potocka heard that his end was near, she hurried back to Paris. "It was to enable me to see you that God has postponed calling me to Him," Frederic said when he saw her. He asked Potocka to sing for him. She sang Stradella's "Hymn to the Virgin," Marcello's Psalm.

During the second song, Chopin began to cough uncontrollably. Within two days, on October 17, 1849, he was dead. He was only 39.

After his death, his heart was cut out and taken to Poland where it was placed among the other relics at the Church of the Holy Cross in Warsaw, while his body was buried at Père-Lachaise Cemetery in Paris. As his coffin was lowered into the grave, a handful of Polish soil was sprinkled over it.

In Longfellow's words:

> He is dead, the sweet musician!
> He has gone from us forever,
> He has moved a little nearer
> To the Master of all music.

11

Vincent Van Gogh: The Unloved Lover

History tells of kings who have lost their thrones; great leaders who have betrayed their followers; ordinary persons who have wrecked their lives—all in the name of love. Some have had a positive view of love, and have given their all to maintain and enhance that relationship. But, to others, the pursuit of love has been the pursuit of a mirage, which they thought was real and within their grasp. Such a person was Vincent Van Gogh, the great Dutch artist.

"Love, and you shall be loved," wrote Ralph Waldo Emerson. "All love is mathematically just, as much as the two sides of an algebraic equation." Few will contradict the profound wisdom of Emerson; yet Van Gogh's life defied its accuracy.

The life story of Holland's great Vincent van Gogh is a never-ending struggle to control deep-rooted melancholy and tragic loneliness. He searched for love and never found it; reached out for people and was repeatedly rejected. He desperately wanted to love and believe, and from the moment he became aware of his pressing needs, his hunger pangs never ceased.

Van Gogh longed for intimacy with others, yet he wanted solitude. The world turned a deaf ear, women rejected him, friends avoided him. His feelings of self-doubt and self-depreciation were intensified. Sorrow was woven into the fabric of his life. Not even his family with the exception of his brother, Theo, understood him.

Throughout his life, Vincent was alone. When he once visited Rijksmuseum in Amsterdam, he told his pupil, Kerssemakers, that he would willingly give 10 years of his life if he could go on gazing at Rembrandt's "The Jewish Bride," a portrait of a man embracing a young woman. Vincent's burning desire was to be united with a woman. When finally he satisfied his hunger, he was criticized for living with a prostitute, Sien. To his defamers, he replied that he preferred death to separation.

His ever-present curse was his loneliness and daily he lived the words of Thomas Stearns Eliot:

> What is hell? Hell is oneself,
> Hell is alone, the other figures in it
> Merely projections. There is nothing to escape
> from

And nothing to escape to. One is always alone.

Vincent tried to fill his lonely hours. He used both art and religion to this end. He once wrote: "I tackle things seriously and will not let myself be forced to give the world work that does not show my own character."

The great Dutch master, whose paintings adorn museum walls the world over, can only be understood and appreciated as we understand that, from beginning to end, this hunger, this depression cast an indelible stamp on his art. Commenting on his own work, he said: "In either figure or landscape I should wish to express, not sentimental melancholy, but serious sorrow." In 1880, he described his paintings as "a cry of anguish."

Sadness is expressed in the glossy atmosphere of Vincent's northern landscapes. Van Gogh equated storm in nature with sorrow in humans. He compared himself to "a prisoner who is condemned to loneliness. . . The worse I get along with people," he wrote, "the more I learn to have faith in nature and concentrate on her." His words were echoed by Theodore Dreiser, the American author, who wrote: "Art is the stored honey of the human soul, gathered on wings of misery and travail."

In a sermon which he delivered when still quite young, he told the congregation, "There is sorrow in the hour of death, but there is also unspeakable joy." Vincent's view of "the almost smiling death," as he once called it, arose from a passionate faith in rebirth and immortality.

Vincent was born on March 30, 1853. At his birth, his father was a 31-year-old handsome and dignified minister of the Dutch Reformed Church in Zundert, a town close to the Belgian border. Vincent's mother, a rather strong woman, was industrious and talented. She could write, draw, paint and sew. She was 32 years old when she married Theodorus van Gogh—three years older than her husband. Their first child, also named Vincent, died at birth, a devastating event that plagued his parents and affected the artist throughout his lifetime.

Vincent, their second child and the future Dutch master, resembled his mother more than his sophisticated father. He was of medium height, stockily built, with blue eyes, red hair, and a freckled complexion. Vincent recalled his youth as unhappy, because the discipline of the home was too strict and moralistic, and because he was always singled out by his parents for "unruly behavior." It was the younger Theo who inherited the refined, handsome features of his father and was regarded as a model child. And it was Theo who became close to his artist brother.

Vincent disliked his home, but he loved the countryside and

its people. He once quoted a passage about Bromwell that applied to himself: "The soul of a land seems to enter into that of a man. Often a lively, ardent and profound faith seems to emanate from a poor and dismal country; like country, like man."

Vincent's longing for love, a longing that was always with him, made of the peaceful countryside a loving, nurturing mother. He delighted in taking long hikes, admiring trees and flowers, birds and insects, and acquiring an intimacy with them that he later transferred to canvas.

His mother's interest in art motivated Vincent to paint, while his uncle's knowledge of art stimulated him to study the paintings and lives of famous artists.

Vincent's earliest known sketches were drawn between his eighth and eleventh years. His formal education at the public school began three months before his eighth birthday. When he was 11, he was sent to Jan Provily's boarding school in Zevenbergen, 14 miles from Zundert. Two years later, he was sent to a second boarding school. Like other men of great talent, he claimed to have learned absolutely nothing in school. It was his great love of reading, and his insatiable curiosity that helped him become well-informed in languages, literature, world events, art and history.

At 16, he went to work for Goupil and Company, art dealers who had branches in Paris, London, Brussels, The Hague and New York. At first, he was assigned to the branch in The Hague. During most of his seven years with that firm, he was diligent, sincere and dedicated. In 1873, he was transferred to London.

In London, at age 20, he fell passionately in love with Ursula Loyer, the daughter of his landlady. Ursula had moved to London from France when her father died. In London, her mother set up a school and took in boarders. Mother and daughter impressed Vincent with their closeness—a closeness that he had never known, and for which he craved. "I never saw or dreamed of anything like the love between her and her mother," he wrote.

In the evenings, Vincent read poetry to the ladies. These evenings were perfect: Ursula was there, surrounded by little children. What a joy it was to watch her! He wanted so much to love her. It would be such incredible bliss to love such a perfect creature. After months of silent devotion, he finally confided to Ursula his great love for her.

Unhappily, destiny had decreed otherwise. Years earlier, Ursula had become engaged to another young man. This eventuality had never occurred to Vincent. Loving her so completely, he could not conceive of her not being in love with him. Her rejection shattered him, and he withdrew from the world of people and buried himself in his books.

Vincent, who was still working at the time, soon lost interest in his job. He turned to religion, and began to devote much time to reading the Bible and drawing. In 1876, he was dismissed by his employer. His unhappiness, his withdrawal, and his obsession with religion changed the course of his life. He searched for closeness with another human being and could not find it. Depression completely enveloped him.

Vincent went to Amsterdam to prepare himself for an entrance examination for a theological school. But his depression remained with him and he could not prepare properly. After a year in Amsterdam, he realized that he would be unable to qualify, and so he decided to become an evangelist. Again, he was inadequate.

From religion he turned his attention to art, and he began to paint peasants and landscapes. His early works were realistic representations of his subjects and objects.

In 1880, he had made up his mind, once and for all, to devote himself to art. He moved into the house of a miner named Decrucq. There, he set up his first studio in a room that served also as a bedroom for himself, and for the miner's children. In October of 1880, he moved to Brussels. After six months, he returned to the Parsonage in Etten where he had previously spent some time. Here he worked hard at perfecting his painting skills.

In Etten, he found love in the person of Kee Vos-Stricker, who had been recently widowed, and was a cousin on his mother's side. She was a little older than Vincent. He had met her in 1877 when visiting her and her husband. Impressed by their happy marriage, he wrote: "I spent Monday evening with Vos and Kee; they love each other truly . . . When one sees them sitting side by side in the evening, in the kindly lamplight of the little living room, quite close to the bedroom of their boy who wakes up every now and then and asks his mother for something, it is an idyl." His emotions were deeply stirred, and jealousy followed admiration.

Vincent had always wanted to taste of the love he saw in that home. Now with her husband gone, the situation was quite different. When he proclaimed his love for Kee and proposed marriage, she flatly refused him, and left at once for her home in Amsterdam. Writing to his brother Theo, Vincent said: "I want to tell you this summer a deep love has grown in my heart for Kee; but when I told her this, she answered me that to her, past and future remained one, so she could never return my feelings."

Vincent did not give up. He tried desperately to change Kee's mind. Not wanting to succumb to depression, he refused to take the rebuff seriously, and preferred to believe she was ill, and would change her mind when she recovered. "But she has loved another and her thoughts are always in the past," he wrote, "and her conscience seems to bother her even at the thought of a possible new love."

Vincent's open pursuit of Kee led to quarrels within her family and within his. Her father, a pastor by profession, launched an attack against Vincent, and forbade Kee to see him. He told Vincent that his daughter would not dream of having anything to do with him; that she was disgusted by him.

Vincent stretched out his hand and held it in the flame of a candle. "Let me see her only for as long as I hold my hand in this flame," he begged his uncle. But the pastor blew out the light and showed Vincent the door.

This episode in Vincent's life was a brutal blow to his ego. He suffered untold anguish. But his passion for his work kept him occupied, and saved him from a recurrence of the severe depression that followed his earlier rejection in London by Ursula.

A short time later, at dinner in a communal kitchen, he noticed a young woman with a little girl. She was rather pale-looking, and a bit sad. Her hands were those of a working woman. She was approachable and Vincent quickly sensed this.

A reservoir of unreleased emotion and energy was bottled up within him as a result of his recent failure with Kee. Kee had not only turned away from his love, but had even denied him the pleasure of helping her out of the tragedy that had befallen her. He yearned, not only to love, but to help.

The young woman glanced up. "Listen," Vincent said to her crudely, "you and I don't need to make ourselves drunk to feel emotion for each other. You'd better pocket what I can spare." She was clearly a prostitute; but he had always felt affection for fallen creatures who were forced into prostitution. How often he envied the man he saw walking along the street with one of them. Prostitutes were like sisters to him; and he visited them occasionally in their brothels.

Van Gogh now began to work in earnest. Working at his craft with diligence was difficult, for he lacked the money for his models, and brother Theo did not always send money at the right time. He tortured himself, aspiring toward perfection in his work. He strove for realism in his painting and noticed that he was slowing breaking through and achieving the desired results. By day he worked, and at night he wrote letters to Theo urging him to take up painting.

In January of 1882, he met up with another prostitute who caught his fancy. Sien was not very beautiful, not very young, she was foul-mouthed and pregnant, and had sunk very low. But

Vincent saw something marvelous in her, and his heart reached out. He wrote of Sien, who was in poor health: With "one foot in the grave when I met her, and whose mind and nervous system were also upset and unbalanced . . . Nobody cared for her or wanted her, she was alone and forsaken like a worthless rag . . . She was a 'whore,' already pock-marked, already withered and prematurely old."

But the artist saw Sien in terms of his own needs: "In my eyes she is beautiful, and I find in her exactly what I want. Her life has been rough, and sorrow and adversity have put their marks upon her. Now I can do something with her." And he captured her tortured soul on canvas.

Sien was ill, and needed surgery. The fact that she was pregnant when he met her appealed to his altruism, to his love of children, and to his desire for a family. He accepted her with all her physical and mental weaknesses, and took over the household chores. Her problems became his problems; her debts, his debts. He took her to Leyden to see a good doctor who might operate on her. The operation over, he nursed her back to health. He was determined to make this unfortunate his wife.

Their closeness grew; they had much in common. She, too, had had an uncaring mother. She, too, had been rejected. When he shared his problems with Sien, he felt less unhappy, less despised. With the beauty which he saw in her, he saw less ugliness in himself. Having been humiliated by Ursula and Kee, he had declared, "I know that what I have to do is retire from the sphere of my own class."

Van Gogh knew what Sien lacked. How could she be good-hearted, if she had never know any goodness? And so he was good to her, and she matched his goodness with her own. She even learned how to sit for him, this in spite of her feeble health. She helped him with his drawings, and to him it was sheer bliss to be able to say "we."

His association with Sien alienated both family and friends. Although he did not consider her an evil woman, he did not take her to meet his parents. He wanted to preserve this newly discovered peace and do his work in peace.

He wrote to Theo, telling him about Sien, and now he awaited his reply. He needed his brother's financial help desperately. If Theo should desert him, all would be lost.

In June 1882, Vincent fell ill. Sien had infected him. He was taken to the city hospital where he stayed for several weeks. His depression was now at its worst since coming to The Hague. Sien had gone to Leyden to a maternity hospital, where she was delivered of her child.

His melancholia prevented him from doing anything properly and made life "the color of dishwater . . . an ash heap." However, as the winter of 1883 wore on, his depression mercifully subsided. He worked to set up a new home—a garret in a suburb of The Hague.

He set up a most comfortable studio. Theo raised his allowance to 150 francs a month, not a tremendous sum to support several people, but a fortune to Vincent. He now had his own home, and he and Sien planned to marry. They set the date of their wedding which would take place as soon as he earned 150 francs on his own.

As he set out to bring Sien home from the hospital, he felt a sense of triumph. Sien was popular in the hospital. The nurses and doctors all knew her and liked her.

At home, she was a little mother, a tame dove. The cradle and baby's clothes delighted Vincent beyond description. He watched over the baby, not giving too much thought to the fact that he was not the child's father.

He cared for them both. He endured her family's nastiness and put up with Sien's own unhappiness from time to time. Yet, the arrangement with her seemed to be working so well that even his brother Theo thought of finding a woman of similar background for himself. Like Vincent, he, too, met a woman who had suffered at the hands of fate, and was deserted and helpless. Like his brother, Theo took her to doctors, arranged for hospital care, and nursed her back to health after her operation. And always, Vincent's sympathy and understanding were there to encourage his brother when it was needed.

In spite of all Vincent's efforts, fate worked against him. Sien failed him. She turned back to her old ways ignoring his pleas and forgetting his devotion. She once again took to the streets. Vincent was shattered. His depression returned, and brought with it a loss of appetite, dizziness, headaches and other such problems that kept him constantly ill and miserable.

Theo's allowance was not sufficient, and Vincent was plagued by poverty. At times, he had no money either for himself or for Sien or her family. Sometimes he was so hungry that he grew faint. Vincent and Sien's personal relationship was poor. He had thought he could make a companion of Sien, but to her, back in her old ways, Vincent was some queer stranger who belonged to another world.

Sien's mother began to prod her daughter to enter a brothel. This is where she belonged, her mother counseled—in a brothel, not in an artist's garret. Vincent fought the idea and decided to take her to the country where they would be among peasants, and where the living was inexpensive. He wanted to work, steadily and uninterruptedly. He had a feeling that not too many years of life lay ahead for him. Sien made no objection to moving, but displayed no enthusiasm. Her prostitute-mother continued to brainwash her, and, in the end, Vincent went alone.

As he bade her farewell, Vincent said: "I don't suppose you will be able to be altogether honest, but be as honest as you can. I'll try to be as straight as I can myself, although I can tell you right away that I shall never get through life as I should like. . . Even if you are only a poor woman and a prostitute, as long as you act so that your children find a real mother in you, in spite of all your faults, you will be good in my eyes. . . I will try, too. I must work hard, and so must you!"

Vincent left for Drenthe in September 1883. It was poor, dreary country with thatched huts shared by both man and beast. For a time, it seemed as if Vincent had found what he was seeking. It did not take long, however, for his self-imposed exile to gnaw at him. He blamed his father; blamed his ill health; even blamed Theo, accusing him of refusing to understand his relationship with Sien. He insisted that this lack of understanding had caused the split between Sien and himself. He attacked his rich uncles. Only when his mother seriously injured her hip, and was bedridden because of it, did his accusations cease; and he cared for her with tenderness and devotion.

Van Gogh struggled with the emptiness within him; it was as if he had come no closer to knowing love than when he was 20. Once again, he yearned for the closeness of a woman and for a deep relationship. This, he felt, he found in a lonely spinster, Margot Begemann, who lived next door to the parsonage. She had helped him nurse his mother back to health.

Margot was 10 years older than Vincent, and was neither beautiful nor gifted. They were drawn together by a common loneliness and the need for companionship. It wasn't long before they were discussing marriage, and Vincent would have married her, had they been left alone.

They took long walks together and Vincent brought her new hope and the chance of a new life. When Margot told Vincent that she wanted to die, he talked to her—tried to help her. He knew that her family relationship was at the root of her trouble. This confused and frightened her. Torn between Vincent and her family, she attempted suicide by taking strychnine, which made Vincent exclaim: "How absurd was the love of these respectable people who took poison instead of struggling with themselves! How absurd was their mysticism which they called religion!" Margot was sent off to a sanitarium in Utrecht. Once again, Vincent had failed to establish a meaningful relationship with a woman.

Vincent's deep melancholia seems to have been present from

his earliest years. He felt that his youth was "gloomy and cold and sterile." He felt he had been deprived of mother-love, and a mother's attention. In all of his letters to his mother, seldom, if ever, is a word of affection to be found. He openly accused his mother of cutting off every opportunity for him to discuss the unhappiness of his life with her.

"There really are no more unbelieving and hard-hearted and wordly people than clergymen and especially clergymen's wives," Van Gogh once said. In later years, he rarely mentioned his mother. In March 1885, he protested that his mother, upon the death of his father, selfishly wanted the whole inheritance transferred to herself.

There was a time, he swore, when he would no longer write to her. Yet, soon after, he included this poem in a letter to her:

> All evil has come from women; obscured rea-
> son,
> Appetite for lucre, treachery . . .
> Golden cups in which the wine is mixed with
> lees,
> Every crime, every happy lie, every folly
> Comes from her. Yet adore her, as the gods
> Made her . . . and it is still the best thing they
> did.

Albert J. Lubin, in his psychological biography of Vincent van Gogh, entitled *Stranger on the Earth*, stated: "Because of the powerful tendency to repeat behavior patterns, a man's feelings about women reflect in some measure his attitude toward the first woman in his life. The mate he chooses, the tendency toward success or failure in love, the kind of love relations he seeks, all bear the stamp of his first love, both in its sweet and its bitter components."

Lubin then relates this generality to Vincent van Gogh's relations with women which ended in disaster. Ursula and Kee's refusal to give him love caused him intense suffering. Sien proved to be completely untrustworthy, and he was forced to forsake both her and her children. Margot's problems added to the turmoil in her family and finally led to her attempted suicide.

Lubin then points out that with Ursula and Kee he placed himself in the position of a child demanding the love of an unloving mother, and with Sien and Margot he reversed the role, becoming a parent whose child could not accept the loving care he offered. In all these relationships, the evidence suggests that Vincent unconsciously sought out situations that would result in disappointment and humiliation.

A study of Vincent's work shows that most of the women he depicted are marked by sadness and tragedy. Early portraits on display at The Hague, Drenthe, and Nuenen show women with bowed heads and downcast eyes—women brought low by the cares and sorrows of a fruitless existence. A.M. Hammacher points out that many of his portraits of women combine the features of the grieving Kee and the miserable Sien.

In Antwerp, Vincent once commented that he preferred painting a woman's figure to possessing it; in that way he was in no danger of disillusionment and depression.

It was in Paris that Vincent's joy as an artist emerged and flourished. There, all his inhibitions vanished. There, everyone appreciated his cool, artistic manner, and there Theo was at his side. In Paris, he found sunshine and warmth, and friendly people everywhere. All discord seemed to have vanished and Vincent felt at home. Life was calm, without turmoil. There was music in the air, and he joined in the chorus. He could never have hoped for such joy and satisfaction.

He now painted flowers; and the beauty of Paris was present in his work. He held Paris in the hollow of his hand like a blossom. He was intoxicated with happiness. Julius Meier-Graefe, in his biography of Vincent van Gogh, wrote: "The Dutchman began to sing melodies from lungs which had nearly atrophied; they were new tunes no one had ever heard before in Paris."

During his two years in Paris, Vincent turned out more oils than drawings: about 200 oils, 10 water-colors, and 40 drawings. Seeing himself as a deteriorating "little old man," he tried to create pictures with youth and freshness.

Included among his vast output were 25 self-portraits. His work in Paris was greatly influenced by the Impressionists. Unfortunately, after a while, Van Gogh became disillusioned with Paris. He wrote: "When I left Paris I was seriously ill, sick at heart and in body, and nearly an alcoholic." He and his brother Theo decided to move to Arles. A friend had described the great beauty that surrounds the plain near Arles; living there was cheaper, and peasant models were readily available.

They arrived in Arles on February 26, 1888. Everything was lovely, including the brothels. Vincent began to paint. He painted 10 pictures of Arles' flowery gardens. He worked hard, never pausing for a moment. At night he was exhausted and hungry. Painting was his life; it was a substitute for people.

At night he often read. He read Zola, the Goncourts, Maupassant—everything he could put his hands on. He devoured literature as he had devoured the shades of light and color each day. But money was scarce and he was hindered in his frantic desire to paint more and more, because he was unable to afford the pigments and canvas he required. His productivity as an artist was at a high level; still, he was assailed by the thought that he did not really know life.

Fortunately, at this juncture he met Gauguin, the French artist who decided to move in with him. Not only did he now have a friend, but others came to visit often. His energy increased, and his dark mood subsided.

Gauguin arrived in Arles on October 20, 1888, eight months after Vincent's arrival. He was a most remarkable man. He was cold outwardly but a warm heart beat within. He was practical, and he could make instant decisions. He was a remarkable artist and could be an extraordinary friend. However, his demeanor was like that of a monarch and everyone submitted to his will.

Gauguin discovered evil moods in Vincent. He saw Vincent as too slovenly, as unable or unwilling to think a matter through.

Gauguin's approach was too stinging for Vincent. They clashed often. Vincent could not endure Gauguin's mud-slinging at others; and, within two months, Vincent's affection for him ended. He failed with Gauguin as he had with everyone else.

On December 23, Vincent wrote: "I think myself that Gauguin was a little out of sorts with the good town of Arles, the little yellow house where we work, and especially with me." That very night Vincent mutilated his ear in a state of violent agitation. The incident caused Gauguin to flee and Vincent was hospitalized in the Hotel Dieu.

The incident of cutting off a piece of his ear and presenting it to Rachel, a prostitute, gave rise to the popular notion that great artists are basically insane. The incident happened at about midnight. A present was handed to a little brunette, as she was dancing. The present was from Monsieur Fou-roux. She stopped dancing and proceeded to open the wrappings, one after another. The last wrapping was bloodstained and contained a piece of canvas which was also soaked in blood. All the girls had gathered around by now. They looked on in amazement. It was a real ear!

Who had brought the parcel? Where was its owner?

When Gauguin returned home, he found a crowd in front of the yellow house. Rumors were flying. It was announced that Vincent was dead, and that the murderer was known. Gauguin, with his usual calm, made his way through the crowd, went upstairs and there found the doctor, the police, and the postman, all gathered around a bloodstained bed.

By this time, Vincent had been bandaged, but he was unconscious. Now and then, he regained consciousness. Theo had been summoned. When Vincent saw his brother, his only thought was to apologize to his brother for spoiling his vacation.

The Dutch psychoanalyst, A. J. Westerman Holstijn has

pointed out that two frustrations contributed to the self-mutilation: Theo's engagement, and the collapse of the relationship with Gauguin. Westerman Holstijn was the first to suggest that Vincent's ear was a phallic symbol and that the act represented castration. Jacques Schnier, art professor and psychoanalyst, agreed that the self-mutilation resulted from aggression turned inward, that the ear was a phallic symbol, and that the act was a symbolic castration. He also suggested that the giving of the ear to a prostitute fulfilled an unconscious wish to possess his mother.

Rachel, the prostitute to whom Vincent presented his ear as a gift, was but one more woman in his life with whom he had had a miserable relationship. In Arles, Vincent's visits to prostitutes was a regular habit. As one observer said, "He was always hanging around in brothels."

To Vincent, "prostitutes were truly human." To Theo, he had written: "And I tell you frankly, in my opinion, one must not hesitate to go to a prostitute occassionally if there is one you can trust and feel something for, as there really are many."

He once confided: "I know full well that whores, frankly speaking, are bad, but I feel something human in them which prevents me from feeling the slightest scruple about associating with them . . . If our society were pure and well regulated, yes, then they would be seducers; but now, in my opinion, one may often consider them mere sisters of charity."

Vincent left the hospital in Arles on January 7, 1889, two weeks after the ear mutilation, and returned to his painting. Early in February, he had another psychotic attack and was incarcerated in a hospital. As Vincent told his brother: "Anyhow, here I am, shut up in a cell all the livelong day, under lock and key, and with keepers, without any guilt being proved or even open to proof . . . So you understand what a staggering blow between the eyes it was to find so many people here cowardly enough to join together against one man, and that man ill."

On May 8th, Pastor Salles took Vincent into the asylum of Saint-Remy. There he began to paint. Vincent had regained some hope that he might recover. He decided that he would search out the causes of his fits. He knew that they were violent because, for weeks after they occurred, he felt shaken, and could only regain his strength gradually.

His illness did not interfere with his painting, however, and he was content to remain an invalid. Dr. Peyron gave him permission to take his easel into the open, and so he painted the fields. It was at this time that he painted the cornfield with the sower and the large sun. Once, while painting, he had a fit during which he screamed so violently that his throat became inflamed and he could not eat for days.

The nightmare of being cloistered at Saint-Remy ended on May 17, 1890. He went to Paris and met Theo and Theo's wife. She found nothing strange about her brother-in-law, except his ear, which she did not dare to look at.

A surge of energy and the desire to paint seized Vincent. He went to Auvers, where he planned to live. He was happy again and said that to be back among painters, having discussions with them, was like a healing balm.

He did not establish close relationships with the other artists, however. It was enough to be in their midst. In Auvers, he painted 70 oils, 30 water-colors and drawings, and one etching. He drove himself faster and faster.

In spite of the accessibility of Theo in nearby Paris, the brothers saw each other only twice during the 70 days Vincent spent in Auvers. Although he pleaded with Theo to spend his vacation with him, Theo and his family left for Holland as planned.

On the afternoon of Sunday, July 27, shortly after Theo returned, Vincent shot himself with a revolver. He was in the fields at the time, and stumbled back to the inn. Two doctors examined him and both agreed that the bullet was inaccessible. Vincent was not in great pain. His mind was clear, and he smoked his pipe throughout the night.

Theo was summoned. When he arrived at his brother's bedside, Vincent said, "Do not cry, I did it for the good of everybody." He died peacefully in Theo's arms at one o'clock in the morning of Tuesday, July 29, just four months after his 37th birthday. His last words to his devoted brother Theo, in Dutch, were: "Now I want to go home."

12

Sarah Bernhardt: The Woman who Captured the Hearts of the World

Sarah Bernhardt, the vibrant, sparkling Frenchwoman, is considered by many to be the greatest actress who ever lived. There was a time when Sarah Bernhardt was known as "The Eighth Wonder of the World." Kings and emperors bowed to her. Royalty showered her with jewels. Admiring mobs placed their jackets on the ground so that her feet would not touch the cold cement. If all newspaper and magazine reviews written about her during the more than 60 years of her career were placed end-to-end, they would stretch completely around the world. And, if all her printed photographs were placed one on the top of the other, they would reach the top of the Eiffel Tower.

The British critic, Arthur Symons, characterized her acting as "an irresistible expression of a temperament; it mesmerized one, awakening the senses and sending the intelligence to sleep."

The poet, Theodore de Banville, said: "One can't praise her for knowing how to speak verse. She is the Muse of Poetry. . . She recites as the nightingale sings, as the wind sighs, as water murmurs. . ."

Maurice Baring, the British man of letters, likened her to "a symphony of golden flutes and muted strings . . . so pure, so tender, so harmonious, that if one fine day Mme. Sarah Bernhardt ceased to speak and began to sing, it would not surprise me."

No actress in the history of the theater ever had more written about her, either as praise or as vicious censure. The gossip spread about her once caused Sarah to declare, "I am the most lied-about woman in the world."

Sarah had numerous lovers. But, none were allowed to interfere with her many and assorted interests and hobbies. At one time or another she took up sculpture, painting, writing, piano playing, sharpshooting, fishing and alligator hunting.

Cornelia Otis Skinner, in her book, *Madame Sarah*, describes Sarah as follows: ". . . Her face, the shape of a young Pharaoh's, was hollow-cheeked and colorless, and she emphasized its pallor with slathers of white *poudre-de-riz*. Her eyes were shaped like a cat's, blue as star sapphires when she was in a good mood; when she was angry, they deepened into a brooding slate color with threatened flashes of green. Her nose was straight and Hebraic.

Her mouth could be passionately expressive one moment and slyly prim the next. Her hair was a reddish blonde mop, thick, fuzzy and completely unruly. She arranged it in a disordered twist held more or less in place with a single heavy pin of carved ivory. If Sarah Bernhardt was no true beauty, she could create the illusion of great beauty. She was so great, so famous, that she was called Madame Sarah, or Dame Sarah, or Sarah the Divine."

She was born in Paris on October 23, 1844, to Judith Van Hard, a Jewish Dutch woman who worked as milliner until she decided to take up a more lucrative, if less respectable, profession. Judith was beautiful, and could turn men's heads as well as their pockets. She was so successful at this line of work that money was no great concern.

She found little time for daughter, Sarah, born out of wedlock.

Up to the age of four, Sarah was raised by a wet nurse, later by her Tante Rosine, and for some time by her mother. At the age of eight, Sarah could neither read nor write. Her mother, desirous of ridding herself of the responsibility, sent Sarah to Madame Fressard's pension for young ladies. Here, Sarah spent two years. She learned how to embroider, write, read, count, and say a few Christian prayers. Over a period of two years, her mother visited her twice.

At ten, Sarah's mother, although steadfastly Jewish, placed her daughter in the convent of Grandchamps at Versailles. This she thought would give her daughter a better chance of penetrating the Parisian smart set. The nuns were very considerate of their new pupil.

From this time on, Sarah was raised as a Catholic, but she never forgot her Jewish origin. She had the courage to defend Dreyfus, and she never permitted an anti-Semitic statement to be made in her presence. When asked if she was a Christian later in life, she replied: "No, I'm a Roman Catholic, and a member of the great Jewish race."

Sarah's formal education lasted about six years. Her adult education was derived from conversations with brilliant men and women. She was a good listener and could quickly absorb what was being said.

The first hint that Sarah would become an actress occurred when Sarah's mother was discussing the youngster's future with two gentlemen. Sarah said that she wanted to be a nun. One of the men present ridiculed her, and Sarah put on her first dramatic scene. She screamed, she scratched, she tore fistfuls of hair from the gentleman's head. It was then that Duc de Morny, who witnessed the scene, remarked: "The girl's a born actress."

"An actress! she cried. "Never!"

That night she was taken to the theater. Seated next to Duc de Morny and Alexandre Dumas, Sarah again put on a dramatic scene which convinced Dumas that she was indeed cut out to be an actress.

Slowly, Sarah accepted the idea of becoming an actress. She took speech lessons from Monsieur Meydieu, and Dumas coached her as well, putting her through rigorous rehearsals. Sarah's audition at the Conservatoire was successful, and she was enrolled as a pupil.

Her debut as an actress was by no means sensational; it wasn't even good. She was seized with a terrifying attack of stage fright which made her performance utterly amateurish.

For almost four years, Sarah was eager to be on the stage, but the stage did not call her. There were simply no roles for her. It was during this time that Sarah began taking on lovers. It seemed the proper thing to do. Her mother and aunt had set the example, and it came to her quite naturally. In fact, they at once toyed with the idea of training her for this financially rewarding but precarious profession.

Her first lover was Emile de Keratry, an officer of hussars. He was goodlooking, had a good sense of humor, and wore a uniform—which helped make him irresistible. Their affair was short-lived. She was then just 18.

In Belgium, she met her next lover, the father of her child. She first saw Henri de Ligne at a masked ball. She was dressed as Queen Elizabeth; he, as Prince Hamlet. Henri knew just what he wanted. He didn't hesitate, he didn't procrastinate. The following day, he lifted the blushing Sarah and drove her directly to his palatial estate. She was not seen by her friends for the next eight days. She was completely incommunicado. The Queen and the Prince were having their own ball.

It was soon afterwards that Sarah found herself pregnant. She let no one in on her secret. And it was only when her state of pregnancy became more and more apparent that she decided to tell her mother.

Her mother became enraged. She would not permit a bastard to be born under her roof! She seemed to have forgotten that she, Judith, had mothered three bastards, each from a different father.

Sarah moved into her own apartment and found a job as an actress playing small walk-on parts. Her financial problems were solved by the arrival of Prince Henri de Ligne. When Henri learned that he was the father of Sarah's unborn child, he was delighted. He was in love with her and she with him. In fact, after a month of blissful togetherness, he decided to tell his parents of his intention to marry her. They reacted sharply and negatively, as might be expected of a titled family receiving news of their son's plan to marry a Jewish actress whom he had impregnated. The affair was promptly terminated!

Once again Sarah turned to the theater and found a place in the Odéon, a repertory theater on the Left Bank. She signed a contract for 150 francs per moth. Her big break came in 1868 with the revial of *Kean*. Sarah was cast in the leading female role, playing Anna Damby. She was a great hit, and, for the first time, ardent fans waited at the stage door, cheering and tossing flowers. This happened again and again—after each performance—and Sarah became one of the most popular actresses of the Odéon.

As her success expanded, so did the rumors about her. Her name was linked to the emperor's cousin, Prince Napoleon, son of King Jerome. Following a performance which Prince Napoleon's sister, the Princess Mathilde, had set up as a command performance, and which was attended by Louis-Napoleon himself, the emperor sent Sarah Bernhardt a magnificent brooch bearing the imperial initials in diamonds.

In early summer of 1870, when Sarah was 26 years old, war broke out between Prussia and France. Sarah got permission to set up a 32-bed hospital in the foyer and lobby of the First National Theater to attend to the needs of war casualties. She then set out to solicit her influential acquaintances for medical supplies. She worked like a trojan, performing all kind of duties, including that of head nurse. Her endurance and her fortitude were phenomenal, and she won the respect of the French people.

Late in 1871, the Odéon management decided to produce Victor Hugo's *Ruy Blas*. Sarah Bernhardt was to be the star. After her performance on the night of January 16, 1872, the house went wild. The audience, which included the Prince of Wales, Victor Hugo, and any number of other celebrities, acclaimed her as the First Lady of the theater.

With Sarah Bernhardt playing the role of the Queen, *Ruy Blas* was the hit of the season. She was offered a contract of 12,000 francs a year by Emile Perrin, the administrator of the Française. She accepted although it meant paying 6,000 francs in damages to the management of the Odeéon for breach of contract.

Sarah's star continued to rise, and, as it did, so did the rumors. It was whispered that at 11 Boulevard de Clichy, orgies of an immoral nature were going on equal to those of the *Quat'z Arts Ball*—and that Sarah attended them. It was also claimed that because of her interest in sculpture, she undressed her guests. There was talk about the coffin she kept in her bedroom, the coffin her mother had bought her when she was a girl. Sometimes she slept in it. It was said that once or twice she allowed a few intimate friends to see her lying in it. The stories knew no bounds.

Sarah then met her next lover. He was Jean Mounet-Sully, an exceptionally good-looking actor. Both had been members of the Odéon company at one time, and Sarah was completely taken in by his masculine beauty. This love affair lasted for many months, with the approval of the public. How the Parisians loved the affair between the greatest male and female stars of the time!

During her years with the Française, Sarah's health was anything but good. Yet she continued with her acting career. She starred in *Zäire*; played the title role in *Phèdre*—a performance which was considered unexcelled artistry. In 1877, her outstanding role was her Donna Sol in Victor Hugo's *Hernani*. Victor Hugo after attending a performance, wrote to Sarah:

> Madame, you were great and charming; you moved me—me the old warrior—and, at a certain moment when the public, touched and enchanted by you, applauded, I wept. This tear which you caused me to shed is yours. I place it at your feet.

The "tear" he sent her was a single perfect diamond attached to a delicate gold chain bracelet.

In 1879, in England, she met her friend Oscar Wilde. They had met earlier in Paris and were old friends. He adored her and wrote *Salomé* especially for her. Before it was produced, Wilde's star broke and he found himself in Reading Gaol. He needed both money and the support of his friends. Although Sarah was not among those to come to his aid at the time, he nevertheless continued to love her. And, shortly before he died, he told a friend that "the three women I most admired in my life are Sarah Bernhardt, Lily Langtry and Queen Victoria."

Sarah met with success in England, and, while there, she was told she could make a fortune in the United States. With this encouragement, she set off to conquer the new world. And conquer it she did! Madame Sarah had become a *must* among theatergoers. In play after play she brought down the house, taking curtain call after curtain call. The box office at Booth's Theatre was enjoying a thriving business.

One evening, as a publicity stunt, the management arranged a meeting between the most famous man in America, Thomas Edison, and the most famous French woman, Sarah Bernhardt. Edison received her with polite formality; but she soon captivated him. Writing in her memoirs about this visit, she stated:

> His marvellous blue eyes, more luminous than his incandescent lamps, permitted me to read all his thoughts. I realized that I must conquer

him, and my combative spirit summoned forth
all my seductive forces to win over this shy and
delightful scholar . . .
A half hour later we were the best of friends.

Sarah Bernhardt's successes in the United States and Canada
were fantastic. She was serenaded by Harvard students; she met
with Henry Wadsworth Longfellow, then 73, as well as with
Oliver Wendell Holmes. Everywhere she went, she was *the*
woman of the hour.

It was no different in Montreal where her performances met
with hugh success. Everywhere, she was received by tremendous
crowds, and box office receipts reflected her popularity.

Sarah's reputation as a great lover continued as new leading
men came to play opposite her and were captivated by her mys-
tique. One reporter asked her, "Is it true that you have had four
children and never one husband?" "Certainly not!" she retorted.
"But at least that would be better than the case of some of your
American women who have had four husbands and never any
children."

When she returned to New York from Canada, she had given
157 performances in 51 cities. It was a triumphal return. She gave
a final New York performance, and then sailed for France. Sarah
Bernhardt, who did not believe in checks or in banks, had demanded that she be paid for her performances in gold coins, and
in her baggage was a strong metal chest containing $194,000 in
gleaming, gold coins.

Her return to Paris was a joyous occasion. Her son, Maurice,
met her on the dock along with crowds of well-wishers. But, once
the joy and excitement of homecoming was over, Sarah wanted
to work. Her life was acting, and not one play was being offered
her. She knew that her $194,000 would not last too long—not
with the way she and Maurice were accustomed to spending
money.

To help change the situation, Sarah contrived a plot. The
noted actress, Madame Agar, was to appear in the *Spirit of the
Marseillaise*. One of Madame Agar's maids, who joined with
Sarah in her intrigue, informed the Madame that her handsome
officer had suffered a bad fall from his horse, and had been taken
to the hospital. Madame Agar bounced out of her seat and was
on the first train bound for Tours so she could be with her captain. Before leaving, she told her maid to notify the Opéra Gala
that she could not appear that evening, and that a substitute
should be hired for the evening.

The maid conveniently forgot to give the message to the
theater.

When Sarah Bernhardt appeared in the wings of the Gala,

she was greeted with indifference. Smiling, she informed the managers that Madame Agar had gone off to the bedside of a dying relative, and had requested that Sarah take her place. Then, turning to the male star, her former lover, she said, "Mounet, *mon cher*, will you kindly help me off with my wrap?"

Mounet acted as if hypnotized. When he saw Sarah in her dazzling white robe, he was spellbound. Within minutes, she was on the stage before a silent audience. After her appearance, the house went wild. "Sarah! Our Sarah!" they shouted. After a prolonged absence abroad, Sarah had made her comeback.

Madame Agar was not at all angry with Sarah for having deceived her. She had found her captain alive and well, and ready to make love . . . which they did with abandon.

Once again Sarah went on tour, and once again she was successful wherever she appeared: London, Northern Italy, Greece, Hungary, Switzerland, Belgium and Holland. Everywhere, she was received with unbridled enthusiasm.

She arrived in Russia in the dead of winter, and it was here that Sarah Bernhardt met Jacques Damala—the cause of the great tragedy in her life. Eleven years younger, he was an Adonis; he was also vain, haughty, and despicable. His reputation was that of a Don Juan who had women at his beck and call, and whom he treated with utter disdain. Women lost their heads when meeting him. The scandal columns were full of stories about his love affairs and wild escapades—many of which were brought on by his addiction to morphine.

When the divine Sarah set eyes upon him, she succumbed no less that the other women. She, who had had numerous love affairs; she, who had handled men of royalty and men of wealth with ease, acted like a fool with Jacques Damala. He swept her completely off her feet; and, at the same time, made her forget that she was Sarah Bernhardt, adored by all of France, if not the whole of Europe. To her, this love was the grief of passion—a middle-aged woman's desire to be with a younger man.

Damala knew how to handle this love-struck woman who was eleven years his senior. He was casual, didn't flinch in her presence, was totally poised, and completely impersonal. Infatuated by his goodlooks, disarmed by his casual, sophisticated manner, she offered him a role in her next play. He reacted evasively, keeping her in a state of uncertainty about his intentions and feelings. He was warm and cordial one day, formal and impersonal the next. He was like an expert fisherman who knew how to let the reel go slack, and knew exactly when to pull it in.

During this entire period, Sarah's heart ached for a positive sign from Jacques. Summoning all her talents as an actress, she turned on all her womanly charms, charms which had in the past caused men to become her slaves.

Damala was unmoved and unimpressed. Not once during this entire period did he attempt to embrace or kiss her. He went no further than to kiss the back of her hand in bidding her farewell. He followed this with a whisper: "Come to St. Petersburg. I'll be waiting for you."

Sarah was overcome by hunger for this seducer of women. She wanted him more than she had ever wanted anybody. Her current lover—a gifted actor named Philippe Garnier—did not interest her. She hungered only for Damala. Sarah went about rearranging her schedule so that she could play in St. Petersburg in January—the earliest booking she could manage.

In St. Petersburg, the Bernhardt-Damala affair started at a furious pace. They were seen all over town together. Sarah would accept no invitation that did not include Damala. At one performance, she was invited to supper by the Grand Duke. When she demanded that Damala be invited as well, the invitation was withdrawn.

Sarah was in love—madly, insatiably in love. She was infatuated, befuddled, fascinated by this lover of hers. But Sarah was soon to discover the great truth of Antoine Bret's observation: "The first sign of love is the last of wisdom."

If Sarah Bernhardt didn't care about her reputation, her former lover, Philippe Garnier, did. His pride was hurt over being summarily dropped from her life, and he could not bear the sight of so great an actress becoming the tool of this debased "youngster." Quietly, he resigned from the cast of *Froufrou*, using the excuse that the Russian winter was too severe for him. Sarah promptly saw to it that this leading spot was given to Damala who now played the lead of Sartorys. Damala was a rank amateur. He had nothing to offer but his good looks. His lack of technique, his poor timing and his atrocious accent made his lines almost unintelligible.

Despite all these shortcomings, Sarah unquestioningly believed in him and thought him to be a genius. She was convinced he would prove to be one of the most brilliant newcomers to the theater. She was completely blind to his lack of talent, as well as to his poor character. She refused to acknowledge the truth about Damala even when she saw him openly flirting with other young actresses in the cast.

Sarah, now almost 40, watched him as he made advances to younger women, and she decided that she did not want to lose him. Against all logic, she proposed to Damala who lost no time in agreeing to marry her. Thus the great Sarah Bernhardt and the nonentity Damala were united in marriage. This was both the joke and the calamity of the age.

Soon after the marriage, Sarah gave a benefit performance of *La Dame Aux Camelias.* Her husband was cast in the same play. The reviews praised her performance, and severly criticized his. Damala was enraged and blamed Sarah for his poor showing. Although she attempted to placate him by showing him her own poor early notices, it did little good.

A few weeks later, Sarah played *La Dame* in London. Damala was given the male lead. Again, Sarah was praised generously. The Prince and Princess of Wales attended one of the performances and personally congratulated her. As always, the audiences went wild over Sarah. Damala was ignored.

None of this pleased Damala, who was beginning to doubt the wisdom of having married Sarah. He was upset and irritated, and was taking still larger doses of morphine. To placate him once again, Sarah signed a lease for the Ambigu Theater, and installed her son as the managing producer and director.

She searched and found a play in which her husband could star: *Les Mères Ennemies.* This time the reviews were kind, and Damala was somewhat pacified. But it did not last for long.

At the time that Damala was appearing in his play, Sarah opened in another play: *Fedora.* She was superb, and received excellent notices. One day, Damala, who had come to pick up Sarah, arrived early enough to see the final act of the play. He saw the crowds stand up and cheer at the end of the performance. He noticed the bouquets of flowers that were piled high in the corridors leading to her dressing room. Viewing his wife's great triumph was an upsetting experience for him.

From that time on, his attitude toward his wife, never good, turned to sheer disdain. He humiliated her at every opportunity, spent her money to send gifts to other women, charged her with pushing him into an unwanted marriage, and finally declared that he wanted freedom from his marital slavery.

One evening in particular, their feud was louder and longer than usual. The next morning, he departed for North Africa to enlist in a company of Algerian guards. He notified no one, not even the theater where he was playing a role in a current production.

Damala's sudden desertion at last touched Sarah's pride. She had permitted Damala to make a fool of her and this was extremely damaging to her ego. In addition, the Ambigu Theater had proven to be a financial disaster. She had sunk 200,000 francs into this venture. She lost another 400,000 francs producing a play at the Ambigu, which received good reviews but ran for only 50 performances. Her love for Damala had cost her money, pride, and embarrassment. Longfellow judged such a situation wisely when he wrote: "Love gives itself; it is not bought."

Sarah decided to close her own play and go on the road. She believed that a tour of European cities would be more rewarding financially. She also took on a new lover, Jean Richepin, a playwright.

He, like Damala, was a healthy specimen of a man with broad shoulders and an outgoing personality. He was handsome, bearded, and casual in his dress. He was an outdoor man who could be found any early morning bicycling around the lake.

Jean had held down several jobs in the past: as stevedore, boxer, wrestler, weightlifter, even poet. At one time, he had lived with a band of gypsies.

He was like a breath of fresh air, and it didn't take long before Sarah's spirits and energy were restored.

Their affair was an open secret. In Copenhagen, George Brandes wrote, "Sarah the Divine was here with her shadow, Jean Richepin, the poet of *Les Caresses*. She was always with him —she dined and slept with him."

A surprise was to greet Sarah upon her return home one evening. Her staff tried to break it to her mildly: Her husband, Jacques, had returned and was now lying on his bed, stark naked, reading a novel. When she entered the room and asked him the reason for his return, he coldly replied that it was his house as well as hers. Having said this, he returned to his reading.

Life became hell once more for Sarah. As she played in the theater, her husband spent time making love to the women he brought home with him. He would often wander around the house in a morphine-induced stupor. At every opportunity, he insulted her; and more than once referred to her as "the long-nosed Jewess."

When Sarah learned that he was openly carrying on an affair with a young girl in her own troupe, she fired the girl. Damala immediately took off with his girl to Monte Carlo where he lost 80,000 francs. He wired Sarah for more money. She sent it to him, and such was her need that she begged him to return. This he did, with his lover—who promptly put in a claim for back wages.

Damala turned more and more to the use of morphine. Sarah searched his room at every opportunity, throwing out the morphine and drugs she found. But it did little good. He purchased additional supplies. Finally, he agreed to go to a sanitarium for treatment, which was partially successful.

Jacques was temporarily cured, and obtained a part in *Maître des Forges*. In it, he scored a personal triumph. But his success was brief, and again he started to drift aimlessly about, seeking solace in drugs. This time, the drugs proved too much, and, in 1889, Jacques Damala, at the age of 34, was dead.

Sarah had his body shipped back to Greece along with a bust she had sculpted of him. It was to be placed on his tomb. At 45, Sarah Bernhardt was a widow, but her new status made very little difference in her life.

She now began to work even harder, and she did many plays, both new and old. In 1891, she went on a two-year tour which took her almost around the world. Her earnings were large —about 3,500,000 francs.

She produced her own plays, and she worked harder and longer than before. Success followed success, but hard work and long hours began to affect Sarah's health. She traveled throughout the United States, making appearances in city after city. In New York's Winter Garden Theater alone—from 1899 to 1915— Sarah Bernhardt appeared in 40 different roles

Her mad pace caught up with her, and, in 1916, Sarah wired Mrs. Campbell, an actress friend:

Doctor will cut off my leg Monday.

Am very happy. Kisses all my heart.

Although she never lied about her age, Sarah Bernhardt could not admit that she was ill and getting older. Nevertheless, when she had recovered sufficiently, she continued her tour. In 1921, she took seriously ill. For a month, she remained on the critical list. But she recovered and for a time kept up with her new scripts. On March 21, 1923 she collapsed, and for five days she remained in a state of semiconsciousness. When she finally opened her eyes, she murmured: "It will be a beautiful spring. There will be lots of flowers."

Sarah Bernhardt was dying. The date was March 25 and she asked if there were any reporters outside. She was told there were. With a smile, knowing that this was the end, she whispered: "All my life, reporters have tormented me enough. I can tease them now a little by making them cool their heels." These were her final words. At 8:00 P.M. of the next evening she was pronounced dead by Dr. Marot.

The news, while expected, shocked Paris. "Their Sarah" had seemed immortal, and now she was dead. Thousands and thousands of people filed by her coffin. Although France did not award her a national funeral, the Parisians did. By following her hearse in great numbers, they conferred upon her the greatest honor possible.

The words of John Luckey McCreery seem appropriate for Sarah Bernhardt:

There is no death! the stars go down
   To rise upon some other shore,
And bright in Heaven's jeweled crown,
   They shine for ever more.

13

Rasputin: The Mad Lover

Grigori Efimovich Rasputin was known by many names: Rasputin, the Holy Devil; Rasputin, the Mad Monk; or, Rasputin, the Seducer of Women. Sigmund Freud, the father of psychoanalysis, in a letter to Réne Fülöp-Miller, one of Rasputin's biographers, commented: "Your book, *Rasputin*, has interested me extraordinarily. His regime is the happy union of sinful satisfaction of instincts and pious suppression of them—the very ideal of pleasure without payment. This is a happy solution of the external conflict between instinct and morality *ad absurdum*. As a matter of fact, everything is carried out which is supposed to be prevented . . ."

Rasputin believed in the doctrine of purification through sin. He was a ravisher of girls who mingled incense and brimstone to write one of the oddest and perhaps most sexually descriptive chapters in religious history. The women who were ushered into his private room never came out the same. They either gave in to his desires with abandon, or emerged screaming "rape!"

Born into an ordinary peasant family in 1871, Rasputin had a hysterical following drawn from all walks of life. He died a violent death: he was poisoned, shot and drowned. No one act by itself was able to do away with this strange, evil, and passionate man.

His enemies called him a hypnotist. When he came to power, he was approximately 40 years old, and, from his peasant's shirt and wide trousers to his heavy boots, he cut a figure of masculine strength. He came to court with the reputation of being a "new saint," a "miracle worker." And, for a while, it seemed as though he could indeed work miracles. When he stared into a person's eyes, after placing their hands in his own broad palms, that person was overcome by a strange, disturbing feeling. Rasputin's eyes seemed to probe and penetrate the innermost chambers of the mind and heart. It was as if he could see right into the soul.

It wasn't long before a wide circle of women from all classes of society—from nobility and wealth, down to maids and peasant women—looked on Rasputin as a higher, divine being. Grigori Efimovich was admired, pampered and worshipped everywhere.

And wherever he saw a beautiful woman and desired her, he pursued her. Few escaped his amorous advances.

There were those who attempted to fight Rasputin's magic. They tried to remain in control, and fought with all their might against his hypnotic eyes and manner. But even the few who succeeded could not completely escape his mysterious power. On the lips of many of the women whom he had ravished was the question, "Was Rasputin a saint or a libertine?" The question is still being asked today.

He could edge close to a woman, and his gentle, monastic gaze would quickly turn to that of a deliberate, diabolical seducer whose hot breath of desire almost scorched the recipient. His eyes, burning with sensual desire, roamed over her body, devouring her breasts, transferring his debased sexual longing to the woman who was compelled to surrender her body and soul to his.

Over the next few years Rasputin had to be called to save the tsar's son on several occasions. Each time he managed to effect a cure. Rasputin's influence at the court increased. He espoused causes which he thought were just. He convinced the tsar, in 1912, not to enter the Balkan conflict. Soon, no one could hope for a ministerial post unless he had been previously submitted to Rasputin for examination, and had passed creditably. In fact, in a conversation with Protopopov, Minister of the Interior, Rasputin boasted, showing his peasant fist, "Between these fingers I hold the Russian Empire!"

As Rasputin's influence grew, his apartment became the meeting place of many Russians. His home was closely guarded by the secret police, and was spied upon by others. Stories about his drinking habits and sexual conquests continued to circulate. When a woman visited him to ask him for help, he would take her into an adjoining room where he would touch her face, cup her breast, and ask that she kiss him. This would serve to prepare her for further ministrations.

Rumors of all Rasputin's involvement with women of all stations continued to surface. There was the prostitute Gregubova, Maria Gill, the wife of a captain in the 145th Regiment; the actress, Varvarova. On yet another occasion, he was discovered drunk with the 28-year-old wife of Yaziniski.

And now it came to be known that Rasputin had a price. He could arrange deals—to get appointments, arrange releases from military service, have prison sentences squashed—but all for a fee. Prices were set in advance.

A long line of favor-seekers came to him with gold and gifts. Women offered not only gold, but their own warm, charming, willing selves. They had learned that, better than with gold, Rasputin could be bought with moist, red, passionate lips. If he liked the seductive figure of a woman who offered herself as a gift, she was accepted with undisguised joy.

Very few female suppliants resisted Rasputin's advances. Many proudly boasted that they had given their bodies to this holy man. These women were eager to be admitted to Rasputin's mysterious "holy of holies." They were convinced that it was wrong for a woman to even consider not offering herself to this "saint." One such case occurred when a young novice refused to accede to Rasputin's advances. One of his disciples, a married woman, asked her in amazement: "Why do you not want to belong to him? How can one refuse anything to a saint?"

"Does a saint need sinful love?" inquired the novice. "What sort of saintliness is that?"

'He makes everything that comes near him holy," was the immediate reply.

"And would you be ready to accede to his desires?" was the next question.

"Of course. I have already belonged to him, and I am proud and happy to have done so."

"But you are married! What does your husband say to it?"

"He considers it a very great honor. If Rasputin desires a woman, we all think it a blessing and a distinction—our husbands as well as ourselves."

Rasputin was called a charlatan, a sex fiend, a seducer of defenseless women, but he was also reputed to be a religious man. He was both a loud drunkard and a pious reciter of psalms.

That he helped many is a fact. That he bedded down many is also a fact. That he made enemies, and was finally assassinated, is recorded in Russian history.

Grigori Efimovich Rasputin (the dissolute one) grew up like all peasant lads. He chased girls, frequented public houses, and led a disorderly and dissipated life. He worked during the day and was dead drunk almost every night.

He married the beautiful fair-haired, slim, dark-eyed Praslpvoa Fedorovna Dubrovina. After marriage, he continued to indulge in sexual intercourse with the village girls who were only too anxious to succumb to his manhood.

Rasputin told the story of how he came to know God's plan for him. While plowing a field, he heard a chorus sing. In front of him he saw an image, the holy Mother of God, swinging on the golden rays of the sun. He heard a thousand angels' voices singing, joined by the Virgin Mary. The entire vision lasted but a few minutes and then disappeared.

His daughter, Maria Rasputin recalled his vivid description:
It was in obedience to a call from the Beyond

that my father separated himself from his family and withdrew from the village of Pokrovskoie. He was already over 30 when he first heard the voice of God . . . At the time he could neither read nor write, but he departed to acquire religious training from monks and certain pious and learned men who taught verbally. With them, he passed several months in different monasteries. His first pilgrimage was made to the monastery of Balak, in Siberia.

Later, Rasputin visited the holy starets of Markari. There, Father Markari told him: "Rejoice, my son, for among many thousands the Lord hath chosen you. Great things lie before you. Leave your wife and children, leave your horses, hide yourself, go forth and wander! You will hear the earth speak and learn to understand its words. Then, and not till then, return to the world again, and proclaim to men what the voice of our holy Russian earth says to them!"

He did just that, encountering all sorts of men in his wanderings. He penetrated the deep secrets of the soul of the Russian people. In his intercourse with these people, he deepened his knowledge of theology, and acquired a skill in the use of Biblical texts that continued to amaze great men of the cloth.

Soon, stories began to filter back to the ears of his wife, stories that told of strange "services" in the forests with pretty young girls and women. Her husband was teaching the Gospel in a novel if not unusual way. Once his devotions were over, he would hug and kiss the women, explaining that it was part of the divine service. He did more than merely caress his "sisters," as he called his female disciples. Amidst their dancing, he would cry out in a strange voice: "Abase yourselves through sin! Try your flesh!" And he helped them try their flesh and abase themselves.

There were times when he took baths publicly and displayed himself to the women; he then made them undress as well. They would wash his feet, explaining that this action killed off the last remnants of their pride and self-righteousness.

Soon, stories were told about his miracles. He could curse a locale by preventing rain from falling for an extended period of time. He could cure the sick and bring solace to the troubled. Indeed, he was a miracle worker.

It wasn't long before Rasputin, now known as "the Siberian muzhik," appeared before the high priests at the Petersburg Seminary. There, he made a tremendous impression with the clarity of his thinking and with the logic of his words. He was interrogated for more than an hour and emerged as a great scholar. He was better able to explain the meaning of the Gospel than any of them—and with greater clarity.

Rasputin came to the tsar's attention at a most dramatic time. The tsar's son suffered from hemophilia, that terrible disease in which the slightest injury could prove fatal. Alexei, the son, was not permitted to ride a bicycle, play tennis, or indulge in most activities. The life of the future heir to the Russian throne was, from the beginning, a series of torments. He never dared to run or romp, and always he heard the voice: "Alexei, take care, you will hurt yourself."

Alexei's parents, although royalty, were no different from other parents. They consulted every doctor, every miracle worker, every saint, every magician; still, their son was not freed of the malady with which he was afflicted. Then, one day, Grigori Efimovich Rasputin appeared at the bedside of the unfortunate boy.

Alexei was very ill. Alexandra Fedorovna, Empress of Russia, sat by the bedside of her sick son. She gazed at his pale face, clenching and wringing her hands. She had not left his side for hours, and was agonized with worry.

The youngster had injured himself in an accident which, under normal circumstances, would have gone unnoticed. He was now bleeding internally, slowly. Doctors had been called. Consultations had been held. But all had to confess their impotence. The potions of a Tibetan magician had failed entirely, and magic herbs had not helped the sufferings of the young tsarevich. Alexandra threw herself down on her son's bed, imploring God to work a miracle and save her son from death.

Suddenly, a knock was heard and her sister entered. The empress listened as her sister told her of the miracle worker, the simple muzhik, Grigori Efimovich, who was endowed by God to help those in need. She had witnessed just such a miracle the other day, she said. He, if anyone, possessed great healing powers and could cure hopeless invalids.

For the first time in many days the empress smiled. She had found a new source of hope and her son could be saved. Without hesitation, she expressed a desire to meet this unique man.

The empress did not have long to wait. Grigori Efimovich was soon brought to court. During his initial visit, he wore a long, black caftan, the typical garb of a peasant. To the amazement of the nurse, Rasputin walked over to the imperial couple, embraced them and kissed both the tsar and his consort. Then, he prayed before the sacred ikons in the room. Finally, he went over to the child's bed, and made the sign of the cross. In a melodious voice, and stroking the boy from head to foot, Rasputin kept repeating, "Look, I have driven all your horrid pains away. Nothing will hurt you any more. Tomorrow you will be well again. Then, you will see what jolly games we'll have together." The boy's color seemed to return, and he no longer felt any pain. It appeared that a miracle had taken place.

As Rasputin was about to leave the sickroom, the empress seized his hands and kissed them. Rasputin was now a hero, and become one of the welcome visitors in the court of the tsar and tsarina. Soon, he was involved in all their troubles, and everyone confided in him. The entire imperial family loved and idolized Grigori Efimovich, and soon he acquired the nickname, "little Father Grigori."

But peace and joy did not reign in the court for long. Jealousy began to assert itself. The first to attack Rasputin was the governess of the tsar's daughters. She objected to Rasputin entering the girls' room when they were in bed. A flood of gossip now circulated among the ladies of the court—both old and young. It was reported that Rasputin had seduced and even raped the children's nurse, Vishniakova. Again and again, reports of his drunkenness and exploits with young girls and women were discussed. Incontrovertible, incontestable, unmistaken proof of his debaucheries were presented to the tsarina, but her faith in her friend, Rasputin, was unshaken.

Rasputin brought an end to the frustrations that plagued many women. To them he was a reincarnation of the Lord, and sexual intercourse with him could not possibly be sinful.

As far as Rasputin was concerned, women belonged to one of two groups: those with whom he could be intimate; and those yet to be initiated as an object of his lust. One of his most faithful women was the nun, Akulina Nikichkina, known as "the holy one." She was completely devoted to Rasputin because of her belief that he had banished Satan from her body. Now she was devoting her life to him.

Olga Vladimirovna Lokhtina, the wife of State Councillor Lokhtina, was a second member of his charmed circle. A truculent monk, Iliodor, had tried to seduce her when she was visiting the monastery at Tsarytsin. She resisted, and Iliodor proclaimed that a demon had entered her. The experience left her in a distraught, depressed condition which she could not shake off. Then she met Rasputin, and he cured her. She boasted that she had shared Rasputin's love. "What a saint does is holy, what he touches is blessed," she proclaimed, "what he loves attains the holiness of Heaven. Believe me, my sisters, the body of anyone who surrenders herself to this God becomes itself divine by contact with him."

A mother and her young daughter: Madame Golovina (a widow) and Maria, were disciples of Rasputin. Maria, as well as her mother, gave themselves to Rasputin. Whenever young Maria saw him, her cheeks flushed, her eyes glistened, and her entire body began to tremble.

There was an opera singer who regularly went to bed with Rasputin. Her husband knew of the affair, but did not object, convinced that intercourse with the holy man could only benefit his wife. She returned again and again.

Many women came to Rasputin because the fires of passion burned too brightly in their hearts, fires they could not extinguish without pangs of conscience. Rasputin helped them. He said: "God has granted me freedom from passion; I touch a woman, and it is as if I touched a bit of wood. I have no desires, and the spirit of passionless calm passes from me to the women with me, so that they, too, become pure and holy." To this holy form of intercourse, these women subscribed happily.

One of these women was Masha, a tall girl who attracted much attention because of her beauty. Often, she was observed visiting the apartment of Rasputin. Another was Princess Dolgo-rukaia, who left her home and children for Rasputin, as did Princess Ahakhovskaia.

Rasputin had even convinced his own family of his power to banish the devil, the carrier of sensual desire. Rasputin's wife, aware of her husband's infidelities, calmly and patiently accepted them. She, too, believed that he was entrusted by God with a higher mission, and that his debaucheries served a holy purpose. She served her husband like a faithful servant, as did Rasputin's daughters. Rasputin seemed to have everything: the power of the court; the loyalty of his family; and a long list of women, who were ever ready and eager to satisfy his every need.

Each day, when he returned to his "holy of holies" a line of women awaited him. Upon his entrance, they surrounded him, caressed him, kissed him. They swooned with happiness when he touched them. Whatever he did, they did, catering to him with unreserved fidelity. If he ate, they ate. If he drank, they drank. If he spoke, they listened. If he commanded, they obeyed.

While eating, he would take a beautiful girl on his knees, and softly stroke her hair. "You believe I pollute you; I do not pollute you, I rather purify you," he would say. He would stop and then continue: "If God sends us a temptation, we must yield to it voluntarily and without resistance, so that we may afterwards do penance in utter contrition." Looking around at his women, he would proclaim, "How can we repent if we have not sinned?" And he was even ready to lead them to sin and subsequent repentance.

When he would see an especially attractive woman among his disciples or petitioners, he would send her to the "little room" to wait for him. There was much gossip about "the little room." When Rasputin was in the "little room" with a woman, no one was allowed to enter. In fact, he was not to be disturbed by anyone or anything—except for a call from the royal court.

Many a young girl left the room with a happy, excited, radiant face. Some, however, rushed out, their clothes disarranged and crumpled, weeping and claiming they had been attacked. Not every pretty woman petitioner understood the "value" of this "holy" man. Some even complained to the police that Rasputin had raped them. The police noted the complaint, but took no action. They realized that Rasputin had protection in higher places.

Day and night, Rasputin was engaged with his ladies and suppliants. His strength never seemed to wane, nor did his appetite.

Bera Alexandrovna Shukovskaia related what went on when she found herself in the "little room" with the single window. The room was sparsely furnished. There was a plain-looking bed with a bulging mattress. No sooner did Rasputin enter the room when he sat down opposite her, taking her legs between his knees. As he brought her legs closer and closer to him, he stroked her face and said: "Listen to what I am going to say to you. Do you know the psalm: 'From my mouth up the lusts of the flesh have tormented me; Lord Jesus Christ, do not condemn me therefore?' Do you know it?"

"I know it well," she replied.

He then began to stroke her shoulders as he continued to speak: "Come to me often, little honey bee, love me and then you will understand everything. Love is the most important thing. From the loved one every word is clear; but so long as I am a stranger to you I may say what I like, and it will only go in at one ear and out the other." He then kissed her and continued: "Now I shall not let you go again. Once you have come to me you will not escape again! Understand clearly, I will do nothing to you, only come, my juicy cherry."

They spoke for a few minutes about sin. When she questioned him, he asked: "Do you want me to show you?" He then kissed her very gently and with some dignity. He asked her to come again Saturday evening, saying repeatedly, "You like me, don't you, so come. Will you come?"

"I will come," she said and then she departed.

Saturday evening brought Alexandrovna Shukovskaia back again. When she saw Rasputin, he wore a blue shirt, plush trousers, and brightly polished boots. He greeted her warmly, putting his arms around her shoulders. He bent down to kiss her. He then helped her off with her things and led her into the dining room where other women were present, 10 women to be exact, and one young man. Some were young and beautiful, one was pregnant, some had red eyes from constant weeping, several elegantly dressed.

The table was laden with heaps of foods, and Rasputin began to coax his guests to eat. He shelled hard-boiled eggs, and offered them to the outstretched hands of the women at the table. Rasputin, himself, ate with his fingers, wiping his hands on the tablecloth.

He then explained to the women that Alexandrovna was a difficult person. Before long, Rasputin was being kissed wildly by Madame Lokhtina. She covered him with kisses, all the while repeating: "Oh my dearest . . . vessel of blessing . . . Ah, your lovely beard . . . Your delicious hair . . . me, the martyr . . . You precious pearl . . . you precious stone . . . you my adored one . . . my beloved!"

Rasputin pushed her aside, and Madame Lokhtina, breathing heavily, sank on a nearby divan saying, "And yet you are mine, and I have lain with you. I have lain with you. Oh, my life! It belongs to you; now for the first time I see how beautiful it is. I belong to you and to no other. Whoever may come between us, you are mine and I am yours. However many women you take, no one can rob me of you. You are mine! Say, say, that you cannot suffer me! And yet I know that you love me, that you lo-ove me!"

"I hate you, you bitch," replied Rasputin. "I tell you I hate you; I do not love you. The devil is in you. I'd like to kill you. I'd like to smash your jaw."

"Soon I will lie with you again," cried Madame Lokhtina.

During the confusion, Alexandrovna slipped through the kitchen to the back landing. There, she met a woman who related her story. "He told me to go to Holy Communion and then come back to him, cleansed from all sin . . . I did it, and visited him in the evening after the Holy Sacrament, as he ordered.

"I went to him out of curiosity, impudent and vulgar curiosity, with the body of the Lord in me. And he winked shamelessly at me, as if he were asking me whether I knew what he wanted from me. He was waiting for me alone in his best clothes, seized me, pulled me into the bedroom and tore off my dress as we went. I felt his hot, burning breath on my neck . . . He forced me to kneel down and whispered in my ear: 'Let us pray.' The next moment he was nothing but savage, animal desire . . . The last thing I remember is his tearing off my underclothing, then I lost consciousness . . . I awoke and found myself lying on the ground torn and defiled. He stood over me shamelessly naked."

Alexandrovna tried to calm the woman, who kept repeating, "I come every day to ask him why he did this to me; why did he defile me?"

Rasputin loved to eat and dance. More than one banquet turned into an orgy. Rasputin's enemies did not hesitate to report all his debaucheries to the tsar and the tsarina. He continued to take bribes and boast about the many favors he had bestowed upon others. Secret agents reported all this to the tsar. Rasputin's enemies now began to hatch a plot for his assassination.

Khvostov, the Minister of the Interior and Supreme Head of the Police, decided that Rasputin had to die. He had too much influence within the court. Khvostov was going to plan the murder so that no suspicion would fall on him. He proposed to entice Rasputin to the house of one of his female admirers. He would arrange for Rasputin to enter a car which would later be held up by two masked men. They would render him insensible with a cloth soaked in chloroform, and then strangle him. However, this plan was not carried out. It was then decided to poison him. The poisons were prepared, but news of the attempt leaked to Rasputin, and he was on guard at all times.

Prince Felix Yusupov was now brought into the plot. The prince had wormed his way into Rasputin's affections. Prince Felix Yusupov was angered over the fact that Munia Golovina had permitted Rasputin to make love to her. She had been betrothed to Yusupov's dead brother. How could she allow Rasputin to take the place of his beloved brother? The prince hated Rasputin with his whole heart. It was not difficult to interest the prince in entering a plot to kill the miserable Rasputin.

The more Prince Felix thought about Rasputin and his sexual and drunken orgies, the more convinced was he that the monk had to die. However, the tsar and tsarina favored Rasputin. They felt he had enemies only because of his deep friendship with the rulers of Russia. Rasputin, more than once, said: "So long as I live, the imperial family will also live; when I die, they will also perish." The tsar and tsarina believed this prophecy.

After some planning, the plot was hatched. Rasputin would be poisoned. His body would then be put in chains and sunk in the frozen waters of the Neva.

Rasputin was completely unaware that his "little friend," Prince Felix Yusupov was plotting his execution. Rasputin was invited for tea to the home of Prince Felix. However, Rasputin was called away and could not accept the invitation.

Another meeting was quickly arranged between Munia and Rasputin. This time they were going to meet at the Golovina's house on the Winter Canal. Prince Felix was asked to bring his guitar so that he could entertain with gypsy songs. The prince arrived with his guitar and played song after song. It was a wonderful evening for Rasputin. Again, the plot failed.

On the morning of December 16, 1916, Prince Felix prepared himself for the murder of Rasputin. It was going to be done in the underground room of the Yusupov Palace. The question was how to get Grigori Efimovich there. Since Grigori had long cherished the wish to meet the beautiful wife of Prince Felix, she was going to be used as the inducement.

Prince Felix wrote to Rasputin, telling him that his wife, who was ill, wished to meet him and be treated by him. The invitation was for December 16th. Prince Felix asked Rasputin to come at a late hour, and not to tell anyone where he was going.

The underground room selected for the murder had to look as though it had been lived in. So, the prince secretly furnished the room complete with curtains, and a roaring fire burned in the hearth. All the conspirators were present. Doctor Lazovert arrived bearing the cyanide of potassium. With rubber gloves, he rubbed some crystals into the upper layers of the chocolate cakes that were prepared, and scattered a large quantity of poison over the under layers. He put in enough poison to kill the entire party.

In the meantime, Rasputin was readying himself for the night. He donned his new blue silk shirt embroidered with cornflowers. He devoted extra care to all his clothing, and had his boots polished again. He was quite excited about meeting the beauteous Irina Alexandrovna and trying his healing art on her.

As he was about to leave, His Excellency the Minister Protopopov came in. He pleaded with Rasputin not to leave the house, indicating that there was danger in his going out alone. "I entreat you to be cautious," he said, "don't take a single step unaccompanied; do not visit any public place; go nowhere, for I fear some evil."

Rasputin refused to accept the warning that could have saved his life. The beauty of Irina Alexandrovna and the anticipated treatment motivated him and excited him.

Rasputin was called for by car and soon arrived at the home of the prince. Everyone sat around the table where there were harmless pink cakes and poisoned brown ones. First, Rasputin was given a harmless pink one; then, he was given a poisoned brown one. Rasputin devoured several, one after the other. All waited for him to fall dead. They had been told that cyanide acted immediately. Rasputin did not seem at all affected. He was then given a glass of wine which was amply doctored with cyanide. Rasputin drained several glasses. All watched him, waiting for the cyanide to take effect, but the expression on his face did not change even a bit.

Could it be that he was a saint? Or, a devil? He had eaten enough poison to kill a whole company of ordinary people, yet he seemed quite unaffected.

The prince decided that as a last resort he would have to shoot Rasputin.

When Rasputin's body was finally found, caked in the frozen ice of the Neva, it showed numerous bullet wounds and knife wounds. In spite of the poison, in spite of the bullet and knife wounds, Rasputin was still alive when his bound body was thrown into the Neva, for one arm was half out of the rope, and the lungs were full of water. He had almost freed himself.

The murder was traced to Yusupov, who, after a hearing, was banished to a distant estate. There were many who repeated Rasputin's prophecy: "If I die, the emperor will soon after lose his crown."

This actually did happen! On March 15, 1917, the tsar handed his formal abdication to the emissaries of the Duma. On March 22, the ex-emperor became the prisoner of the new government. On the nights of March 22 and 23, a crowd of rebel soldiers broke into the Park of the Palace, tore open Rasputin's grave and seized the coffin. They erected a great pyre, soaked the decomposing body of Rasputin in petrol, and burned it.

Maria Rasputin, the daughter of the Mad Monk, defended her father in her book, *My Father*, with these words: "If he had faults and made mistakes, it was because he was only a man—even if he were a "man of God"—and not a saint. Let him who is without sin cast the first stone. He never sinned through pride or ambition . . . he was a good father and a good husband."

Such was the magic, hypnotic power of Rasputin, the mad lover.

14

Isadora Duncan & Her Lovers

Isadora Duncan was a genius—one of the greatest performing artists that the United States had ever produced. She was described as a goddess by the greatest of poets, and roundly criticized by members of the Church. The great artists of America and Europe watched her body movements with delight as she gracefully danced across the stage, while the aristocratic crowd (whose minds and hearts were in the gutter) were shocked by her performance.

In 1902 in Munich, she was termed "goddesslike," and students harnessed themselves as horse to her carriage, to drive her home from the theater, serenading her most of the night. Poets wrote tributes to her dancing. Critics lauded her as original and soulful.

Men vied for her love. Among her lovers and the fathers of her children were Askar Beregi (she called him her Romeo), the handsome Hungarian; Gordon Craig, famed stage designer; Paris Singer, a millionaire; and the Russian poet, Sergei Esseni.

Isadora, with her lively imagination, spun varied tales of her ancestors and her birth. Sometimes her stories were more imaginary than factual. However, her grandparents were outstanding men of the mid-18th century. Her grandfather, Thomas Gray, landed in Baltimore from Ireland when he was just 16. He fought in the Black Hawk Wars and met up with a fellow volunteer, Abraham Lincoln. Subsequently, he became a member of the Missouri State Legislature, and later was appointed by President Polk to the post of Federal Collector of the Port of St. Louis.

Some years later, Thomas joined a train of covered wagons and made the journey to San Francisco, where he raised a large family. President Lincoln awarded him a federal appointment, but war broke out and Thomas Gray enlisted. When he was released, he was given a federal post as Naval Officer of the Port of San Francisco. Subsequently, he was elected three times to the California State Legislature.

It was during this time that his youngest daughter, Mary Dora, married Joseph Duncan. Mary's father did not favor the match. Joseph Duncan was much older than his new bride. Moreover, he had already been married and was the father of four children. He was somewhat of a Bohemian—a charmer with lively tongue and pen, who dabbled in poetry. He was a direct descendant of General William Duncan of Philadelphia who fought with Washington in the Revolutionary War. The exact date of the marriage is not known because all such records were destroyed during the earthquake and great fire of April 1906.

Isadora was born on May 27, 1878 at a time when the family was in dire financial straits. At birth, she was called Dora, after her mother. Later the name of Angela was added. It is not clearly established just how the name of Isadora came to be. In fact, her name, as it appeared on the program in the first Daly production on Broadway, was Sara Duncan.

Isadora liked to say that she was born under the astrological sign of the Twins, and that she really began dancing in her mother's womb. She began to improvise her own style of dancing while still a very young girl.

When she was already famous, she related that her first clear recollection of her early days was of being thrown out of the window of the house in which she was born, as it was going up in flames. "Always," she wrote in the first draft of her autobiography which she began in Moscow in 1923, "always fire and water and sudden fearful death." Without knowing it, she was predicting her own sudden, bizarre, violent death.

When Isadora was still quite young, her father deserted the family and the mother became the sole means of support. She gave piano lessons, but the monies received were not adequate to support the family. The Duncan family shifted from one apartment to another, always one step ahead of the collectors. At an early age, Isadora knew the difference between the children who were the "haves" and children who were the "have-nots." Poverty, however, neither dampened her courage nor her disposition.

Misery was forgotten when the entire family gathered around Mrs. Duncan as she played the piano, or read poetry. Isadora's first dancing steps were motivated by her mother's rendition of Chopin's waltzes and mazurkas, and Mendelssohn's *Songs Without Words*. Both she and her sister, Elizabeth, were soon teaching dancing to neighborhood children. Later, they began to have "regular-paying" pupils, and, after awhile, they opened a dancing school, and, with their brothers, began to give theatrical performances in the spacious barn in back of the house where they lived. The pages of the Oakland telephone directory of 1892-3 list Dora and Elizabeth as dancing teachers.

While Isadora was growing up in San Francisco, she attended many theatrical performances. She saw Sarah Bernhardt, Henry Irving and Ellen Terry. Sitting way up in the top seats of the upper gallery, she resolved that one day she, too, would have

198 • Secret Love Affairs

a brilliant career in the theatrical world.

She did not have much luck in California, so she decided to move east—to Chicago, to New York and, possibly, even to Europe. Her family believed in her—believed that she had something new to offer the world of dance and supported her.

Mother and daughter arrived in Chicago with some jewelry and old lace. They stayed in inexpensive rooms and ate meager meals. Isadora made the daily rounds of theatrical managers, for whom she danced to Chopin's waltzes and mazurkas. All they could tell her was that she was a pretty girl, but they needed someone who could kick high and do unusual things.

She finally got a job at the Masonic Roof Garden. She was engaged for three weeks as "The Californian Faun," in a vaudeville show. It was during this time that she met Ivan Miroski, a 45-year-old Polish poet and painter. Soon they were taking long, unchaperoned walks into the woods and, one day, as they strolled, Miroski asked her to marry him. But the time was not right; Isadora was too busy trying to get the attention of Augustin Daly, one of the greats among theater managers. She finally made her contact, and Daly had only to see her dance for a few minutes, whereupon he engaged her for his show in New York. Isadora and Miroski now pledged eternal love to one another, and off she went to begin a dancing career.

The play was *Miss Pygmalion*, a pantomime with music by Francis Thomé. The leading lady was the temperamental Mademoiselle Jane May. Isadora disliked her part, which she felt was stupid and unworthy of her ambitions and ideals. The play was not a success and closed quickly, and Isadora went on to play a series of new parts.

In 1896, she joined Daly's Shakespearean repertory company. She then got a small part in Daly's *The Geisha*. She danced in a production of *Much Ado About Nothing*. In 1897, she danced in the Prologue of *Meg Merrilies*. After that, she left for England and studied dancing with Ketti Lanner, the famous leading dancer of the Empire Theater in London. She was all of nineteen years of age.

Financially, things were far from satisfactory for Isadora, but a chance meeting with Mrs. Patrick Campbell, who had seen her dance, made for a change. Mrs. Campbell invited Isadora to her own home, and then gave her a letter of introduction to Mrs. George Wyndham, whose home was the meeting place of the London artistic and literary world. It was there that Isadora met tall, slender, gray-haired Charles Hallé, a well-known painter. Through him she met most of the prominent men in the arts. He also conceived an idea for a series of performances to be called *"Evenings with Isadora Duncan."*

The first of the three evenings was given on March 16, 1900. *The Times* described the entertainment as "entirely new to the public, and a pronounced success." She was described as a young dancer of remarkable skill whose art had an elegance of its own.

Isadora now looked towards new worlds and, at the close of 1900, she and her mother packed their few belongings and left for Paris, the city which was to become home for the rest of her life.

Isadora, her mother, and her brother Raymond moved to a bleak loft above a printing plant in the heart of Montparnasse. Together with her teacher, Charles Hallé, who had come to France from London, Isadora frequented the cultural spots of the city. She attended theatrical performances of all kinds. Hallé introduced her to some important people who were in a position to further her career. Isadora was invited to a musical evening at the Saint-Marceau house of the Boulevard Malesherbes. Soon after, she was besieged with a succession of invitations to entertain at the town houses of the leaders of society.

Isadora and her mother now opened a school for the children of the rich. Mrs. Duncan would play the piano as Isadora taught the children to dance at $5.00 a lesson. She was now also dancing publicly and winning great praise. She was admired, congratulated and cheered. Her happiness, however, was not complete. She was hungry to be loved.

From among her three young admirers, Isadora at first selected André Beaunier. He was witty and intelligent, but fat and short. For a while they spoke about art, and books. They took long nature walks. But Isadora wanted more than a platonic relationship. She offered him ample opportunity to take her physically. But André fled from each opportunity. Finally, in desperation, she turned to Charles Noufflard, who although not nearly as witty and intelligent as André, understood what she wanted and eagerly wanted to give it to her. They had a champagne supper, then went to a room reserved for *Monsieur et Madame*. No sooner there, he covered trembling Isadora with kisses and caresses. Suddenly, Charles fell crying to his knees by the side of the bed; he could not commit such a crime. Isadora had to remain pure. He asked her to put on her clothes and be taken home. Isadora later states that she turned to art to give her the joys that love withheld.

In 1902, Isadora danced to sell-out crowds at a theater in Budapest. All in all, she gave thirty performances to very enthusiastic audiences.

It was at this point in her life that Isadora met her "Romeo," as she called Oscar Beregi, a talented young actor in the Hungarian National Theater. After seeing her dance, he invited Isadora and her mother to see him play Romeo in Shakespeare's *Romeo and Juliet.* Their friendship and love affair then began.

Isadora writes about her feelings in her memoirs. She describes her emotional and physical state, as follows: "My breasts, which until now had been hardly perceptible, began to swell softly and to astonish me with charming but embarrassing sensations. My hips, which had been like a boy's, took on another undulation, and through my body I felt one great surging, longing, unmistakable urge, so that I could no longer sleep at night, but tossed and turned in feverish, painful unrest."

She continued to describe her meeting with Beregi: "One afternoon, at a friendly gathering, over a glass of golden Tokay, I met two large black eyes that burned and glowed into mine with such ardent adoration and Hungarian passion that in that one look was all the meaning of the spring in Budapest. He was tall, of magnificent proportions, a head covered with luxurious curls, black, with purple lights in them. From our first look, every power of attraction we possessed rushed from us in a mad embrace. From that first gaze, we were already in each other's arms, and no power on earth could have prevented this."

To him she lost her virginity. But passion wasn't enough to keep them together. He had his theater, and she had her dancing. Neither was prepared to give up the art they cherished. Thus, when Isadora's tour in Hungary was over, she left for Vienna. It was there that she took seriously ill. She spent several weeks in a hospital and Beregi came to stay with her, sharing her hospital room. Later, he left for Budapest, and she went to convalesce in northern Bohemia.

From her dancing successes in Austria-Hungary, Isadora went to Munich, the art center of Germany. There she was welcomed by the leading painters and sculptors. She danced right into the hearts of the Germans.

Isadora Duncan had now become newsworthy in the American press. What made her particularly newsworthy was what the audiences called her "near nudity." This was something new to all audiences, who were accustomed to seeing dancers clothed from head to toe.

Stories were being circulated (all without foundation) about Russian grand dukes who were showering her with jewels. What was happening and what pleased Isadora was that she was now able to accumulate thousands of gold marks.

At this time the illustrious Heinrich Thode fell in love with Isadora. He was an art historian and was married to Cosima Wagner's daughter. Each night, he would come to Isadora and recite poetry, or read from a manuscript he was writing. These intellectual sessions did not remain solely intellectual. Thode would caress and kiss Isadora, but his kisses only left her frustrated since Thode went no further, and remained sexually faithful to his wife. She complained in her memoirs: "He never caressed me as a lover, never tried even to undo my tunic, or touch my breasts or my body in any way, although he knew that every pulse of it belonged only to him. Emotions I had not known to exist awoke under the gaze of his eyes. Sensations so ecstatic and terrible that I often felt the pleasure was killing me, and fainted away, to awaken again to the light of those wonderful eyes. He so completely possessed my soul that it seemed it was only possible to gaze into his eyes and long for death. For there was not, as in earthly love, any satisfaction or rest, but always this delirious thirst for a point that I required."

The long, frustrating nights spent with Thode began to affect Isadora both physically and mentally. Once again she took ill.

Prior to her tour of Russia, she met Gordon Craig, the famous English stage designer. The year was 1904.

Gordon Craig was a stage designer and director. He was 32; Isadora was 26. Isadora described him as tall and willowy, with a face resembling that of his mother, Ellen Terry. Max Beerbohm describes Craig: "He is not an easy man to define. But one thing about him is certain. He is a man of genius . . ."

Craig saw her dance and was enraptured. He said: "I remember that when it was over I went rapidly round to her dressing room to see her, and there too I sat still and speechless in front of her for awhile. She understood my silence very well; all talk being unnecessary . . . After a while, she put on a cloak, and shoes and out we went into the streets of Berlin, where the snow looked friendly and the shops still lighted up, the Christmas trees all spangled and lighted, and we walked and talked of the shops. The shops, the Christmas trees, the crowd—no one heeded us."

Isadora was drawn to his studio. As she expressed it: "I was drawn towards him, entwined, melted. As flame meets flame, we burned in one bright fire. Here at last was my mate . . ." A few weeks of impassioned love-making followed. However, art called again. She went on her Russian tour and he to his drawing board.

When Isadora returned from Russia, she and Craig were inseparable. Craig wrote: "We were indeed full of admiration for each other." Craig now took care of her finances. He accompanied her on her tours through Germany, Belgium, and Holland.

In 1906, Isadora gave birth to a little girl. It was September 24. Craig was in Rotterdam but he hastened to be with Isadora. The birth of the child moved Isadora to write: "Oh, women, what is the good of us learning to become lawyers, painters or sculptors, when this miracle exists . . . Oh, where is my Art? My Art or any Art? What do I care for Art? I felt I was a God, superior to any artist."

They called the child Deirdre, "beloved of Ireland."

After the birth of her daughter, Isadora returned to Berlin. After checking on the progress of her pupils, she left with Craig for Florence, Italy. Here, Craig created sets for a production that immediately earned him a great reputation. He announced his creative independence, and, at that moment, Isadora felt he would soon lose interest in her. For the first time in her life, she experienced jealousy. She wrote: "Visions of Craig in all his beauty in the arms of another woman haunted me at night, until I could no longer sleep. Visions of Craig explaining his art to women who gazed at him with adoring eyes—visions of Craig being pleased with other women—looking at them with that winning smile of his—the smile of Ellen Terry—taking an interest in them, caressing them—saying to himself, 'This woman pleases me. After all Isadora is impossible.' "

Although she was always desired by many men, she began to doubt her physical attractiveness.

To escape from this feeling of insecurity, she took up with Pim. Pim was a young, blond, pretty, blue-eyed homosexual. He carried with him 18 trunks of clothing when he accompanied Isadora on her 1907 trip to Russia. This was a short episode in Isadora's life, an episode that put an end to her passionate affair with Gordon Craig. They were never lovers again. In his notebook, Craig, many years later, wrote: . . . "All's past . . . all's said . . . all's done. What now? It seems that all has not been said. I loved her—I do still—but she, the complex she, might have wrecked me, as she wrecked many—and finally herself."

During this Russian tour, Isadora was received as an honored guest by Stanislavsky and the Moscow Art Theater. It was in Russia that Isadora tried to seduce Stanislavsky in her hotel room.

Stanislavsky was astonished and cried, "But what should we do with a child?"

"What child?" Isadora asked him.

"Why our child of course . . . You see I would never approve of any child of mine being raised outside my jurisdiction, and that would be difficult in my present household." Isadora burst out laughing.

Isadora danced in England, then left for the United States where she performed on Broadway. In New York, she vainly sought to conquer George Grey Bernard, a famous sculptor. She danced before President Theodore Roosevelt, who applauded her vigorously. However, the newspapers still gave her bad publicity based on the activities in her private life. Free love was not looked upon with approval in those years.

Isadora felt more and more homesick for Paris and, on the

last day of December 1908, she sailed for France to be reunited with her daughter, Deirdre. She was now 31 years of age and in the ninth year of her European career as an artist. She was greeted in France with great enthusiasm. Henri Lavendan, one of the leading French dramatists, wrote almost affectionately of Isadora. He described her as "a young woman, vital, beautiful . . . able, without the air of artifice and without uttering a word, to hold an audience for two hours in one of the largest theaters of Paris . . ."

The novelist, Edith Wharton, wrote: "I've never seen dancing as I inwardly imagined. And then, when the curtain was drawn back . . . and before a background of grayish-green hangings, a simple figure appeared . . . then suddenly I beheld the dance I had always dreamed of, a flowing of movement into movement, an endless interweaving of motion and music, satisfying every sense as a flower does, or a phrase of Mozart's."

Great artists, as they watched her dance, sketched Miss Duncan's bodily movements. The great sculptor, Bourdelle, sculpted her in marble. Jean-Paul Lafitte and the more famous artist, Dunoyer de Segonzac, did complete albums of her. Isadora was at the height of her fame. And it was at this time that a desirable millionaire entered her life.

He was Paris Eugene Singer, the youngest, but one of the 3 children born to the American sewing machine magnate, Isaac Singer. He had all the attributes of a story-book Prince Charming. His manners were polished; he was tall, handsome, with an excellent physique. He was already the father of five children. He was an intimate friend of Queen Alexandra. He had mansions both in London and Paris.

He entered her dressing room after a performance, bent down to kiss Isadora's hand, and, in a shy and charming voice, said: "You do not know me, but I have often applauded your wonderful art."

Paris Singer turned out to be generous and openhearted. He took her and her pupils to the French Riviera where he had both a villa and a beautiful yacht. In early 1910, Isadora sailed with Paris Singer on his yacht, *Iris*, to Egypt. They were going to sail up the Nile. She wrote to one of her friends: "We have one magnificent day after another of blue sky and sun. It is as close to Paradise as anything ever could be . . . The only thing we miss here is music; it's true that we always have with us the sound of water wheels and the songs of the Arabs, but we long to hear Bach. It's funny, but Bach and the Egyptian temples would go very well together.

Paris Singer was passionately in love with her. He had romance in his soul. When they reached Pompeii, he conceived the idea of having Isadora dance for him in the Temple of Paestum by moonlight. Their love-making went on and on. One day she remembered that she had to fulfill her engagement in Russia and insisted that they return immediately to Paris.

When they returned to Paris, Isadora gave several very successful performances at the Gaite-Lyrique in June. And her Russian performances were received with tremendous enthusiasm.

Paris Singer soon introduced her to a luxurious life. He dressed her in gowns designed by Paul Poiret, the leading Parisian designer. She was led by her elegant escort to the most fashionable restaurants and night clubs. They seemed to be an admiringly happy and distinguished couple.

But an element of jealousy existed in the relationship as well. Singer disliked the attention Isadora paid to Stanislavsky. She tried to placate Singer by having both men present for dinner. They went to an elegant restaurant and Singer seemed more amiable. He went so far as to invite Stanislavsky to extend his visit.

In September, Isadora discovered that she was pregnant. This presented her with a problem. Was she ready to have a child fathered by a man she loved but whose future with her was uncertain? Secondly, should she take time off from her art to have this child? She consulted her physician, and spoke to one of her friends, but it took time for her to decide. Finally, she telegraphed Paris, and, after returning to Venice, took Deirdre into her arms and whispered: "You will have a little brother."

In October, one month later, she left with Paris Singer for the United States to fulfill her engagements with Walter Damrosch and the New York Symphony. She received great notices in the United States press, but it was soon becoming obvious to her audiences that she was pregnant. She had to cancel the rest of her tour and return to France.

Paris Singer was a happy expectant father. He took Isadora and Deirdre on a long journey to Egypt, and he gave Isadora luxuries of which she had never before dreamed. He even engaged Hener Skene, a young and talented British pianist, to play Beethoven and Bach on a beautiful Steinway grand.

After the long voyage to Egypt, Paris Singer brought Isadora and Deirdre to a palatial villa in Beaulieu Sur Mer, on the French Riviera, where, as Isadora recalled in her diary: "On the first day of May, a morning when the sea was blue, and the sun was burning, and all Nature bursting into blossom and joy, my son was born."

The father himself selected the name of Patrick, the same name as another of his sons, born by his first wife.

Isadora recuperated quickly and once again returned to Paris. Singer now proposed marriage, saying, "You would not have to make tours if we were married."

"How stupid for an artist to be married," she replied.

Singer proposed that they try living *as if* they were married. If after three months she liked it, they would be married.

Isadora agreed to the test.

They entertained, went yachting, gave huge parties, spent money freely. But their relationship was in great difficulty. Writing in her diary, she indicated: "Even today I simply cannot comprehend how little he understood me and my work. You see . . . can you imagine me no longer being Isadora Duncan, but Madame Singer—well, I couldn't." Isadora could not merely entertain and be entertained. She was too alive, too involved in her art. She lived only when she was engaged in artistic creation. She wanted to dance. She *had* to dance.

At the beginning of 1913, Isadora once again toured Russia. She was welcomed in St. Petersburg and in Moscow. In the town of Kiev, at the close of her Chopin program, she insisted that her pianist play the "Funeral March" movement of the *Opus 35 Sonata in B-flat Minor*. It was a kind of premonition of what was to come.

On Saturday afternoon, April 19, 1913, shortly after 3:30 in the afternoon, her two children and their Scottish nurse lay at the bottom of the Seine. It seemed that her chauffeur, in a freak accident, forgot to apply the brakes and the car rushed downhill and crashed into the waters of the Seine.

The news of her children's death left Isadora crushed. Her heart was broken and all her emotions seemed to be at their breaking point. Singer rushed to her side, weeping bitterly along with her. Flowers were sent by friend and stranger alike. The childrens' bodies were cremated, and Isadora was taken by her family to the island of Corfu in the Adriatic.

Singer came down to spend time with her, but Isadora's grief did not diminish. She went for long walks, but kept hearing the voices of her two dead children. She wrote to her friends: "I have always known that my children were the best part of my life. All the joy, the strength and the inspiration of my art. Now I feel that my life and my art died with them."

Death and destruction was soon to rage all over Europe in a World War conflict. Isadora lent her prestige to fund-raising events. She danced for the first time since the death of her children. She sailed on the French liner, *Lafayette,* first to the United States and then to South America.

It was early in 1917 that the break came between Isadora and Singer. Isadora claims he left her because he was jealous of a dance she was doing with a beautiful young boy "and in a fashion one does not exhibit in public." He never came back again. Letters to him went unanswered. He ceased sending her money. She was in debt and had to pawn or sell the gifts he had given her—a diamond necklace, an ermine coat, an emerald. It was at this time that Isadora moved (with her six dancing girls) to a small beach cottage in Long Beach, Long Island. Soon, her home became a meeting place of artists, musicians, and dancers.

Isadora Duncan did not believe in marriage, yet, on May 2, 1922, she married Sergei Essenine, the young Russian poet. Not one of Isadora's friends would have waged a single ruble on such an outcome.

Sergei was a blue-eyed, golden-haired young man, 10 years younger than Isadora. He had already been married twice. As a young man, he had tended horses on his uncle's farm. He was educated by the local priest who was attracted by his intelligence. Later, he was sent off to school. In St. Petersburg, he became the disciple of the poet, Klouieff, and was presented to the tsarina who took more than a passing interest in the handsome peasant.

His mother was an illiterate, who, in her later years, tried unsuccessfully to learn how to read so that she could enjoy her son's poetry.

His father kept reproaching Essenine for not doing the work of a peasant, and for spending what little money he had on books and magazines.

To his co-workers, he appeared conceited and arrogant, and was very much disliked.

Essenine was often invited to salons of St. Petersburg society. In addition to writing and publishing his poems in magazines, he took every opportunity to introduce them publicly by reading them at literary gatherings, which were held quite frequently. It was said in Russia that Pushkin "thought in verse," that Mayakovsky "loved in verse," but that Essenine lived "excited by his heart and his verse."

This was the Essenine that Isadora met, fell in love with, and married. Prior to her visit to Russia, she had gone to a fortune-teller who had told her that she would be married within the year. Isadora left the fortune-teller with a laugh. She was sure that she would not marry.

There are several versions as to how Essenine and Isadora actually met. The most popular states that their mutual friend, Ilya Schneider, brought Isadora to a party at the home of the well-known Moscow painter of theatrical scenery, George Jakuloff. Later, Schneider took both Isadora and Essenine home in his carriage. She had listened to his poetry, and while not understanding Russian, she later stated that she had heard the music in it. In the carriage, Essenine did not let go of her hand.

They became good friends. Although Essenine appeared to be bored with her dancing at private parties (much to the dismay of Isadora's friends), he loved to dance himself and would say that he could do better. Then, to the accompaniment of his friends' accordions, he would let loose with a typically Russian folk dance.

Isadora was falling in love with Essenine with all the passion of a woman who was past 40. Although he would be patronizing to Isadora in public, still, she was the pursuer. It was a challenge to her femininity to conquer—if not with her dancing talent, then with her personal charm. She was charmed by him—by his youth, by his golden hair, by his enthusiasm. She took him with her to Petrograd where she was to give a performance.

Sergei was drunk a good part of the time. His friends, who did not want him to deepen his relationship with Isadora, made sure of that. They feared that his growing love for Isadora would keep him away from his activities in their literary enterprises. They went so far as trying to persuade him to go abroad.

Isadora wanted to remove Essenine from his old crowd. She also wanted to leave Russia and take Essenine with her. She was sure that in New York she could earn enough money to maintain her school. Her telegraph to Sol Hurok in New York brought a reply that he would be happy to arrange a tour for her, but not before the fall of the year.

Isadora's problem was how to bring Essenine with her. She recalled the furor that Maxim Gorky created when he dared visit America with a female companion who was not his wife. The problem was a vexing one and Isadora decided that she would give up her hatred of the legal ceremony and marry her poet lover. It was explained to her that the legal ceremony was just mere formality.

And so, on the day following the May Day festival, at the Moscow Registry of Civil Statistics, Isadora Duncan and Sergei Alexandrovitch Essenine were married. He gave his age as 27, and she, possessing no legal birth certificate to contradict it, gave hers as 37. (Closer to the truth is that she was 15 years older than her lover.)

They left on a honeymoon to western Europe, first having composed her will in pencil on a penny notebook. It read:

> This is my last will and testament. In case of my death I leave my entire properties and effects to my husband Sergei Essenine. In case of our simultaneous death then such properties to go to my brother, Augustin Duncan.
> Written in clear conscience.
> Isadora Essenine-Duncan

Witnessed by: I. I. Schneider
Irma Duncan
May Ninth, 1922, Moscow.

The following day, they took off from the Trotsky Flying Field. They arrived at the Templehof airport in Berlin on May 11. It did not take long for Essenine to find his place in Berlin. He located his friend Maxim Gorky who lived there, and another old friend, the poet Koussikoff. He was soon giving public readings and he began to plan a volume of his poems which were to be translated into French.

Isadora never realized the tremendous burden she had undertaken in marrying and separating a man from his homeland. He was drunk, though a poet. A collection of his poetry, published in France and financed by Isadora, was entitled *Les Confessions d'un Voyou* ("The Confessions of a Roughneck, or Hooligan").

Essenine's behavior *was* that of a hooligan. Coming into their hotel room after he had done considerable drinking, he found Isadora weeping over an album which contained portraits of her two children, Deirdre and Patrick. With no regard for the moment or her feelings, he tore it from her hands and tossed it into the fire, screaming in a drunken rage: "You spend too much time thinking of these . . . . children!"

The Essenines began to travel. They went to Ostend in Belgium and later to Brussels. Essenine tried to stay sober and wrote to Schneider: "If you could see me now you would probably not believe your eyes. It is almost a month now since I've taken a drink. On account of a heavy neuritis and neurasthenia, I made a promise not to drink until October, and now they are over."

From Belgium, the couple went to Paris, to Venice and then back to Paris until it was time for the American tour. In the meantime, Essenine became even more jealous of Isadora's popularity. Again and again, he tried to assert the superiority of literature over the dance by telling Isadora that the dance ceases to exist when the dance is ended; while poetry (and he meant his own) would live forever.

He was also jealous of her admirers, even though she assured him that they were homosexuals. Isadora, too, was jealous. She, her maid and her secretary watched Essenine's every move.

On October 1, 1922, Isadora, standing on the deck of the *SS Paris*, saw the Statue of Liberty. First she was informed that neither she nor her husband would be allowed to set foot in New York. It had to be ascertained that they had not come to spread Communist propaganda; their case had to be further investigated. However, they were spared humiliation by being treated as the guests of the ship's captain.

Isadora ridiculed the fears of the government, saying, "Nonsence! We want to tell the American people about the poor starving children in Russia and not about the country's politics. Sergei is not a politician. He is a genius. He is a great poet. . . It is only in the field of art that we are working. We believe that the soul of Russia and the soul of America are about to understand each other." The following day, they appeared before the Board of Review on Ellis Island and were permitted to enter the United States. Isadora told the reporters, who were also waiting for the outcome of the review: "I feel as if I were acquitted of murder. They seemed to think that a year's residence in Moscow had made me a bloodthirsty criminal ready to throw bombs at the slightest provocation. They asked me silly questions such as: 'Are you a classical dancer?' I told them I didn't know; my dancing is quite personal. They wanted to know what I looked like when I danced! How do I know? I never say myself dance."

All this did the box office much good. Whereas, before, few tickets had been sold, within 24 hours, all performances were sold out. Essenine had signed a written statement that he would not sing the *Internationale* during their stay in the United States, and Isadora promised Hurok that she would leave speeches to the politicians and would only occupy herself with dancing. Her promise would not be upheld.

Isadora's tour of the United States was going to be wrecked by Isadora herself. Her dancing was received with enthusiasm, but her speeches to the audiences regularly caused riots.

Once, from the stage of the Symphony Hall, pointing to the replicas of Greek statues all around, she cried: "Those are not Greek gods—they are false and you are as false as these plaster statues. . . You once were wild here! Don't let them tame you. If my art is symbolic of any one thing, it is symbolic of the freedom of woman and her emancipation from the hidebound conventions that are the warp and woof of New England puritanism. To expose one's body to art; concealment is vulgar. When I dance, my object is to inspire reverence; not to suggest anything vulgar. I don't appeal to the lower instincts of mankind as your half-clad chorus girls do. I would rather dance completely nude than strut in half-clothed suggestiveness as many women do today on the streets of America. Nudity is truth, it is beauty, it is art. Therefore, it can never be vulgar; it can never be immoral . . ."

Then she tore her tunic down to bare one of her breasts and cried out, "This—this is beauty." The Bostonians hurriedly left the hall, but the Harvard University students cheered.

In the meantime, Essenine was growing bored. He was neglected by the American public and he craved attention. He would attend Isadora's performances dressed in colorful Russian costumes. He would wear a Cossack's uniform, a large silver sword dangling from his belt, high soft black boots, and a large fur hat. Once he waved a red flag and, in Russian, yelled, "Long live Bolshevism!"

The Boston incident set the tenor of the rest of the tour. Isadora danced to packed theaters and gave inciting speeches to audiences in Chicago, Milwaukee, and Indianapolis. Billy Sunday got into the act, saying, "That Bolshevik hussy doesn't wear enough clothes to pad a crutch. I'd like to be Secretary of Labor for 15 minutes, I'd send her back to Russia and her Gorki. . ."

Isadora had created a political storm and there was a rush of cancellations. Her manager pleaded with her to stop making speeches. Isadora replied: "My manager tells me that if I make more speeches the tour is dead. Very well, the tour is dead! I will go back to Moscow where there is vodka, music, poetry and dancing." Her final dance performance was given on Saturday evening, January 13, 1923.

As January ended, she was tired, weary, and financially broke. Her husband was in poor mental and physical health due to the quantities of bootleg liquor he had consumed. Sailing on the George Washington with money borrowed from Paris Singer, she set out for Europe telling the reporters who had come to see her off: ". . . I am not an anarchist or a Bolshevik. My husband and I are revolutionists. All geniuses worthy of the name are. . . So good-bye, America! I shall never see you again."

Back in Paris, things did not go too well. Essenine had begun to consume great quantities of vodka. One night, he arrived at the hotel and started to smash all the mirrors and woodwork. The police were called in, and, with much difficulty, finally removed him to the nearest police station. The newspapers made much of the incident.

The newspaper reports and Isadora's defense of her husband made the management of the Crillon cancel her engagement. Finally, using all the influence she could, she had her husband released from jail. They went off to their favorite hotel in Versailles. Because she feared that he would get into trouble with the police, she urged him to go to Russia. This he said he would do.

Essenine got as far as Berlin and then returned, saying he did not want to go to Russia without his wife.

The Isadora-Essenine relationship was deteriorating. Essenine did not relish the attention his wife was getting. At a party in his own home, in a childish fit of jealousy, he shouted to the guests in Russian: "Band of bloated fish; mangy sleigh rugs; bellies of carrion; grub for soldiers; you awoke me. He then picked up a candelabrum and smashed it against a mirror which crashed to the floor.

Acting on the advice of friends, Isadora had Essenine hospitalized. She was accused by her husband's friends of having committed him to a common asylum. This was untrue. He had been sent to one of the extremely high-priced hospitals on the outskirts of Paris. Whatever can be said about Isadora, she never failed to exhibit great loyalty and love for her wild, drunken poet-husband.

Isadora's interest once again turned to Russia. She rented her home on the Rue de la Pompe, sold what little furniture she owned, along with some of the robes and suits made especially for her by Paul Poiret. She piled up her library in the attic and left for Moscow. When they arrived there on August 5, 1923, Essenine fell to his knees and kissed the Russian soil. Isadora is said to have remarked: "I am bringing this child back to his country, but I will have nothing more to do with him."

This was more easily said than done. Isadora loved Essenine, and her love could not be turned on or off at will. Time after time, after a quarrel, she would be found sitting on his bed gently stroking his forehead. Tearfully, he would ask her why she tolerated him. And she would answer with tears in her eyes, "Ah, Sergei, you are too young to understand it."

Something new and more serious now entered their lives. Ever since their trip to the United States, Essenine had been stealing money from Isadora—such large amounts, in fact, that despite her large earnings in the United States, she had had to borrow money from friends for their return trip to France.

Essenine would sometimes go on a clothes buying spree. Being idle for the most part, he spent a good deal of his time shopping. He not only made purchases for himself, but he bought expensive presents for his friends. Isadora took his spending in stride, saying, "the child has never had anything like that in his life." With these words, she cheerfully paid the bills he contracted.

However, his stealing went further than the mere purchase of clothes. He had a metal box, which he claimed contained his manuscripts and a loaded revolver. He threatened that he would kill anyone who dared open this box. Packed inside was crumpled American currency and coins amounting to two thousand dollars. Hurok, Isadora's American manager, could not understand why they had to borrow money for their return trip to France when she had earned considerable money on her American tour. A look into Essenine's beautiful trunks would have provided the answer. Those trunks contained thousands of dollars' worth of expensive clothes. Secreted in his trunks was some of her expensive clothing as well.

Although Isadora was never concerned about money, this disclosure brought her to the realization that the relationship between Essenine and herself had to be terminated.

Isadora was badly in need of a rest, and her friends were urging her to temporarily change her surroundings. It was decided that Essenine would follow in a few days. Instead, he sent her a letter indicating that he was going to earn a great deal of money from a publication he was sponsoring.

Isadora was further stunned when she received a telegram, stating: "Do not send more letters or telegrams to Essenine. He is with me. He will never return to you. Galina Benislavskaya."

She had never heard the name Galina Benislavskaya. She investigated and learned that the telegram had been sent with Essenine's knowledge. She telegraphed Essenine: "Received telegram probably from your servant Benislavskaya saying not to send any more letters or telegrams to your address have you changed your address please explain by telegram love you very much Isadora."

No reply was ever received.

Years later, when both Essenine and Isadora were dead, among Essenine's papers was found the original reply to Isadora.

In the first draft of his reply to Isadora, he wrote: "I told you in Paris that in Russia I would leave you. You unnerved and incited me. I love you but will not live with you. Now I am married and happy. I wish you the same. Essenine."

He was never married to Benislavskaya, nor was she responsible for sending the telegram. He had fallen in love with the 32-year-old Augusta Miklashevskaya, an actress to whom he dedicated a series of seven love poems. All this was unknown to Isadora.

Although she knew her marriage was over, she continued to hope that Essenine would return. The final curtain of the marriage fell after Isadora's first performance at the Bolshoi.

Somehow, Sergei had managed to enter backstage to watch Isadora dance. The police had tried to oust him, but he beat his chest and cried, "I am Duncan." When she finished her dance, she heard Sergei whispering "Isadora . . . Isadora." His hands were outstretched and his eyes were pleading. She fell into his arms, crying in a broken voice, "Darling . . ."

Sergei insisted that they go out for supper and that she listen to his sister, Katya, sing. "She is a genius like you," he kept insisting.

At dinner, he drank incessantly, insisting that his sister sing. Essenine was fast getting drunk. When Isadora tried to restrain him, he struck the table with his fist and walked away. He then picked up a bust of himself and ran out into the street. Isadora Duncan never saw her husband again.

There was much talk about Isadora's relationship with her

husband. Comments were heard that Sergei resembled her dead son, Patrick. Essenine once explained: "When we first met, Isadora was stunned by my resemblance to her dead boy. This was the main thing that brought us together, but I saw something unnatural in it. Very soon I came to my senses."

Isadora now toured Russia with great success. Essenine was now out of her life. Success followed success. Everywhere, enthusiastic crowds greeted and applauded her.

In the latter part of 1925, the shattering news of Sergei Essenine's death by suicide came to Isadora. He had killed himself in the very room in the Leningrad hotel where he had first lived with her in elegance. He had severed the vein of his left wrist. He left the following poem:

To a FRIEND

Good-bye, my friend, good-bye!
You are still in my breast, beloved.
This fated parting
Holds for us a meeting in the future.
Good-bye, my friend, without hand or word;
Be not sad nor lower your brow.
In this life to die is not new,
And to live, surely, is not any newer.

He then hanged himself.

On January 27, 1926, Isadora wrote to a friend: "I was terribly shocked about Sergei's death, but I wept and sobbed so many hours about him that it seems he had already exhausted any human capacity for suffering. Myself, I'm having an epoch of continual calamity that I am often tempted to follow his example, only I will walk into the Sea. Now in case I don't do that, here is a plan for the future . . ." The future concerned itself with a new combination of school and studio.

Isadora had never recovered from the death of her two children and, with this grief in her heart, she now found it difficult to go on living. One morning, she arose with her eyes swollen and red; she had wept all night long. Turning to her good friend, Mary Desti, she said, "Mary, I cannot go on like this. For 14 years I have had this pain in my heart. I cannot go on . . . You must find some way for me to end it all. I cannot continue to live in a world where there are beautiful, blue-eyed, golden-haired children.

Little did she realize what the future held in store.

She was awaiting the arrival of a handsome Italian who was to give her a ride in his racing car. When the knock on the door came, Isadora took her heavy silk-fringed shawl, wound it about her neck, and danced to the door to welcome Falchetto. Her friend suggested that she put on warmer clothing.

"Nonsense," she scoffed, "I shall be quite warm in my red shawl."

Falchetto walked towards the car. Isadora followed. As she was about to step into the seat beside the driver, she turned and waved to Mary Desti, saying in French, "Good-bye, friends, I'm off to glory!"

Before the car started, she was seen to throw the long-fringed end of the shawl, which was wound twice around her neck over her shoulder. The car darted forward and the shawl seemed to trail alongside. Once seated, Isadora again settled the shawl around her neck, unaware that the heavy fringe had fallen into the spokes of the wheel at her side—for the wheels had no mudguards. As the driver set the powerful motor in motion, the very first revolution of the rear wheels broke Isadora's neck. Death was instantaneous.

Isadora's early premonition of violent death was realized.

Sobbing and frantic friends tore the thick silk from about the wheels, and raced the dancer to St. Roch's Hospital where she was pronounced dead. Her body was brought back to her former studio which was now a mortuary chamber. Grief-stricken friends came from everywhere. Paris Singer was singularly distraught.

Covered with the purple cape which she had always worn while dancing to Liszt's "Les Funérailles" and Chopin's B Minor Sonata, the casket was placed on the train to be taken to Paris.

On September 19, 1927, her body was escorted to the Père La Chaise crematorium. The mourners were led by Raymond, her brother; Vitya, her lover; and Doughie, her friend. As the coffin was taken from the hearse to the furnace room, the music in the chapel began. Ralph Lawton played Liszt's "Les Funérailles;" the Calvet Quartette played a Beethoven Andante; and Gracia-Marsellac sang Schubert's "Ave Maria." Ferdinand Divoire, a well-known poet, delivered a moving oration, which was followed by a baritone singing Beethoven's "In Questa Tomba Oscura:"

> In this dark tomb
> Let me be at rest.
> When I was living,
> Then it was you should have
> Thought of me,
> Oh, ungrateful world.

Her ashes, sealed in a small casket, were placed in the wall of the columbarium near two marble slabs which bore the simple names: Deirdre. Patrick.

Isadora had passed on to eternity.

15
Mary Queen of Scots:
A Woman of Passion

Whether or not she was an actual participant in the planning of her husband's death, the truth is that no sooner was he assassinated than she ran off and married her lover, the father of her unborn child. For crimes she claimed she did not commit, she was nevertheless found guilty and was beheaded. Whether it was for genuine love or for passion alone, the unhappy Catholic Queen of Scots lost her kingdom and her life.

Mary, Queen of Scots, possessed just about everything. She had dazzling, luscious beauty, bewitching charm, unflinching courage, and brilliant wit. She was born to reign; and she ruled during an age of violence and treachery. She was born on December 8, 1542 and was executed on February 8, 1587. Her personal motto—"In My End is My Beginning"—tells the story of her life.

As a ruler she was impulsive, and her impulsiveness was her downfall. It brought scandal to herself and her people. Her impulsiveness manifested itself in the overt expression of her passions, and it was here that she was betrayed by a brutal and powerful man whom she shamelessly loved. The price was her throne and her life.

Mary's father, King James V, died at the age of 30, when Mary was just six days old. Historians have credited him with the characteristics and qualities of King Arthur—high-spirited, gay, and able to fire the imagination of his subjects. But he was ruthless, and spared neither another man's wife nor an uncommitted maiden—neither prior to his marriage nor after.

Mary's mother was Mary of Guise, King James's second wife. She was the daughter of a noble French family. When she married James, she was a young widow, tall, well-built, and, though not especially beautiful, wise, courageous and intelligent.

At the age of nine months, Mary was crowned in Stirling Castle as Queen of the Scots. When Mary was one year old, the political play between Scotland and England began to take new form. However, not before four and a half more years had elapsed was it thought safe to send the young queen to France without the fear of harm befalling her. It was a time when bloody violence had erupted between England and the Scots, and it was felt that the queen should be safely tucked away.

In safe company, Mary landed on the coast of France on

August 13, 1549, and, for the next 13 years of her life—from six to 19—she lived in exile. In France, she was hailed as a romantic figure, a brave queen who had been forced to flee the barbaric Scots and the cruel English. The French adored her.

In France, Mary met her future husband, the Dauphin Francis. She was six years old at the time; he just five. She was a bouncy healthy girl; he, a timid, sickly boy whose health had already been the matter of much concern. His sickness worried Mary's family. But, by March of the following year, the health of Dauphin Francis had improved and the relationship returned to normal.

With the passing of years, the young boy had developed into a sullen person whose height was stunted and whose health was always poor. He had a weak aptitude for learning, but he loved hunting. He exhibited genuine signs of love for his future bride. She was romantic, beautiful and radiant. She responded to his love with a love of her own.

On Sunday, April 24, 1558, Francis, Dauphin of France, age 14, and Mary, Queen of Scots, age 15, were married. The waiting onlookers were thrilled as they watched the procession on its way to the cathedral. The parade of dignitaries included bishops, cardinals, abbots, as well as gaily-clad minstrels and Swiss halberdiers. All eyes, however, were focused not on the unattractive groom, but on the beautiful bride. She wore a crown, a white robe with intricate decorations and elaborate adornments. Her immensely long train was borne by two young attendants. Mary looked like a goddess. The diamonds around her neck sparkled, and the golden crown garnished with pearls, rubies, sapphires and other precious stones on her head kept all eyes peeled on her. She carried herself like the young royal lady she had been trained to be.

When Henry II of France was killed in a tournament, Francis II and Mary Stuart became king and queen of France. He was 15 years, six months; she was 16. On September 18, 1559, at Rheims, young Francis was solemnly crowned king of France.

It was doubtful that Francis would be able to rule without advice and help. His health was poor. In fact, his sickly appearance was so appalling that circulating rumors claimed that he had leprosy. He suffered from bleedings, and there were times that medical aid was of no help and divine aid was sought for his recovery.

Mary spent the last weeks of her husband's life nursing him as he lay in a dark room. The end was inevitable. A month before his seventeenth birthday, Francis II was dead. Mary grieved over the loss; it had come just six months after the loss of her mother.

Tradition demanded that she mourn for 40 days, and she

observed the custom with sincerity. When the mourning period had ended, she had to make a choice: to consider a second marriage or to return to Scotland. The choice was not a simple one; Scotland was now ruled by a Protestant regime with both John Knox and the queen's half-brother, Lord James Stewart, in power.

Mary, the widow, was suddenly a new person. Her days of seclusion and caring for a sick husband had strengthened her. Her resilient spirit returned as she moved out into the light among those who loved and admired her.

Many potential suitors were suggested. The most promising from Mary's point of view was a marriage to Don Carlos of Spain. She felt that the Spanish throne held better prospects than the throne of Scotland. Besides, Don Carlos was also a Catholic.

It was only after Mary was convinced that marriage to Don Carlos would not materialize that she decided to leave for Scotland. Safe-conduct passage through English waters had to be obtained. When permission was delayed, Mary exhibited real courage by leaving for Scotland without such approval.

She found ruling Scotland difficult. Firstly, there was James, her half-brother who felt he should rule. Because he was a bastard, he knew that the crown rightfully belonged to his younger sister.

Secondly, there was John Knox—the leading evangelist in Scotland. He denounced her Catholic faith. He was a revolutionary, an egoist, a cunning politician who openly preached violence. He was not going to surrender to the young queen who had lived most of her life in France.

The star under which Mary was born was not a bright one. Again and again, she was the unexpected recipient of a tide of devastating events beyond her control. These included intrigue, jealousy, and much plotting to dethrone her, or at least to weaken her power. Mary seems always to have been surrounded by misguided advisors.

Despite the devastating early years of Mary's rule in Scotland, she succeeded in her attempt to establish wholesome conditions of government. Her youthful spirit and great enthusiasm were critical virtues in this respect. She was a linguist, with a sensitive feeling for poetry and music. She played the lute and was a graceful dancer. Many of these attributes, especially the latter, were fiercely condemned by John Knox. To him, dancing was an invention of the devil.

Mary loved beautiful clothes. The inventory of her wardrobe made at Holy Rood in February 1562 included 131 entries: 60 gowns of cloth of gold, cloth of silver, velvet, satin and silk. There were 14 cloaks, five of which were designed in the Spanish fashion. There were two royal mantles: one purple velvet and the other furred in ermine. Also in the collection were 34 *vasquines* and 16 *devants* or fronts (stomachers), mainly of cloth of gold, silver and satin.

The inventory of her jewels made in 1562 contained 180 entries—an increase of 21 over the inventory of the queen's jewels made at the time of her departure from France. New acquisitions included a cross of gold set with diamonds and rubies, and some new Scottish pearls from Edinburgh reputed to be the finest in Europe. This inventory did not include Mary's special earrings which consisted of 23 pearls, plus a precious collection of rings, necklaces and other earrings.

Mary Stuart was truly beautiful, attractive, regal and wealthy. What a dowry for a husband! Yet, it was difficult for her to find one who would meet the requirements of king. Some felt that not she, but the people, should choose a husband for her, since, after all, her husband would be *their* king. Still, Mary had no intention of leaving such a personal matter to the whim of her subjects.

Her most pressing problem was that of religion. Should she marry a Catholic or a Protestant? The second question was: should she marry an independent prince with a kingdom of his own, or should she marry a subject without a kingdom? The views of Queen Elizabeth had to be considered as well. Mary saw marriage in terms of power politics.

In March 1564, Lord Robert Dudley, Queen Elizabeth's own favorite lover, was presented to Mary. At first, her outward reaction was noncommital. She listened graciously, and suggested that a conference be held at Berwick between the English and Scots. Finally, he was absolutely rejected by Mary. She was not interested in taking the queen's lover for her husband.

It was in February 1565 that Lord Darnley was secretly granted permission to travel to Scotland. He was young, eligible and handsome, and had royal blood in his veins. Queen Elizabeth, herself, pleaded with Mary to receive him. At the time, it was felt that Elizabeth was launching Darnley in order to trap Mary into a demeaning marriage. Darnley, although outwardly attractive, was a weak individual.

Elizabeth, who knew Mary's weakness for masculine beauty, believed that Mary would fall for him. When Darnley arrived, he looked like a young god, with his golden hair, his perfectly-shaped face, the neat oval chin, and his fine figure. Yet, looking closely at Darnley, one sensed a streak of cruelty. His height was his great attribute. His elegant physique could hardly have failed to sweep vulnerable Mary off her feet.

Darnley could ride a horse, hunt, dance gracefully and play

the lute extremely well. He had a single purpose in life: the pursuit of pleasure. He was the product of an adoring mother and a doting father. He was spoiled, headstrong and ambitious. He wanted the crown and the power, but none of the responsibilities of ruling. He had a quick temper which made him incapable of assessing any person or situation. The most honest judgment made of his character was that of the Cardinal of Lorraine. He considered Darnley "an agreeable nincompoop."

Queen Mary did not notice the serious defects in Darnley's character. She saw merely a handsome man, and her reactions were immediately romantic. Her love for Darnley was overwhelmingly physical. Fulfillment of her passionate, pent-up longings, unfulfilled in her first marriage and certainly unfulfilled during her period of celibacy since Francis's death, became uppermost. All logic, all concern about the reaction of her subjects was shunted aside. Romance engulfed her.

Mary was impressed with Darnley, but not so the Scots. They opposed the match; but Mary listened to no one, nor did she wait for her own Parliament to give Darnley the coveted title of "King." She bestowed it upon him herself.

They were married and Mary announced that Darnley's new title was to be "King Henry." She happily proclaimed that henceforth all documents would be signed by them jointly as Mary and Henry: ". . . set forth in the names of both their Majesties as King and Queen conjunctly." The queen's proclamation was not looked upon with favor by the Scottish noblemen.

The July marriage, which began at the peak of love and passion, did not survive the chilly autumn and winter that followed. Darnley mainly sulked, demanding sums of money for self-enjoyment.

The marriage soon soured. Darnley, a spendthrift who shunned responsibility, became a tool of Mary's enemies. They incited him, telling him that his wife was the mistress of David Riccio, her small Italian secretary. A plot was hatched to execute Riccio in the queen's presence with the hope that this would cause her to miscarry.

The bloody murder was carried out, and the conspirators took charge of the castle. Mary was now a virtual prisoner. Fortunately, one of her supporters escaped and gathered an army of 4,000 men to come to her aid. Nine days after the murder of Riccio, Mary led an army of 8,000 men and re-entered Edinburgh.

Mary now began to rely on James Hepburn, Earl of Bothwell, for advice. She mistakenly saw in Bothwell the image of a strong, wise protector, able to solve her problems by his ability to control the other nobles.

Bothwell was not a stupid man. He had been well educated, spoke French, and was well-traveled. He was adventurous by nature and his relations with women followed the same pattern as his career. His name was linked with an array of women. He regarded lust as a simple need to be gratified quickly. Marriage, on the other hand, was a more serious business to be undertaken for positive gain.

Mary's instincts led her to Bothwell. He had served her well and she owed him much. She loved him not only because he had exhibited no greed but because she felt a passion for him that she had not felt in a long time. Her first husband had been a boy, her second was a boy, and Bothwell was a man. His reckless courage, his gaiety, his ability, his masculinity—all were factors which contributed to her infatuation with him.

Rumors began to spread about her interest in Bothwell, and relations with her husband worsened. She refused him conjugal rights and this humiliation was too much for Darnley.

Mary, however, persuaded Darnley to return with her to Edinburgh. She promised him that if he left with her they could resume full marital relations. Mary's coldness as a wife had long been one of Darnley's complaints. It hurt his vanity as a man and threatened his status as a king.

Darnley took up residence in a house on the outskirts of Edinburgh. This was to be his last week alive. In the days that followed, Mary visited her husband daily, nursing him tenderly and even entertaining him.

It was Lord Robert Stewart, Mary's half-brother, who visited Darnley and advised him: "Quit this place or it will cost you your life."

Darnley confided his fears to Mary who put his mind at ease, but little did he know that soon he was to be murdered.

Some hours later, the king thought he heard keys grating in locks. He moved quickly. Not waiting to put on his slippers, he jumped from the window of his house. Soon he was surrounded, and although he fought frantically to free himself, he could not. "Pity me, kind men," he cried. "Pity me for the love of Him who pitied all the world." But they didn't. They strangled him. At the age of 21, Darnley died a pathetic and unheroic death.

Mary ordered the court into mourning. She embarked on the traditional 40 days of mourning for her husband. A reward of 2,000 pounds was offered for discovery of the murderers. Only one man seemed to move easily about the palace, and that was the Earl of Bothwell. This increased the talk about his love affair with the queen, and he was denounced as the murderer.

As far as Mary was concerned, she couldn't show remorse about Darnley's death; she herself, had wished him dead often.

Soon, placards appeared showing her as a mermaid, naked to the waist, with a crown on her head, and Bothwell as a hare—the crest of the Hepburns crouching in a circle of swords. This implied that she was a siren, or, in other words, a prostitute.

Despite Mary's claims to have had no part in the plot to murder Darnley, she was found guilty. Historians differ as to the justice of the verdict. Some writers feel that Mary was innocent of participation in Darnley's murder. Others feel that she was very much involved. Her role, they state, was to lure him out of his father's house; else, what was the sense in her removing an invalid in the winter from his protective father's house and bringing him to Edinburgh. One historian wrote: "That Mary had no hand in the actual murder does not clear her, if she knew it was to take place and if it were through her cooperation that it did take place. I believe there is enough evidence in her behavior both before and after the calamity to convict her."

The famous Casket Letters, which later were used to doom her, are incriminating pieces of evidence. The "Casket" was a small, oblong, silver casket covered with green velvet, and bearing a king's crown and the monogram F. It contained several letters and sonnets purported to have been written by Mary. There were also documents relating to their marriage.

There is one letter, referred to as Letter Two, which was written by Mary to Bothwell. It is direct evidence that she was in love with Bothwell, that she hoped to marry him, that she had come to Glasgow for the sole reason of winning her husband's confidence in order to lead him to his doom.

The reaction of her subjects caused Mary to panic. Where she could have shown real leadership, she almost collapsed. She sought advice and counsel, but honest counsel was hard to come by. Who could advise her? Bothwell was hardly the one. He himself had ambitions to become the ruler of Scotland.

Bothwell's wife now hovered at the brink of death. His finances were in awful shape, and his future had to be considered. He began to court Mary with regularity.

There were demands made of the queen that Bothwell be brought to trial, which was done. However, since there was no accuser, Bothwell was acquitted. He reacted characteristically to his acquittal: He challenged anyone to doubt his innocence.

Bothwell's next move was absolutely in keeping with his character and the conditions of the time. He entertained 28 noblemen with a lavish banquet. At the end of this momentous supper party, Bothwell produced a long document proving his innocence in the murder of Darnley. It also stated that the queen was in need of a husband, and that he was the best choice. He asked them to sign the document. With it he followed the queen to

Seton and there suggested that he be selected as her husband.

This direct request threw the queen into a state of confusion. Her chief nobles pleaded that she accept Bothwell. Some time later, Bothwell took matters into his own hands. When the queen was returning to Edinburgh, he appeared with a force of 800 men and told her that since danger awaited her in Edinburgh, he would conduct her to the castle of Dunbar. She allowed herself to be taken about 40 miles through the heart of Scotland to Dunbar.

Rape was not the sort of duty from which Bothwell was likely to shrink. Once within the castle, Bothwell made his second planned move. He decided to complete his abduction of Mary by taking possession of her body as well. He wanted to make sure that the queen would have to marry him. Melville, one of the queen's followers, who was present in the castle at the time, was certain that the ravishment had taken place. Melville later stated, "The queen could not but marry him, seeing he had ravished her and lain with her against her will." It was also Melville who said that Bothwell had already boasted that he would marry the queen: "who would or would not; yea, whether she would herself or not."

Several weeks later, the queen herself explained her hasty marriage to Bothwell: "Albeit we found his doings rude, yet were his words and answers gentle."

There was talk that the entire abduction scheme had been rigged and was intended to save the queen's face. There was further talk that Mary found a sexual satisfaction with Bothwell which she had not experienced with either of her previous husbands.

The queen kept silent. There were many reasons for the marriage other than the fulfillment of her sexual needs. There were practical matters in which Bothwell could serve her well. He could settle the religious situation in Scotland. He would provide her with an able and masterful consort—someone with whom she could share the strains of government.

Practical political ambition had moved Bothwell to woo this elegant, graceful, flirtatious queen with her red-gold hair, and beautiful figure. Her courage and ability to make quick decisions appealed to Bothwell as well.

Now that he was accepted by the queen, Bothwell had to rid himself of his own wife. This did not prove difficult. Jean Bothwell raised no objections, and their marriage was annulled by the Catholic Archbishop Hamilton.

When Mary returned to Edinburgh, she received an offer of rescue from one of her lords, but this she firmly rejected.

Queen Mary moved around now as though she were in a trance. The aristocrats were furious that Bothwell had made himself a virtual dictator. A party of dissidents who had gathered at Stirling vowed to set the queen at liberty. Bothwell was charged with adultery, rape, collusion between him and his wife, and suspicion of murdering the king. They were aghast that their dream figure, their beautiful young queen had recklessly and carelessly allowed herself to be trampled in the mire of Bothwell's ambition.

Shortly thereafter, Mary named Bothwell Duke of Orkney and Lord of Shetland and placed the ducal coronet on his head with her own hands. She moved like a mindless corpse under the power of Bothwell's authority.

Twelve days after his annulment and just over three months after the death of her own husband, Mary and Bothwell were married in the great hall at Holy Rood. The fact that the ceremony took place according to the Protestant rite was evidence of the queen's loss of control of her own destiny. There were no rich presents for Bothwell as groom as there had been for Darnley. Nor did she wear expensive attire.

Bothwell was not an ideal husband. He was jealous if his wife so much as looked at anyone but him; he accused her of being fun-loving; he used filthy language when speaking to her. There was talk that Mary suffered tortures of jealousy because Bothwell's former wife, Lady Jean, still remained installed in his own Castle of Crichton. Gossip had it that Bothwell loved his former wife more than he loved the queen.

It was necessary to explain the hasty marriage to both the French and English courts. Mary, in her letters to the courts, stressed Bothwell's loyal service to the Scottish crown. She emphasized the fact that Bothwell had won her hand over other nobles. In addition, she described her own helpless and broken spirit; she felt too weak, she said, to deal single-handedly with the Scottish situation.

However, by the end of May 1567, the clouds of war were gathering over Bothwell's head with such menace that the queen and duke were constrained to summon their people to meet with them.

On June 6, Bothwell took Mary from Holy Rood to the Castle of Borthwick. Here, too, Bothwell was surrounded by insurgents. Bothwell, with his military knowledge, realized that he could not withstand a siege and so slipped away through a side gate and escaped. He left the queen to hold off the besiegers.

The insurgents called on her to abandon her husband and accompany them back to Edinburgh. This she proudly refused to do. She had suddenly regained her old spirit. Disguising herself as a man, she escaped to neighbors where she knew Bothwell would be hiding. From there, both made their way to Dunbar.

They assembled a force and prepared for a pitched battle.

At 2 A.M., Sunday morning, June 15, 1567, the confederate lords marched out of Edinburgh to meet Bothwell's band. At the head of the procession was a white banner showing a green tree, with the corpse of Darnley lying underneath it, and the infant son kneeling before him, with the legend: "Judge and avenge my cause, O Lord."

It was a blazing hot day as the troops faced one another, not knowing what to do. At this crucial moment, the French ambassador, deputed by the rebels, came forth and begged Mary to abandon Bothwell. Should she do this she would be restored to her former position. This Mary furiously declined to do, feeling that Bothwell, with all his faults, had proven himself loyal to her throughout her adversities. In addition, she knew that she was pregnant with his child.

Bothwell, feeling that their cause was hopeless, asked Mary to ride with him to Dunbar where they could rally additional support. Mary declined. With a trust in her own people, Mary bade farewell to the man for whom she had sacrificed her own honor and reputation. They embraced in full view of both armies. At sunset, Bothwell mounted his horse, and, after five weeks of power, galloped away down the road to Dunbar. Mary never saw him again.

Now completely alone, Mary made her way into the camp of the rebels. She was greeted less than graciously. The soldiers shouted crude insults at her: "Burn her, burn the whore, she is not worthy to live . . . Kill her, drown her!"

Amazed, almost stunned, the queen allowed tears of shock and humiliation to pour down her cheeks. For the first time, she understood the consequences of her reckless action in marrying her husband's assassin. To her subjects she was no longer their young and beautiful queen; she was an adulteress—an adulteress who had subsequently become the willing bride of a murderer.

She was brought to the house of the Laird of Craigmillar where guards were posted even in her bedroom. By the next morning, Mary had lost all self-control. She appeared at the open window—her hair hanging down about her face, her clothes torn open so that the upper half of her body was almost bare, her beauty gone. Who was this wretched, near-demented creature, half hanging from the window of an Edinburgh prison, partly naked, her bosom exposed? Was this their beautiful queen? It was only four weeks since Mary's marriage to Bothwell, and not two years since her marriage to Darnley! What a misfortune had befallen her! And them!

On June 16, a warrant for the queen's imprisonment was signed by nine lords. Much of her wealth was confiscated, and

Mary, rightfully felt betrayed by those who claimed they wanted to free her from Bothwell. In the meantime, Bothwell was still at liberty. When he learned that Mary was imprisoned, he went forth with the hope of raising some sort of support for her.

Mary absolutely refused to consider divorcing Bothwell. Her reasons were twofold: her pregnancy by Bothwell, and her suspicion of the lords' motive in suggesting this course of action.

Imprisoned in the castle, she was allowed neither pen nor paper. Writing material was smuggled in to her and she wrote to Catherine de Medici in France, pleading with her to have compassion and send troops to deliver her.

Meanwhile, plans for the queen's escape were being formed. One day, a pearl earring was pressed into her hand, a sign that George Douglas, a loyal follower had made all preparations necessary for her escape. And escape she did. Once she reached Niddrie Castle, she could not eat or sleep. She wrote to her uncle and gave instructions to kinsmen of Bothwell to seize the Castle of Dunbar and then go to Denmark to notify Bothwell of her escape. Yet, she knew there was really no safety for her in Scotland. Her hope was to go to England, to her cousin Elizabeth. Elizabeth was a sister sovereign, her own flesh and blood.

When Mary crossed over into England, Elizabeth had reigned for some nine years. She hated Mary. Mary's life had now become a spider's web: the more she struggled to free herself from it, the more hopelessly she found herself entwined. Mary was now a prisoner in England. Instead of a haven, England had proved to be a trap; instead of a protector, Elizabeth had revealed herself to be a destroyer. But hope took long to die in so joyous a heart.

The trial of Queen Mary was held in Fotheringhay Castle. Mary entered the great hall at nine o'clock with an escort of soldiers. She wore her chosen garb of the many years of captivity —a dress and mantle of flowing black velvet, her traditional white headdress with its widow's peak, and a long white gauzy veil.

She entered the courtroom supported by her French physician on one side, and her Scots master of the household on the other. She looked at all the counselors and judges, all Englishmen, and said, "Alas! how many counselors are here, yet not one for me."

For two days, she ably matched wits with the best brains in England. Her knowledge of English law was searching, and she had an answer for every question. "My crimes," she stated, "consist in my birth, the injuries that have been inflicted upon me, and my religion. Of the first, I am justly proud, the second I can forgive, and the third has been my sole consolation and hope under all my afflictions."

She asked for an advocate to plead her cause, for one more day to be allowed for consideration and preparation of her defense. She was refused both. She then demanded to be heard in Parliament in the Presence of the Queen of England and her Council. Abruptly, the court dismissed itself.

Sentence of death was passed on her four weeks later. From then on, she was spared no indignity. She heard them working in the hall erecting the scaffold. Her room and bed were hung with mourning, signifying that she was already a dead woman. The night before her execution, she did not sleep. At six in the morning, she rose, handed over her will, distributed her purses, and gave her women a farewell embrace. Her men servants were given her hand to kiss. Then, she prayed. Later, accompanied by her women servants, she entered the great hall in silence. Three hundred spectators were on hand to watch the execution. After 19 years of imprisonment in England, the moment they awaited had come.

They saw the tall and gracious woman who at first sight seemed to be dressed in black. She walked with dignity. Her serenity and composure made her still beautiful. Above all, her courage was matchless. A great axe lay ready. Mary, Queen of Scots, was led up the three steps to the stage; she listened while the commission for her execution was read aloud. Her expression never changed. She kneeled and prayed. When her prayers were finished, the executioners asked her, as was customary, to forgive them in advance for bringing her death. Mary answered immediately: "I forgive you with all my heart, for now I hope you shall make an end of all my troubles."

She quickly undressed. Stripped of her black garments, she stood in her red petticoat, and it was seen that above it she wore a red satin bodice, trimmed with lace, the neckline cut low at the back; one of the women handed her a pair of red sleeves, the liturgical color of martyrdom in the Catholic Church.

The time had come to bind the queen's eyes with the white cloth embroidered in gold which Mary had chosen for the purpose. The queen, without even the faintest sign of fear, knelt down once more on the cushion in front of the block. In Latin, she recited a psalm: "In you Lord is my trust, let me never be confounded." Then, feeling for the block, she laid her head down upon it, placing her chin carefully with both her hands. The queen stretched out her arms and legs and cried: "Into your hands, O Lord, I commend my spirit."

The first blow missed the neck and cut into the back of the head. The second blow severed the neck, all but the smallest sinew, and this was quickly severed.

It was approximately ten o'clock on the morning of Wednesday, February 8, 1587. The queen was 44 years old, and in the nineteenth year of her English captivity.

Bothwell? He had been captured earlier and died in jail—a madman.